"Do we need another book about Bruno and his inquisitorial trial? In the case of this new volume the answer is unreservedly yes. Germano Maifreda brings new interpretations and documentary evidence along with a fresh point of view to the conversation. Taking up the perspective of post-Tedeschi historiography and building upon the work of Tom Mayer and others, Maifreda demonstrates that although the Black Legend may be exaggerated, the logic and rule of law in *ancien regime* Europe was definitely not that of the twentieth century, and that it makes absolutely no sense whatsoever to try to make the distinction between legal and moral justice in that past world of factionalism and power politics."

Simon Ditchfield, *University of York*

"Germano Maifreda is a leading scholar of the Inquisition, as his new book on the trial of Giordano Bruno shows. Thanks to groundbreaking archival research, he gives a convincing reappraisal of the power dynamics and the religious repression that brought the philosopher to death. Further, *The Trial of Giordano Bruno* is written like a true spy story: engaging and surprising!"

Simone Maghenzani, *University of Cambridge*

The Trial of Giordano Bruno

In 1600, Giordano Bruno, one of the leading intellectuals of the Renaissance, was burned at the stake on the charge of heresy by the Roman Inquisition. He is remembered primarily for his cosmological theories, particularly that the universe was infinite with the Earth not being at its centre. Today, he has become a symbol of the struggle for religious and philosophical tolerance.

The Trial of Giordano Bruno, originally published in Italian in 2018, provides English audiences with a complete and updated reconstruction of the inquisitorial trial by analysing the accusations, witnesses, and legal proceedings in detail. The author also gives a detailed profile of Bruno as well as the body which arrested and accused him – the Inquisition.

This book will appeal to all those interested in the life and death of Giordano Bruno, as well as those interested in Early Modern legal proceedings, the Roman Inquisition, and the history of religious and philosophical tolerance.

Germano Maifreda is Professor of Economic History at the Università degli Studi di Milano.

Routledge Research in Early Modern History

The Politics of Obscenity in the Age of the Gutenberg Revolution
Obscene Means in Early Modern French and European Print Culture and Literature
Edited by Peter Frei and Nelly Labère

Losing Face
Shame, Society and the Self in Early Modern England
Ilana Krausman Ben-Amos

Brokerage and Networks in London's Global World
Kinship, Commerce and Communities through the experience of John Blackwell
David Farr

The Early Modern State: Drivers, Beneficiaries and Discontents
Essays in honour of Prof. Dr. Marjolein 't Hart
Edited by Pepijn Brandon, Lex Heerma van Voss, and Annemieke Romein

The Making of the Modern Corporation
The Casa di San Giorgio and its Legacy (1446–1720)
Carlo Taviani

The Trial of Giordano Bruno
Germano Maifreda

A Genlis Education and Enlightenment Values
Mrs Chinnery (1766–1840) and her Children
Denise Yim

For more information about this series, please visit: https://www.routledge.com/Routledge-Research-in-Early-Modern-History/book-series/RREMH

The Trial of Giordano Bruno

Germano Maifreda

Translated by
Paul M. Rosenberg with
Loretta Valtz Mannucci

Routledge
Taylor & Francis Group
NEW YORK AND LONDON

First published in English 2022
by Routledge
605 Third Avenue, New York, NY 10158

and by Routledge
4 Park Square, Milton Park, Abingdon, Oxon, OX14 4RN

Routledge is an imprint of the Taylor & Francis Group, an informa business

Translated by Paul M. Rosenberg with Loretta Valtz Mannucci

Published in Italian by Giuseppe Laterza & Figli 2018

Library of Congress Cataloging-in-Publication Data
A catalog record for this title has been requested

ISBN: 978-0-367-45913-0 (hbk)
ISBN: 978-1-032-28679-2 (pbk)
ISBN: 978-1-003-02608-2 (ebk)

DOI: 10.4324/9781003026082

Typeset in Times New Roman
by codeMantra

The Open Access version of this book was funded by Dipartimento di Studi Storici "Federico Chabod".

I would like to dedicate this book to the dear memory of Loretta Valtz Mannucci, to whom I am indebted for long conversations and her encouragement for me to embark on areas of research that were, in more ways than one, "heterodox."

Contents

Preface

This text presents the English edition of my book *Io dirò la verità: Il processo di Giordano Bruno*, published in Italy by Laterza in 2018. The original text has been revised in places, particularly with the addition of a new Introduction aimed at allowing the reader who is not familiar with the political-religious history of 16th-century Italy to orient themselves in the rather complex events which I have tried to reconstruct and interpret. The original references were preserved, apart from indicating the English editions of texts that were originally consulted in their Italian translations, and in a few cases adding information where it seemed useful to provide some brief indication to the English speaking reader wishing to pursue further insights.

The genesis of this book is in itself, I believe, significant. Several years ago I did research on the economic structure and logic of the Roman inquisitorial tribunals, the results of which were presented in a volume published by Routledge in 2017, *The Business of the Roman Inquisition*. While browsing the many account books of the Roman prisons of the Holy Office in the early modern era I was greatly surprised when my eye fell on the receipts for the prison upkeep of an obscure Capuchin friar named Celestino da Verona. I discovered that the friar, imprisoned in 1599, had been given food, provisions, and clothing in incomparably greater proportions (and of a very different type) than all the other prisoners whose names I had identified in the registers – including Giordano Bruno. Who was this obscure figure, who at the time was unknown to me? Why had he merited this exceptionally favorable treatment? Curiosity pushed me to learn more. I thus discovered that Celestino da Verona had always been a genuine black hole in the historiographical reconstructions of an affair that has in many ways distinguished the history of Italy and of Europe in the last centuries: the trial of Giordano Bruno. Several historians before me have investigated him. I believed that these new documents I had discovered could shed light on this mysterious and opaque figure.

The unpublished research and documents (a good deal of which were in Latin) that emerged from my first approach to the story of Celestino and his relations with Bruno were presented in my book *Giordano Bruno e Celestino da Verona: Un incontro fatale*, published in Italian by Edizioni della Normale in 2016. However, I felt that this story deserved to be presented to a larger public than that reachable with a scholarly text offering the first results of an erudite documentary survey. The trial of Giordano Bruno needed to be studied further and deeper in light of the events and information which I had discovered, and the events had to be placed in their broader historical context, offering an overall interpretation that accounts for dynamics larger than solely those of the trial itself. These considerations matured into my decision to answer those needs, and write this book.

Acknowledgements

I would like to thank Paul M. Rosenberg, without whose professionalism and collaboration it would have been difficult to bring this project to what is for me a happy outcome. In addition to working on the translation, he also played the role of cultural mediator, helping me present this very specific text and subject to a non-Italian public.

The translation itself was financed in part by funds granted to me by the competitive project of the Italian Ministry of Universities and Research (PRIN 2015-prot. 2015NA5XLZ) and in part by the Department of Historical Studies of the Università degli Studi di Milano. Figures 12.1, 12.2, 12.3 in chapter 12 are published with the kind permission of the Italian Ministero per i Beni e le Attività Culturali e per il Turismo (further reproduction is prohibited).

My thanks to Editori Laterza for having graciously granted the rights to the Italian edition, and to Max Novick for having accepted this book to be one of Routledge's publications, as well as for the understanding he showed when the delivery of the manuscript experienced delays during the complicated period of the pandemic in which it was prepared. I am also grateful to Simon Maghenzani for his suggestions, encouragement, and availability he has shown me over the years.

Finally, I would like to thank Simon Ditchfield for his scientific review of the text in its final stages, which he graciously did out of friendship and a longstanding admiration for the subject matter.

Abbreviations

ACDF:	Vatican City, Archivio della Congregazione per la Dottrina della Fede (So: *Sant'Officio*; St.st.: *Stanza storica*)
APCVM:	Mestre, Archivio provinciale dei cappuccini veneti di Venezia-Mestre
ASFi:	Florence, Archivio di Stato di Firenze
ASR:	Rome, Archivio di Stato di Roma
ASV:	Vatican City, Archivio Segreto Vaticano (now Archivio Apostolico Vaticano)
ASVe:	Venice, Archivio di Stato di Venezia
BAV:	Vatican City, Biblioteca Apostolica Vaticana
Processo:	Luigi Firpo, *Il processo di Giordano Bruno*, edited by Diego Quaglioni, Rome, Salerno editrice, 1993, followed by page numbers.

Introduction

It is well-known that Giordano Bruno, perhaps the most important Italian philosopher of the Renaissance, died at the hands of the Roman Inquisition on February 17, 1600. Bruno could have avoided that sentence by simply abjuring his positions – albeit before a tribunal whose legitimacy he rejected and whose moral authority he disdained. Why, then, did Bruno choose to be burned at the stake? What really happened during the long years of his trial that could have led him to such an extreme decision? The "secular martyrology" around the figure of Bruno that arose in the first decades of unified Italy, which interprets the philosopher's death as an act of heroic intellectual consistency in the face of the Holy Office, has long deprived investigations into Bruno's motives for this decision of historiographical dignity.[1]

In this book I will argue that Bruno conceived of his trial as a political enterprise: during the eight years of the proceeding he lucidly attempted to save the fundamental nucleus of his philosophy, both by trying to set up an intellectual debate with the inquisitors, as well as by declaring on multiple occasions, both in the Venetian phase (1592–1593) and in the Roman phase (1593–1599) of the proceeding, his full willingness to abjure: that is, the formal act of retracting one's thoughts that would have saved his life.

The recent revival of historiographical interest in Giordano Bruno's thought and biography has also led historians – mostly historians of philosophy – to return to the evidence which emerged during the inquisitorial process that ended tragically, with the death of the Dominican friar from Nola. However, this renewed attention has not, I believe, created an authentic dialogue between the new history of the Roman Inquisition (of which a brief account must be provided here) and the study of the Bruno trial, for which the documentary evidence has largely been investigated in view of answering philosophical, more than strictly historical questions.

As Michele Ciliberto has concluded,

> in over eighty months of imprisonment – first in Venice, then in Rome – Bruno conducted, day after day – and with all the tools available to him – a bitter struggle to not succumb, to not abjure, to not die. [...] Bruno decided to turn the tables, and chose to go to the stake, when he

DOI: 10.4324/9781003026082-1

> sensed that he was definitively trapped, without any real possibility of saving himself or his philosophy.[2]

Bruno therefore reversed himself only at the end of a long process, only after he realized the failure of his plan to use the trial – and the proximity it gave him to the summit of Catholicism – as a platform to launch the political project (of a religious, philosophical, and magical nature) he had developed during his long years of religious exile in France, England, and Germany. But when did he make this decision? What exactly happened at that moment and in what way? And ultimately, after having fought for so long, why did Bruno – unlike several of his well-known contemporaries, among who were Tommaso Campanella and Galileo Galilei – decide to close himself in obstinacy, accepting not only the inquisitors' condemnation of his thought and censorship of his books, but even the agony of being burned alive? These are the main questions addressed in this volume.

Reconstructing Bruno's intellectual itinerary in the courts of Europe and analyzing the various stages of the trial through previously unpublished documents, I will first of all formulate the hypothesis that Bruno was prejudicially manipulated by the Holy Office. I suggest that the Inquisition wanted to make an example with the sentencing of the philosopher, who was believed to be loyal to the heretic king of France Henry IV, at a turbulent international political juncture. I believe this desire led the inquisitors to make use of a spy, a certain Capuchin friar, Celestino da Verona, who in turn – and not by coincidence – was later sentenced to burn at the stake in Campo de' Fiori a few months before Bruno. In this regard I will raise the problem of the direct relationship between Celestino's imprisonment and death sentence and the final developments in the Bruno trial. I will further suggest an overall and unsettling interpretive hypothesis which, should it be confirmed, would explain the mysterious temporal coincidence between Celestino da Verona's return to the Roman inquisitorial prisons and Bruno's final decision to refuse abjuration, sending himself to the stake.

The reconstruction of the dynamics of events in one of the most famous inquisitorial trials of all time demonstrates how, although the Black Legend may be exaggerated, the logic and rule of law in Old Regime Europe was definitely not that of the 20th century. Thus as we look at the trial of Giordano Bruno from new perspectives, it makes no sense to try and apply the modern distinction between legal and moral justice to that past world of factionalism and power politics. As we will see, the justice of the faith moved in much different ways than what we are used to today.

§

First, let us set the scene in which the final steps of the Bruno trial unfolded. It is December 19th, 1598. Pope Clement VIII returns to Rome after spending several months in Ferrara, which had been annexed into the papal domains following the extinction of the main branch of the House of Este. A few days later a powerful sirocco wind and torrential rain are unleashed on the area, culminating in the catastrophic flood of the Tiber on Christmas day 1598.

It is believed that on the day the Tiber's waters, prevented by the winds from flowing into the sea, reached the highest levels ever recorded, at some points approaching the 20-meter mark. By evening two of the Palatine bridge's arches, which had been overwhelmed by floods many times before, and just as often rebuilt, were already damaged: people were quick to note that cardinal Pietro, the pope's nephew, had crossed that very point only minutes earlier. The swirling waters invaded the city's low-lying quarters first – the Jewish ghetto, the port of Ripetta, the Pantheon, Trastevere – and then swallowed most of the rest of the city. In the shops, all closed for Christmas, benches, meat, bolts of cloth, precious stones, jewels, paintings, and statues were all swept away. The poor who slept in basements and cellars died first, then, gradually, the people living on the higher floors. The dead were in the thousands. The city and the surrounding countryside were transformed into an extensive swamp, upon whose surface floated, we are informed by chronicles of the time, carts, buffalo, oxen, household goods, trees, and barrels, alongside the remains of disinterred corpses.[3]

The astrologers and the Roman people did not hesitate to blame the calamity on the iniquities and nepotistic excesses of the increasingly disliked papal family of Aldobrandini. The previous year their aggressive foreign policy had culminated in the excommunication of Cesare d'Este, a cousin of the late Duke of Ferrara, Alfonso II, and the son of a union which the Church of Rome insisted on considering illegitimate. Despite this, Alfonso had designated him as his testamentary heir to lead the Duchy, and the succession had been recognized by the Emperor, Rudolf II. Ferrara, however, was a papal fiefdom; the Pope's approval was indeed required. Clement VIII's firm opposition led to the deployment of the papal army at Faenza to dissuade the aspirant duke from attempting to claim what he considered to be his right. Backed by 20,000 foot-soldiers and 7,000 riders, cardinal-nephew Pietro Aldobrandini made his triumphant entry into Ferrara in January 1598, and began to organize the solemn arrival of his uncle, the pope, with his court and dozens of cardinals, facilitating the provisioning of grain and more refined foods.[4]

The Este family line died out, Cesar became duke of Modena and Reggio, and Ferrara was ceded the Papal State. But the Roman people had not forgotten, and continued to blame the Pope and his family for the weather's devastation. The fact that the Jewish ghetto was miraculously saved, despite being located in one of the areas that was most vulnerable to the flooding of the Tiber, was also interpreted as a sign against the Aldobrandini family. In fact, since the early months of his papacy Clement VIII Aldobrandini had resurrected all of the bulls by issued his predecessors that oppressed the Jews. He additionally prohibited any contact between Jews and Christians.

But most grievously, the new pope ordered the Jews to surrender all copies of the *Talmud* to be burned in the public square.[5]

The Christmas flood of the Tiber would repeat in the first days of 1599, with another wave of flooding between January 9th and 10th. On January 23rd, with the bad weather at last at an end, the Pope issued the bull *Manus Domini manus Patris*, condemning the popular opinion that God was angry with the papal family, and instead admonishing Romans to atone for their sins.

It was in this tense atmosphere in January 1599 that the conclusion of the heresy trial against philosopher Giordano Bruno da Nola – who had been arrested in Venice seven years earlier – began to take shape in the Roman palazzo of the Holy Office, situated next to St. Peter's basilica. The context of the trial, one of the longest in Inquisition history, was quite intricate, and there was disagreement among the judges over the procedure to follow in reaching a sentence. The tribunal, almost certainly with the direct intervention of the Pope, entrusted the task of re-examining all of the documentation from the lengthy trial to the Jesuit scientist, Roberto Bellarmino in early 1599. The Jesuit he was, at that moment, on the eve of the decisive event of his career: he would be created a cardinal by Clement VIII on March 3 of that year.[6]

Upon completion of this examination the Jesuit, basing his conclusions on the largely sloppy work carried out by the censors of Bruno's books from 1595 to 1597, proposed that the tribunal present Bruno with a list of eight clauses which had been judged heretical for him to abjure – that is, to solemnly recant – or be sentenced to death. Unfortunately, this list has not survived; we only know that it was delivered to the prisoner on January 18, 1599, with six days granted for a decision.

Had he agreed to formally repudiate his positions, the philosopher would have saved his life, though the gravity of the accusations would have resulted in a sentence of prolonged incarceration, with the possibility of a future reduction in duration. But condemnation by the Holy Office would have undermined the foundations of Bruno's philosophical system, and would undoubtedly have been a prelude to the censoring of his books and a prohibition on teaching or publishing theories that coincided with or were linked to his abjured opinions. The clauses Bellarmino collected most certainly included some of the crucial nodes of Bruno's work. We can infer from the surviving documentation that they definitely included Bruno's conception, contrary to the Thomist doctrine, which saw the soul as mankind's "form." They also very likely included "Copernicanism," issues concerning the Trinity, the doctrine of universal animation, and that of the rational soul of the earthly globe.[7]

At that point an extreme alternative was placed before Bruno: officially renounce belief in his own truths and save his life, or accept his death sentence and the total censure of his philosophy. Neither choice would have saved his thought from oblivion or from being forgotten for eternity, since the Roman Church believed the power of its laws and its Courts was everlasting, and would endure until the end of time.

Faced with an alternative that would have seen his work dissolve either way, Bruno refused both possibilities, and tried to build a third way with his bare hands.

On January 25th, after having read the eight clauses, Bruno appeared before the Inquisitors and declared himself to be "willing to revoke them." However, at the same time he presented a written brief, whose contents are unknown to us, which he claimed was pertinent to his defense. Here is the tactic he had devised and would keep alive for some months: take note of the charges made by the judges aimed at dismantling his system of thought, while at the same time attempting to open up a dialogue with them through written argumentation in order to limit the theoretical and practical damage inflected by abjuration.

It is impossible today to know whether in Bruno's mind this effort was simply dilatory, or if it really was an attempt to establish a dispute with the leaders of Catholicism. Luigi Firpo, one of the finest Italian historians of the 20th century, has restored philosophical dignity to this desperate decision, defining it as "a debate," "an effort at persuasion," and "hope in the recognition of his own valid reasoning."[8]

On February 15, 1599 Bruno openly declared himself "to acknowledge the said eight propositions to be heretical and to be ready to detest and abjure them in the place and at the time which pleases the Holy Office."[9] It seemed to be an unconditional surrender. At that point, the cardinals charged the Commissioner with collecting the instances of heretical clauses in the trial depositions and in Bruno's books to be incorporated in the sentence and in the act of abjuration. However, on April 5, 1599 Bruno returned to applying his strategy, presenting a second brief during one of the inquisitors' periodic visits to the prisons; in all likelihood this was meant to reduce the extent of the abjuration as much as possible. Clearly Bruno still believed it was useful and possible to gain time by trying to reopen a "dialogue" with the judges, who for their part had no choice but to look for new information in Bruno's document. The contents had to be analyzed.

At this point it must have become increasingly evident to the inquisitors that Bruno's intelligent plan had them trapped in a vicious circle. On the one hand, brief after brief, a process which had already lasted seven years was further prolonged, with the risk that it would drag on without end: the exceptional breadth of Bruno's philosophy could act as a palette for a potentially infinite range of nuances. On the other hand, the judges could not prevent Bruno from unburdening his conscience, producing new criminal evidence, or even indicating accomplices. The only way to close that endless trial was to eradicate the philosopher's obstinacy in defending his own positions: his spasmodic search for confrontation that sounded at the same time both derisory and accusatory.

The patronizing philosopher had to be made to understand that the era of disputation had definitively passed, and that the Renaissance was over. Italy had entered the age of the "courts of conscience."[10]

§

Over four centuries after the end of the Inquisition's proceeding against the major Italian philosopher of the Renaissance, the circumstances of his death continue to raise questions.

One of the major scholars of Giordano Bruno's work and biography has recently pointed out the need to "break down the screen between us and [Bruno], the game of mirrors that continues to hide his face and obscure the profound reasons for his decisions, even in the moment of extremity": that is, the decision to refuse abjuring his ideas, at the cost of his life. Meeting this need requires "a fresh look at this very complex affair – "naïve," a philosopher would have said – to the extent this is possible."[11]

The task is made desperately difficult by a great number of documentary and interpretive obstacles, not the least of which is the fact that the documentation from the Roman trial of Giordano Bruno has never been found, and may well be lost forever.[12]

Our knowledge of the Bruno trial, which took place between Venice and Rome from 1592 to 1600, is in large part owed to the reconstruction of the few surviving documents done over 60 years ago by one of the great Italian historians of the 20th century: Luigi Firpo. His essay *Il processo di Giordano Bruno* appeared in two installments in the pages of "Rivista Storica Italiana" on the 400th anniversary of Bruno's birth, between 1948 and 1949, along with the publication of a rich trove of documents. The republication of this work in 1993, edited and integrated by Diego Quaglioni, remains the reference edition of these sources.[13] The editor was able to match Firpo's publication to all the accessible originals, which are preserved at the Archives of the State of Rome and Venice, the Secret Vatican Archive (today Vatican Apostolic Archive) and the Vatican Apostolic Library. Quaglioni was not able to get access to documents in the Archive of the Holy Office, which did not open for consultation – under the name and form of Archive of the Congregation for the Doctrine of the Faith (*Congregazione per la dottrina della fede*) – until 1998.[14]

A large part of the documentation published by Firpo consists of the so-called *Sommario* of the Bruno trial, found among the personal papers of Pope Pius IX and published for the first time in 1940 by the Prefect and custodian of the Secret Vatican Archive, Angelo Mercati. The identification of a long manuscript with a summary of the Bruno trial documentation, complied no earlier than 1597 for use by the then Assessor of the Congregation of the Holy Office, was accepted by Firpo, who curated the publication, but it has recently been challenged.[15] However, by all accounts the document represents a source of primary relevance for knowledge of Bruno's struggle with the Inquisition. In these pages we will continue to refer to it using the conventional nomenclature of *Sommario.*

Studies on Bruno in the second half of the 20th century were greatly enriched by this source, but were also, I believe, limited by it. In fact, the *Sommario* has imposed a dyadic approach to the historiography of the trial by restricting the scope of studies to observation of the relationship between the defendant and the judges. Investigating sources and episodes which have until now been disregarded, simply because they are lateral to the central elements of the trial, can in fact bring new elements to light – as I will try to demonstrate in the following pages – that are very useful for understanding not only the arc of the trial in its strictest sense, but also the strategies of self-defense employed by the prisoner. The opening of the *Archivio della Congregazione per la dottrina della fede* – the Archive of the Holy Office – in 1998, and the subsequent development of studies on the Inquisition now offers the possibility of reconsidering old questions about Bruno's trial and death, starting from this newly available documentary evidence about the *modus operandi* of the Holy Office in the early modern era.[16]

In the earlier period of the renewal of studies on the Inquisition, between the 1970s and 1980s, perhaps partially as a reaction to the excessive distortions of the *leyenda negra*, historians – while becoming aware of the possible distortions ensuing from the cultural and linguistic gaps that often separated judges and defendants – tended to place too much faith in the overall transparency, procedural consistency and operational unity of the Holy Office and its processes. The Inquisition's penchant for averting abuses ("Suggestive questioning [...] was to be scrupulously avoided"; "Testimony [...] was to be reported verbatim") and record keeping is well summarized in the distinguished scholar John Tedeschi's foundational work. To the question he himself poses, "Could not inquisitors have attempted to suppress or distort information so that their activity would remain from contemporaries and posterity alike?" Tedeschi answered: "On the contrary, it was strict Holy Office practice to preserve detailed records of all its proceedings from first summons to the final sentencing." It was also easy to believe these records were inclusive and complete because "the inquisitors did not feel that they had anything to hide."[17]

However, the fact is that the faith traditionally placed by scholars in the legal consistency and overall transparency of the application of inquisitorial procedures conflicts not only with what we know about the fluidity of judiciary procedures in the early modern era, but also with the growing amount of information emerging about the daily functioning of the *officium fidei* in the context of a culture and an idea of rights that were quite different from today. Judges were empowered with very broad procedural discretion in that period, and freely used the concrete procedural "exception" as a tool to redefine the rules and general legal principles of the detailed, and often cumbersome, framework of canon law and procedures that presided over the activities of the Inquisition, an inheritance from the medieval past. As Thomas Mayer has observed:

> Although the Inquisition had lots of rules, and regularities can be observed in its procedure, it was also rife with almost infinite variations and subtleties, and the rules were constantly subject to reinterpretation. The complete process by which the Congregation managed its decision making is obscure, and likely to remain so. [...] To say that any act in a Holy Office case was illegal or improper is an almost meaningless statement. As the ambassadors to the pope never tired of complaining, it could be hard to predict what the Inquisition might do, and almost impossible to discern the principles behind its actions.[18]

Furthermore, we now know that heated conflicts regularly took place both within the Congregation of the Holy Office and between it and the papacy, ever since its establishment by Pope Paul III in 1542. These clashes were bitter at times, moved by pride of identity, strenuous defense of the arguments for orthodoxy, broad autonomy of address, providential ideology, and personal rivalries and jealousy. The leaders of the Holy Office were willing to manipulate both procedures and evidence, even and especially when it came to choosing a new pope – as we will see, this is what happened to Cardinal Reginald Pole in 1549 and Cardinal Giovanni Morone in 1555. In the middle decades of the 16th century the institutional secrecy of the Holy Office and its tribunals rendered it effectively free of any form of control, and therefore able to carve out an almost absolute autonomy with respect to papal authority.[19]

Accepting this evidence does not imply acceptance of the representation of the Roman Inquisition as a bloody machine of death, lacking any legal dignity and moved by blind and irrational punitive spite. This updated historiographical knowledge made available from the Inquisition's archives does, however, make it possible to state that when researching a trial it is no longer possible to assume that all of the elements of the trial are present in the documentation, even where it appears to be complete. Neither can we hypothesize that the judges of the faith made their decisions based solely on the current legal standards or on evidence that emerged in the trial, working as they did in the context of a procedural consistency that, compared to today's standards, scarcely existed even at the height of the era of codifications.

§

This book was written to argue several hypotheses that contribute to reopening the historiographical debate about the death of Giordano Bruno. It does not systematically present a collection of studies on his trial, nor does it present the full panorama of sources and open problems. I only take results from the available material that I consider useful for reopening old questions and proposing new ones, at the same time developing some conjectures to be examined in further research. In particular, I intend to shed light here on the role played in the Bruno trial by the one who was, on a factual but also methodological level, an external "spy."[20] A character who until now has been regarded with suspicion, but has remained at the margins of historiographical reconstructions: the Capuchin friar Celestino da Verona, who was in prison with Bruno during the Venetian phase of the trial (1592–1593), and who emerges as his key accuser. Celestino, in turn, for unknown reasons, also ends up falling victim to the Holy Office, being condemned to death as a relapsed heretic in September 1599: four months before Bruno's execution.

The text is divided in three parts, building on both published and unpublished documentation. Part 1 rereads the inquisitorial trial against Giordano Bruno, recalling unresolved problems and questions, and proposing an overall interpretive scheme. Part 2 recapitulates what is known about Celestino da Verona, enriched by unpublished documents, and formulates a new interpretation of the Capuchin's relationship with the Holy Office during the Bruno trial in the 1590s. Part 3 is dedicated to a detailed look at the events of 1599, the final year of both Celestino and Bruno's lives, and follows the parallel developments in each figure's story.

It is said that there are no coincidences. If we apply this perspective to the case of Giordano Bruno, which on its surface appears rife with coincidences, then we must accept that human actions and decisions are behind everything that took place, incomprehensible or unpalatable though they may be, and that many of these remain – and likely will remain – unknowable. However, when the trial itself is placed in the broader context of culture, politics, religion, and the newly accessible view of the inner workings of the Roman Inquisition, it is at least possible to draw some very plausible hypotheses about what happened to Giordano Bruno. That is what this book sets out to do, and in doing so, to restore the image of Giordano Bruno to something closer to what must have been the reality – a brilliant, idealistic, prolific, provocative, and even reckless philosopher, caught up in a system that was set up against him from the start and worked by its own rules, in strict secrecy – the Roman Inquisition. In the tribunal of the Holy Office, at the height of the Counter-Reformation, Giordano Bruno's proud and fierce self-defense, "I will tell the truth," was in fact the warrant for his own death sentence.

Notes

1 On the construction of the "martyriology" around the figure of Bruno between the *Risorgimento* and Liberal Italy – which had at its base the conflict with the popes' claim of temporal power over the Italian peninsula – see Anna Foa, *Giordano Bruno*, Bologna, il Mulino, 1998 and Massimo Bucciantini, *Campo dei Fiori. Storia di un monumento maledetto*, Turin, Einaudi, 2015.

2 Michele Ciliberto, *Bruno, il processo, la morte*, in «Rivista di storia della filosofia», 2012, n. 1, now in Id., *Italia laica. La costruzione della libertà dei moderni*, Roma, Edizioni di storia e letteratura, 2012, pp. 143–167, p. 146. Complete historiographical accounts on the 'Bruno Renaissance' may be found in Id., *Giordano Bruno*, Rome and Bari, Laterza, 2005[2], pp. 259 sgg.; Id., *Bruno tra mito e storia*, in «I Tatti Studies. Essays in the Renaissance», 1997, n. 7, pp. 175–190; Id., *Morire «martire» e «volentieri». Interpretazione del processo di Giordano Bruno*, in *Humanistica. Per Cesare Vasoli*, edited by Fabrizio Meroi, Elisabetta Scapparone, Florence, Olschki, 2004, pp. 172–205, now in Id., *Pensare per contrari. Disincanto e utopia nel Rinascimento*, Rome, Edizioni di storia e letteratura, 2005, pp. 325–363; Id., *Introduzione*, in *Giordano Bruno, Le ombre delle idee. Il canto di Circe. Il sigillo dei sigilli*, translation and notes by Nicoletta Tirinnanzi, Milan, Rizzoli, 2006[4]; Id., *Il sapiente furore. Vita di Giordano Bruno*, Milan, Adelphi, 2020[2].

3 Michele Carcani, *Il Tevere e le sue inondazioni dall'origine di Roma fino ai nostri giorni*, Rome, dalla Tipografia romana, 1875, pp. 53 ff.; Margherita Fratarcangeli, *Giovanni Fontana e la sua stirpe: edifici d'acqua e inondazioni del Tevere*, in *Studi sui Fontana. Una dinastia di architetti ticinesi a Roma tra Manierismo e Barocco*, edited by Marcello Fagiolo, Giuseppe Bonaccorso, Rome, Gangemi, 2009, pp. 339–354, p. 341.

4 Tiziano Ascari, *Cesare d'Este, duca di Modena e Reggio*, in *Dizionario biografico degli italiani*, Rome, Istituto della Enciclopedia italiana, 1960–2020, vol. XXIV, 1980, *ad vocem*.

5 See Franco Motta, *Bellarmino. Una teologia politica della Controriforma*, Brescia, Morcelliana, 2005, p. 568. On Clement VIII's politics towards Jews see Marina Caffiero, Anna Esposito, Tersilio Leggio, *Gli ebrei nello Stato della Chiesa. Insediamenti e mobilità (secoli XIV-XVIII)*, Padua, Esedra, 2012.

6 F. Motta, *Bellarmino*, cit., p. 569.

7 See the overall interpretation proposed by Luigi Firpo in *Il processo di Giordano Bruno*, edited by Diego Quaglioni, Rome, Salerno editrice, 1993 (hereafter *Processo*).

8 Ivi, p. 111.

9 Ivi, p. 94.

10 The reference is to a volume by Adriano Prosperi which marked a turning point in Italian historiography of the Counter-Reformation: *Tribunali della coscienza. Inquisitori, confessori, missionari*, Turin, Einaudi, 2009[2].

11 M. Ciliberto, *Italia laica*, cit., p. 145.

12 As argued by the then-prefect and custodian of the Vatican Secret Archives Angelo Mercati, in *Il sommario del processo di Giordano Bruno. Con appendice di documenti sull'eresia e l'Inquisizione a Modena nel secolo XVI*, Vatican City, Biblioteca apostolica vaticana, 1942, p. 1.

13 See Luigi Firpo, *Il processo di Giordano Bruno*, in «Rivista storica italiana», 1948–1949, n. LX, pp. 542–597; n. LXI, pp. 5–59, and the *Processo*. An updated reconsideration of the history of the trial is the entry *Processo* by Laura Fedi in *Giordano Bruno. Parole, concetti, immagini*, scientific direction by Michele Ciliberto, 3 vols., Pisa, Edizioni della Normale, 2014, volume II, *sub voce*.

14 See the *Avvertenza* of the editor in *Processo*, p. xxiv. On the multiple "difficulties and obstacles" encountered by Firpo in the course of his research see Diego Quaglioni, *Il Bruno di Luigi Firpo*, in *Giordano Bruno. Note filologiche e storiografiche. I giornata Luigi Firpo 3 marzo 1994*, Florence, Olschki, 1996, pp. 37–55.

15 The document was published for the first time by A. Mercati (who discovered it) in *Il sommario del processo di Giordano Bruno*. It was considered "the *sommario* of the Brunian trial" also by Firpo (*Processo*, p. 3), who corrected errors in the Mercati edition. I will elaborate further on recent historiographical revisions in the text.

16 For an initial balance of the historiographic reassessment produced following the opening of this archive, see Simon Ditchfield, *Of Dancing Cardinals and* mestizo *Madonnas: Reconfiguring the History of Roman Catholicism in the Early Modern Period*, in «Journal of Early Modern History», 2004, n. 8, pp. 386–408; Elena Bonora, *L'archivio dell'Inquisizione e gli studi storici: primi bilanci e prospettive a dieci anni dall'apertura*, in «Rivista storica italiana», 2008, n. 3, pp. 968–1002; Michaela Valente, *Nuove ricerche e interpretazioni sul Sant'Uffizio a più di dieci anni dall'apertura dell'Archivio*, in «Rivista di storia della Chiesa in Italia», 2012, n. 2, pp. 569–592; *L'inquisizione romana e i suoi archivi: A vent'anni dall'apertura dell'ACDF*, edited by Alejandro Cifres, Rome, Gangemi editore, 2019.

17 The reference is to his collections of papers *The Prosecution of Heresy: Collected Studies on the Inquisition in Early Modern Italy*, Binghamton, NY, Medieval and Renaissance Texts and Studies, 1991, quotes from the pp. 48 and 131.

18 Thomas F. Mayer, *The Roman Inquisition: A Papal Bureaucracy and Its Laws in the Age of Galileo*, Philadelphia, University of Pennsylvania Press, 2013, pp. 36–37.

19 Massimo Firpo, Germano Maifreda, *L'eretico che salvo la Chiesa. Il cardinal Giovanni Morone e le origini della Controriforma*, Torino, Einaudi, 2019.

20 On Carlo Ginzburg's 'evidential paradigm' – built on the observation of some similarities in the detective methods of Freud, Morelli, and Sherlock Holmes – as a research strategy based on reading clues and traces embedded in the historical record in order to reveal otherwise hidden information, see the classic collection *Clues, Myths, and the Historical Method. With a New Preface*, translated by John and Anne C. Tedeschi, Baltimore, MD, Johns Hopkins University Press, 2013.

References

Tiziano Ascari, *Cesare d'Este, duca di Modena e Reggio*, in *Dizionario biografico degli italiani*, cit. vol. XXIV, 1980.

Elena Bonora, *L'archivio dell'Inquisizione e gli studi storici: primi bilanci e prospettive a dieci anni dall'apertura*, in «Rivista storica italiana», 2008, n. 3, pp. 968–1002.

Massimo Bucciantini, *Campo dei Fiori. Storia di un monumento maledetto*, Turin, Einaudi, 2015.

Marina Caffiero, Anna Esposito, Tersilio Leggio, *Gli ebrei nello Stato della Chiesa. Insediamenti e mobilità (secoli XIV-XVIII)*, Padua, Esedra, 2012.

Michele Carcani, *Il Tevere e le sue inondazioni dall'origine di Roma fino ai nostri giorni*, Rome, dalla Tipografia romana, 1875.

Michele Ciliberto, *Bruno tra mito e storia*, «I Tatti Studies. Essays in the Renaissance», 1997, n. 7, pp. 175–190.

Michele Ciliberto, *Giordano Bruno*, Rome and Bari, Laterza, 2005^2.

Michele Ciliberto, *Pensare per contrari. Disincanto e utopia nel Rinascimento*, Rome, Edizioni di storia e letteratura, 2005.

Michele Ciliberto, *Introduzione*, in *Giordano Bruno, Le ombre delle idee. Il canto di Circe. Il sigillo dei sigilli*, translation and notes by Nicoletta Tirinnanzi, Milan, Rizzoli, 2006^4, pp. 5–34.

Michele Ciliberto, *Italia laica. La costruzione della libertà dei modern*i, Roma, Edizioni di storia e letteratura, 2012.

Michele Ciliberto, *Il sapiente furore. Vita di Giordano Bruno*, Milan, Adelphi, 2020^2.

Simon Ditchfield, *Of Dancing Cardinals and mestizo Madonnas: Reconfiguring the History of Roman Catholicism in the Early Modern Period*, in «Journal of Early Modern History», 2004, n. 8, pp. 386–408.

Dizionario biografico degli italiani, Rome, Istituto della Enciclopedia italiana, 1960–2020, 100 vols.
Laura Fedi, entry *Processo*, in *Giordano Bruno. Parole, concetti, immagini*, scientific direction by Michele Ciliberto, 3 vols., Pisa, Edizioni della Normale, 2014, volume II, *sub voce*.
Luigi Firpo, *Il processo di Giordano Bruno*, in «Rivista storica italiana», 1948–1949, n. LX, pp. 542–597; n. LXI, pp. 5–59.
Luigi Firpo, *Il processo di Giordano Bruno*, edited by Diego Quaglioni, Rome, Salerno editrice, 1993.
Massimo Firpo, Germano Maifreda, *L'eretico che salvo la Chiesa. Il cardinal Giovanni Morone e le origini della Controriforma*, Torino, Einaudi, 2019.
Anna Foa, *Giordano Bruno*, Bologna, il Mulino, 1998.
Margherita Fratarcangeli, *Giovanni Fontana e la sua stirpe: edifici d'acqua e inondazioni del Tevere*, in *Studi sui Fontana. Una dinastia di architetti ticinesi a Roma tra Manierismo e Barocco*, edited by Marcello Fagiolo, Giuseppe Bonaccorso, Rome, Gangemi, 2009, pp. 339–354.
Carlo Ginzburg, *Clues, Myths, and the Historical Method. With a New Preface*, translated by John Tedeschi and Anne C. Tedeschi, Baltimore, MD, Johns Hopkins University Press, 2013.
L'inquisizione romana e i suoi archivi: A vent'anni dall'apertura dell'ACDF, edited by Alejandro Cifres, Rome, Gangemi editore, 2019.
Thomas F. Mayer, *The Roman Inquisition: A Papal Bureaucracy and Its Laws in the Age of Galileo*, Philadelphia, University of Pennsylvania Press, 2013.
Angelo Mercati, *Il sommario del processo di Giordano Bruno. Con appendice di documenti sull'eresia e l'Inquisizione a Modena nel secolo XVI*, Vatican City, Biblioteca apostolica vaticana, 1942.
Franco Motta, *Bellarmino. Una teologia politica della Controriforma*, Brescia, Morcelliana, 2005.
Adriano Prosperi, *Tribunali della coscienza. Inquisitori, confessori, missionari*, Turin, Einaudi, 2009^2.
Diego Quaglioni, *Il Bruno di Luigi Firpo*, in *Giordano Bruno. Note filologiche e storiografiche. I giornata Luigi Firpo 3 marzo 1994*, Florence, Olschki, 1996, pp. 37–55.
John Tedeschi, *The Prosecution of Heresy: Collected Studies on the Inquisition in Early Modern Italy*, Binghamton, NY, Medieval and Renaissance Texts and Studies, 1991.Michaela Valente, *Nuove ricerche e interpretazioni sul Sant'Uffizio a più di dieci anni dall'apertura dell'Archivio*, in «Rivista di storia della Chiesa in Italia», 2012, n. 2, pp. 569–592.

Part 1

“Because When It Was Time He Wanted to be a Captain”

1 "My Profession Has Been and Is Letters and All Science." Profile of a Defendant

Who was the "small man, thin faced, with a touch of black beard, about 40 years old"[1] arrested by the Venetian Inquisition in the late spring of 1592? Where did he come from? What was he doing within the borders of the Serenissima? Despite the large number of studies about the life and thought of the foremost philosopher of the Italian Renaissance, some questions remain open, and perhaps will remain so forever.

There is a circular relationship between Giordano Bruno's biography, the interpretation of his work, and the conduct of the trial. Bruno's death, the "extreme point which seems to concentrate and resolve his entire destiny,"[2] has inevitably influenced the interpretation of the life and thought of a philosopher who was destined to become a genuine myth, deeply rooted in the European consciousness. From then on secular culture would exalt him as a pioneer of free thought and a martyr of Catholic intolerance. In this "vulgate" his intellectual legacy would be interpreted as the legacy of someone who had liberated thought from religious dogma; to be counted among the foundational moments in the birth of modern philosophy.[3]

All told, sketching the story of Bruno's life prior to his arrest in Venice at the end of May 1592 is certainly not simple. Despite rigorous research carried out in the archives of the many places all over Europe where this tireless traveler lived and worked, the documentation that has emerged remains desperately scarce. Even today, much of what we know still depends on the official record of the trial: that is, on statements made in a situation that was not at all neutral, in which Bruno had every interest in smoothing over the most awkward corners of his life's path – and highlighting others in the hope that they might reassure his accusers.

A Restless Novice

Giordano Bruno linked his work to his origins with great pride: he used the adjective "Nolano" or *Nolanus* to define himself or his philosophy.[4] "My profession has been, and is, that of letters, and all sciences," he declared in his first trial deposition before the Venetian judges. At the same time he stated that his baptismal name was Filippo, and that he had been born in

DOI: 10.4324/9781003026082-3

1548, his father having been a soldier named Giovanni, and his mother being Fraulissa Savolina.[5] Both parents were dead at the time of the trial, and Bruno never mentioned the existence of any brothers or sisters.

At the end of the 1550s Filippo moved to Naples to continue his grammar studies, which he had excelled at in childhood. In the capital of what was then a part of the Spanish empire he studied "letters in humanities, logic and dialectics" and attended lectures by the Aristotelian Giovan Vincenzo Colle da Sarno. He also sought out scholars who taught outside of the university, such as the Augustinian Father Teofilo da Vairano. He probably witnessed his first inquisitorial burnings at the stake here, pressed in among the crowd. Two were carried out in the capital of Naples – at the time the most populous city of Western Europe after Paris, with ca. 200,000 inhabitants – on March 4, 1564, "with a great throng of people."[6] On that occasion Neapolitan noblemen Gian Francesco Alois and Giovan Bernardino Gargnano were sent to their deaths at the conclusion of a second trial for Calvinist heresy, conducted by inquisitor Giulio Antonio Santori. It was Santori, who shortly thereafter became the cardinal of Santa Severina, who 30 years later would lead the proceeding opened against Bruno – and with the same, tragic outcome.

Bruno took the habit of a Dominican novice in June 1565. He chose the name Giordano for himself in honor of Giordano Crispo, former Prior of the local monastery of San Domenico Maggiore in Naples and a teacher of theology and metaphysics. Entering the monastery, the 17-year-old novice joined a community of some 150 monks. They were organized in a "democratic" form that called for the direct election of the principle governing bodies (Master and Chapter Generals, provincial Masters, monastery Priors) and a community vote on the admission of new novices. The Neapolitan community was probably the most numerous of the male monastic communities in a city that was already inherently turbulent. Embezzlement, theft, rebellion against the rules, and escapes from the monastery were the norm before – and for a long time after – the reforms outlined in the Canons and Decrees of the Council of Trent (1545–1563). All this took place alongside the not infrequent instances of assaults, possession of weapons, murders, and incidents of prostitute visits within the monastery walls that emerge from the papers of contemporary trials prosecuted by the provincial fathers.[7]

Isolation and meditation were not, however, the main reasons that normally spurred adolescents to embrace the life of a regular. Thus a greater attraction must have been exerted – including for Bruno – by the authoritative Dominican intellectual traditions and the opportunity to obtain a "*lettorato*," a degree that conferred the right to teach in the Dominican *Studi*. San Domenico Maggiore included the most important *Studium generale* in Southern Italy. Bruno undoubtedly attended the formal course in theology centered on the Dominican Thomas Aquinas' *Summa Theologica*. The most prestigious medieval treatise on the subject, the *Summa* still had a huge influence on the theology of the 1500s. Daytime work hours were rounded out by recitation of the daily Offices, performance of the liturgical chants, study of the Order's Constitution and Laws, and reading devotional books and biographies of exemplary men. The days were broken up by shared meals, and concluded with a few hours of sleep.

In the dialogue *Cabala del Cavallo Pegaseo* (Cabala of the Pegasean Horse), printed in London in 1585, Bruno would recall how various texts of dubious orthodoxy circulated in the Neapolitan community; writings "about every satyr, faun, melancholic, inebriated and infected by other bile," by vaguely defined "writers of dreams" and "nonsense without any design or meaning at all," authors of "grand prophecies, hidden mysteries, of other secrets and divine arcana to revive the dead, from philosophers' stones and other vanities to mislead those who have little brain."[8] Here Bruno offered a lively satire of Neapolitan – and, more generally, Italian – life in the religious Orders, while at the same time highlighting the crisis of scholastic philosophy's cognitive monopoly within those Orders. This resulted in the circulation of cabbalistic, philosophic-magical, and alchemical literature in the monasteries, accompanied by esoteric practices. More than a trace of this emerges in inquisitorial trials.

Bruno was ordained as a priest in 1573, concluding his theological studies two years later with brilliant results in his final examinations. Yet along with this record as a model student, his years as a novitiate had exposed signs of restlessness which were the subject of a disciplinary investigation by his master, friar Eugenio Gagliardo. On that occasion, Gagliardo confessed to the Venetian inquisitors in 1592, Giordano had "given away some images of saints, which I recall were of saint Catherine of Siena, and perhaps of saint Antonino, if I remember well, and kept only a crucifix." In addition, a "statement" prepared by his teacher, and then, according to Bruno, immediately torn up, had recorded a taunt that he had directed at a novice who read the naive *Historia delle sette alegrezze della Madonna*: "I said [...] that I wondered why he wanted to read a book like that, he would do better to read *Vita de' santi Padri*, or some other book."[9] These are stirrings of religious restlessness in which we are more apt today to discern the effects of reading Erasmus of Rotterdam and the centrality of Christ he advocated,[10] rather than the harbingers of future heretical tendencies.

If we are to believe what Bruno told his Parisian confidant Guillaume Cotin in 1585, in his Neapolitan years he was already cultivating one of his great future passions: mnemonics. During the pontificate of Pius V, and therefore from January 1566 to May 1572, Bruno would be summoned to Rome and accompanied in a carriage, to teach them the art of memory to the pope and Cardinal Scipione Rebiba, who already held a prominent role in the Holy Office. If this episode really took place,[11] it would foreshadow Bruno's use of his knowledge of mnemonics – an ancient discipline, sought after by princes and rulers – to gain influential protection; a strategy which the friar deployed throughout his life until his last arrival in Venice.

Towards the end of 1575 the philosopher was once again caught up in a trial brought against him by the Dominicans. This one was based on more serious elements than those that had aroused the suspicions of his teacher in the previous decade. Later, when facing the Venetian Inquisition, Bruno would downplay the incident:

> The Provincial [Domenico Vita] opened a trial against me regarding some articles – though I am not really certain which articles these were, nor on what particular points, except that he told me they were trying me for heresy, and that it had to do with this matter of the novitiate and more.

The episode of the disposal of the images of saints had therefore not been so easily resolved, and faced with new misgivings about the friar the provincial Father had opened an inquiry. When asked by the Venetian inquisitors to try and imagine which "articles" that investigation might have been concerned with, Bruno defended himself by citing the ill will of some of his fellow monks, claiming that they had purposely misrepresented a conversation he'd had with friar Agostino da Montalcino regarding the dogma of the Trinity.[12]

This episode, which is hard to contextualize because it did not have great significance in the overall economy of the trial, nevertheless changed Bruno's life. It was, in fact, at this juncture that he was summoned to be tried at his Order's Roman monastery of Santa Maria Sopra Minerva. That journey was the prelude to the decisive event of his life: "I removed my habit and left religion," or rather the Dominican Order, "as I doubted that I would not be put in prison."[13] While he was in Rome the situation worsened. He received a warning from Naples that forbidden volumes of the writings of saint Jerome and saint John Chrysostom had been discovered in his cell, "with the commentary of Erasmus restored, which I referred to secretly."[14] These books had been prohibited since 1559, when Paul IV had placed the Dutch humanist's entire production in the Index. In *In Praise of Folly* Erasmus had condemned the excesses of the Marian cult, and in *Handbook of the Militant Christian* he had admonished the reader to appeal only to Christ, defining the veneration of saints as "so un-Christian as to end up resembling superstition."[15] Erasmus therefore put his reader – who in this case had taken care to throw these volumes "into the necessary," or rather into the toilet, before leaving Naples[16] – at risk of referral to the Holy Office, and so to the opening of a full-blown inquisitorial trial for heresy.

The idea of throwing his habit in the bushes and fleeing Rome to the north must have developed in Bruno's mind very quickly, and was also spurred on by a bloody episode that took place in the city. Bruno was accused, by whom we do not know, of a homicide that had been committed by a Dominican friar in the swirl of the crowds drawn to the capital of Catholicism for the Jubilee year of 1575.[17] This prompted his final decision to abandon the Papal States and move, in civilian clothes, towards the heart of immense Europe.

In Trouble in Geneva

In the last quarter of the 16th century the confessional rift opened by Lutheran Reform in Central-Western Europe had consolidated, destined to continue to the present day. Even as he immersed himself in the life of a continent wracked by religious conflicts – but also in the cultivation of his own grand intellectual projects, and with them, his intense hopes for an epochal political and spiritual renewal – Giordano Bruno was considered an apostate in the eyes of his own Order, having abandoned his habit and evaded the authority and justice of his superiors. His flight northward from Rome did not coincide with an immediate decision to leave Italy, where he remained for another two years, occasionally living in monasteries and staying with fellow friars. The status of "fugitive" from a religious Order was anything but unusual in that era of spiritual turbulence and anxieties.

Bruno probably lived by his wits for a time, working as a private tutor. In the meantime he began to develop his first publications. He moved to Venice in 1576, where he lived in Frezzaria, the quarter that was home to many printing houses and publishers. There he had "a certain booklet printed, entitled *De' segni de' tempi* (Of the Signs of Time)," which was perhaps his first publication on the subject of astrology and prophesy.[18] Most importantly, it is possible that Bruno began to formulate his plan to seek a position at the court of Henry III of Valois while he was in Venetian territory. Henry had been the first French ruler to travel through Italy peacefully after many decades of war, deciding to pass triumphantly through northern Italy in 1574, on his return from Poland and on the way to his own country. Here he would be consecrated in the cathedral of Reims prior to ascending to the throne after the death of his brother, the weak and sickly Charles IX. Lavishly honored in Venice two years earlier, Henry, the son of Catherine de' Medici, was known as a cultured man and a patron of the arts and philosophy. For years his court had been open to Italian exiles and refugees, where they carried out the most disparate tasks: there were bankers, merchants, writers, musicians, alchemists, cooks, and perfumers. In a France bloodied by religious wars, the memory of the terrible St. Bartholomew night massacre and the weeks that followed lived on. There had been an uncontrolled slaughter of several thousand people, mostly Calvinists. Hopes for pacification by the new king, however, would soon be disappointed.

Having conceived his plan for reaching Paris, Bruno first went to Milan, and then moved towards Lyon through the Mont-Cenis pass. He would tell the inquisitors:

> When I was in Chambéry, I went to stay at the Order's monastery, and finding myself treated very coldly and discussing this with an Italian priest who was there, he told me, "Be warned that you will not find kindness of any sort in these parts, and what's more further ahead you will find even less.[19]

Thus warned about the precarious security conditions on the roads of southern France – due to the military and religious riots which made the *Union des protestants du Midi* a territory that was out of the French crown's control – Bruno decided to temporarily head towards the "Protestant Rome": Geneva.

Despite the tenuous documentation available, the philosopher's tribulations within the borders of Genevan territory can serve as a useful precedent for understanding his attitude towards justices of the faith. Bruno was not a sympathizer of Calvinism, and in any case, the fascination of the Italian exiles with the French reformer's innovations they had once nurtured had by this point become disillusioned. In 1553 Calvin had sent Miguel Servetus and his books to the stake, displaying the same intolerance which in those years was sending the heterodox to their deaths at the hands of the Mediterranean Inquisitions. The climate in Geneva darkened further after Calvin's death in 1564 with the confirmation of the political and religious leadership of his successor, Théodore de Bèze.

For easily understandable reasons, Bruno told the Venetian inquisitors that he had not gone to Geneva to practice Calvinism ("because I did not know what religion it was"), but that he had been attracted only by the Republic's reputation for philosophical tolerance ("and because of this, I wished to be there as soon as possible to live in freedom and be safe, rather than for another purpose"[20]). However, the information that emerges from the Genevan archives describes a different reality. Bruno joined a group of Italian refugees, and found protection from the Marquis of Vico, Gian Galeazzo Caracciolo, a Neapolitan noble who had left Italy in 1551 to embrace Reform. Employed as a proofreader, he formally became a Calvinist and joined the local Italian Church. However, he immediately broke with the Calvinist authorities, and was jailed for printing a slanderous text about a minister of the Geneva Church, Antoine de Faye, in which he pointed out errors de Faye had made during a lesson held at the Academy.

Brought before the Consistory – the body which oversaw ecclesiastical discipline and also functioned as a tribunal of morals and customs – Bruno was sentenced to tearing up the libelous text with his own hands and to acknowledging his wrongdoing, with the penalty of being excluded from participation in the Calvinist Eucharistic rites, and imprisonment. In various hearings, Giordano Bruno reiterated his good intentions, acknowledged his guilt, and asked to be readmitted to the celebration of the sacraments.[21] The sentence handed down in Geneva in August 1579 required, in addition to his retraction in the Consistory and the destruction of the criminal text, that "he ask forgiveness from God and from justice" as well from the Minister he had offended.[22] Some years later, at Paris in 1586, he told librarian Guillaume Cotou of having left the trial in Geneva "bending my knee to the ground." This is exactly the same thing – as we will see – that Bruno would do several years later in Venice before the inquisitors, who in private conversation, Cotin noted, he always called "ignoramuses"; individuals who, being unable to understand his philosophy, would certainly condemn it as "*héretique*."[23]

This episode has important significance. In Geneva, as was later the case in Venice, Bruno was – or declared himself – willing to bow to the dictates of a tribunal of faith to which he attributed no legitimacy at all, as recalled by the contemptuous words reported by Cotin and evidenced in many passages of his works. Retracting – or declaring himself fully willing to retract – his own positions, the philosopher pragmatically placed his personal freedom – or his survival – before intellectual consistency and pride in his own convictions. Something very different occurred in Rome. Here Bruno found himself in the heart of Catholicism, in the presence of the pope, and in one of the most authoritative and influential Tribunals in the world. To Bruno it was the place meant for the concrete implementation of the project of universal political and religious reform which he had been developing during over a decade of travel and research in the most important courts of Europe. As we shall see, he also declared his willingness to abjure in Rome: but he was later denied by the facts. What prevented Bruno from behaving in Rome as he had in Geneva or in Venice? What was different, and what had changed in the interim? We shall return later to reflect on these questions.

After his retraction Bruno left the city of Calvin. He went to Lyon, and then to Toulouse at the end of 1581. Always driven from place to place – as he would tell the Inquisitors – by the chaos of civil wars, he arrived in Paris. "They had me read a special lesson to introduce myself and to test me," he recalled: this was a philosophy lesson concerning Aquinas' *Summa* which would finally bring him fame. Shortly thereafter he was summoned by Henry III, "seeking to discover whether or not the memory I possessed and professed was natural or the result of magical arts."[24] Thus it was mnemonics that brought Bruno close to the supreme political spheres in the French capital: that "art," perched between classical culture and natural philosophy, and not exempt from traces of magic and the occult, was considered useful for effective oratory and persuasion, as well as for victories in diplomatic and intellectual disputes.[25] These aspects could not help but stimulate the curiosity of the king of France and Poland, himself an avid reader of Montaigne. The king had already founded a Court academy where the capital's intellectual and social élites mingled with poets and scholars. "And with what I told him and made him try himself," the philosopher later recounted, the king "understood that [my memory] did not derive from magic arts, but from science."[26]

Protected by the king and supported by a network of friendships, Bruno's intelligence thrived in Paris. The quality of his published work in those years testifies to this: the booklet of mnemonics *Cantus Circaeus* (Incantations of Circe) and then particularly the *De umbris idearum* (On the Shadow of Ideas), a treatise on gnoseology and the memory arts in which Bruno claimed that human knowledge is structurally vague and that truth cannot be known directly.[27] The volume was dedicated to King Henry III in 1582 as thanks for the protection extended to its author and for his nomination as the royal "special and provisioned reader." This office included the honor of directly instructing the king in literary, philosophical, historical, and political matters. Printed in a richly illustrated edition, the *De umbris idearum* remains one of Bruno's most famous works, as attested to by the large number of examples now to be found in libraries across Europe.

The philosopher also delivered *Candelaio* (The Candlebearer) to the presses of the French capital in 1582. This work, written in Italian and laced with profanity, is his only comedy. Bruno parodies the alchemists and pedants, superstitious people and hypocrites who moved within the popular heart of his Spanish Naples. He may have begun writing the work as early as the years of his studies in Naples. The work enjoyed moderate fortune in France, where it was reprinted in 1633 by Pierre Menard, and thus exerted a marginal influence on *Pédant joué* by Cyrano de Bergerac.[28]

The next stop in Giordano Bruno's travels was London. To justify his reasons for this suspicious decision before the Venetian inquisitors – Queen Elizabeth I had been declared a heretic and excommunicated, along with her Protestant subjects, by Pius V's bull *Regnans in excelsis* – he invoked the need to escape from the French religious wars:

> Because of the chaos that arose later, I took my leave and with a letter from the King (Henry III) himself I went to England to stay with His Majesty's ambassador, who is called the lord of the Manciviera, Michel de Castelnuovo by name; in which house I did nothing, other than to stand for his gentleman.[29]

Frances Yates, a leading Bruno scholar, saw in Bruno's departure from France the desire to carry out a specific political-religious mission entrusted to him by Henry. That assignment would have consisted of persuading Queen Elizabeth and her court of the need to promote a spiritual and political reunion of a tolerant Christianity steeped in hermeticism, creating an alternative to the Church of Rome.[30]

This suggestive interpretation is greeted with skepticism in the most recent historiography.[31] Although the idea that Henry III had entrusted his "*lettor straordinario*" with a task to carry out in England cannot be ruled out, it is more likely that Bruno was attracted to crossing the Channel by his intellectual and political curiosity, as well as by the search for employment opportunities at another Italianized court. In 1559 Queen Elizabeth succeeded her half-sister Mary, who had tried to violently restore Catholicism in England after their father, Henry VIII, had brought about the separation of the local Church from Rome. Elizabeth's pride, her sense of royalty, and her will to restore Protestantism as a beacon against superstition and ignorance could not help but seduce Bruno. In London he was introduced into the Queen's inner circles, and had close relations with the poet Philip Sidney and the scholar and translator John Florio, born in England but raised on mainland Europe by his former Franciscan turned Protestant pastor father, Michelangelo, in addition to meeting occultist John Dee.

Giordano Bruno dedicated several of the texts that he printed in London to the nobleman Michel de Castelneau, Henry III's ambassador at the English court. Among these were *Ars reminiscendi*, a return to the theme of mnemonics; the *Explicatio triginta sigillorum* and the *Sigillus sigillorum*, in which he continued his investigation of the knowledge process, which is illustrated as unitary; and the first three philosophical dialogues in Italian: *Cena de le Ceneri* (The Ash Wednesday Supper), *De la causa, principio ed uno* (On Cause, principle and unity) and *De l'infinito, universo e mondi* (On the Infinite Universe and Worlds). Appearing between 1583 and 1584, these works sought to present the central nucleus of Bruno's thought on cosmology, being, physics and ethics. Bruno's vision of the universe as "one, infinite, in motion," not static and distinct from God, is elaborated here. "One therefore is the heavens, the immense space, the bosom, the universal continent, the ethereal region through which everything converses and moves." The goal was to clearly distinguish philosophical research from the boundaries imposed by the Judeo-Christian scriptural tradition, in particular freeing cosmology from any religious influence.[32]

On the political level, however, the work of Bruno's that represents the greatest break with the European situation at the time was the *Spaccio de la Bestia trionfante* (Expulsion of the Triumphant Beast), also printed in 1584. The author was already preparing to leave England, frustrated by his experience in a variety of ways. He felt that his research had been given a disappointing reception across the English Channel, and he had clashed with his colleagues at the University of Oxford, who accused him of having plagiarized *De vita* by Marsilio Ficino while teaching a course. In the *Spaccio*, the Egyptian religion, which he preferred, was directly compared to Judaism and even more so to Christianity, both of which had renounced the knowledge of magic and according to Bruno had thus lost the ability to communicate directly with the divinity in the language of nature, resulting in only darkness and ignorance.[33]

> The [Egyptian] sages knew God to be in things – Bruno wrote in the *Spaccio* – [...] and [they] in all respects, each according to their own reasoning, contemplated the divinity; and they knew how, from the species that are in the womb of nature, to receive the benefits that they desired from it; which like the sea and rivers give fish, from the deserts wild animals, metals from the mines, apples from the trees; so from certain parts, from certain animals, from certain beasts, from certain plants are offered certain fates, virtues, fortunes and impressions.[34]

Underneath its anti-Catholic and anti-Roman shell, the *Spaccio* delivered an invitation to intellectual and moral renewal as an essential requirement of the peace Europe hoped for, and for overcoming the continent's spiritual and civic crisis. Reform is criticized as the manifestation of intellectual atrophy, summed up by the pedantry of the "Lutherans." This is followed by a long indictment against opposing religious extremists and the extremism of the Protestants, in the hope that the political and military defeat of the Calvinists in England, France and Holland would lead to the long-awaited pacification.[35]

Equally radical, and perhaps even more so, is the message contained in *Cabala del cavallo Pegaseo*, published in early 1585. This book contains all of the philosopher's intolerance for Christian dogma, representing – as Michele Ciliberto has observed – the final step in the "radical liquidation of Christianity in its entirety." This was a project that Bruno completed in the years he spent in the English capital, where he saw the local Church riven by conflicts between Anglicans and Puritans (though such labels are here used retrospectively for the sake of clarity).[36] A "lament" about the negative consequences of the victory of Judeo-Christian theology over the "civil" and "natural" religions of the ancient world, the *Cabala* enjoyed very little circulation in its day. Bruno himself ended up "rejecting" it in 1591, on the eve of his return to Italy, because "it displeased the common people without pleasing the scholars."[37]

The last works from the London period were a determining factor in the formation of the durable, as well as inaccurate, image of an atheist Bruno who mocked all faiths. Their development must have fueled his isolation and driven him to the decision to return to the continent after publishing the *Eroici furori* (Heroic Frenzies), his final English text, in which the philosopher returned to the less explosive terrain of gnoseology.

Towards the East

In the last eight years of his life as a free man Giordano Bruno tirelessly traveled across Europe, moving through lands and cities dominated by political conflicts. There he encountered universities internally divided by ideological extremism, populations caught up in outbursts of fanaticism, and princes unable to find stable solutions to the most burning issue of their time: the pacification of religious conflicts. His journeys on the continent constitute the compass for a tireless intellectual search, and at the same time made him an acute calibrator of the era's disagreements.

The first incident Bruno had to face upon his return to France was the excommunication of Henry of Bourbon, King of Navarre, in September 1585. This event also turned out to be fraught with consequences for his inquisitorial troubles. In recent decades this small kingdom at the foot of the Pyrenees had officially adopted the Reformed rite and banned the Catholic rite, thanks to the efforts of Jeanne d'Albret, Henry's mother and a fervent follower of Calvin. After marrying Antoin of Bourbon, Jeanne then transmitted the inheritance of Navarre to the blood prince. Henry succeeded her on the throne in 1572.

The bull *Ab immensa*, issued by Pope Sixtus V to excommunicate the King of Navarre, was a reaction to the destruction of places of worship and Roman ecclesiastical property in the Navarre territories. This branded the future king of France, at that time the leader of a Huguenot faction, as a *relapsed* heretic. In fact, Henry had adhered to Reform in his youth, under the influence of his mother. He then converted to Catholicism in 1572, thus saving his life during the bloody massacre of San Bartolomeo just days after his marriage to the Catholic Margaret of Valois. Catholics considered the union sacrilegious and scandalous because it was formalized without waiting for papal dispensation, even though *reine Margot* was the sister of the current King of France, Charles IX, and therefore a close relative of her husband, as well adhering to a different confession.

Just a few years later the Bourbon was moved to convert back to Calvinism by political opportunism. As a recidivist heretic – and a heresiarch, having abolished the Catholic rite in his domains – Henry of Navarre was essentially subject to a death sentence from the Holy Office. In fact, the bull of excommunication itself was the meticulous work of Giulio Antonio Santori, the cardinal of Santa Severina, who in the future would be the supreme inquisitor for the trial of Giordano Bruno.

Bruno arrived in Paris in the midst of the controversy stirred up by *Ab immensa*. The "Most Christian King" Henry III refused to publish it. In his judgement, Navarre was the only plausible option for succession to the throne in the absence of direct heirs. His namesake blood relative prince had, moreover, spent a good part of his adolescence at court, growing up in the company of the entire royal family, under the watchful eye of the very powerful "governess of France," Caterina de' Medici. The expedience of his prior religious conversions hinted that the Bourbon's ascension to the throne – Henry's ancestry was directly connected to the venerated figure of Louis IX the Saint – would give France a new Catholic king.

Bruno remained in the French capital for about a year; "At my expense, however, for most of the time."[38] During the first phase of the trial, which was underway when the Bourbon was still seen as a relapsed heretic and heresiarch in the eyes of the Holy Office, Bruno tried to minimize his involvements in France with the Venetian inquisitors. But things had not really gone that way.

While the final conflict for succession to the throne of France between the Calvinist Henry of Navarre and the Catholic Henry of Guise was erupting, Bruno had kept close relations in Paris with two Italian Navarrans: Jacob Corbinelli, Henry III's trusted man, and Piero Del Bene, to whom he dedicated two brief works in Latin. These two were important figures on the French political scene, where the moderate party of *politiques* – which counted Jean Bodin as a member – made itself an advocate for tolerance and coexistence between the two religions, Catholicism and Calvinism, supporting the candidacy of Navarre for succession to the throne. In addition to Bruno, Corbinelli and Del Bene also had ongoing relations and political affinities with Giovan Vincenzo Pinelli, a Venetian who led an intellectual circle at Padua which Bruno may have attended when he returned to Italy.[39]

It is very likely that Bruno had hopes for the future King Henry IV – whom he never met – not only for his possible inclusion in a circle of beneficial relationships, but also and more ambitiously in hope of the new King's support in the realization of his project of religious pacification and reform. By now this program was clearly delineated in his mind, in the terms proposed in the works he had published in recent years or reworked during his later stay in Germany. Proceeding from the need to establish religious peace on the continent, now felt by many in a Europe torn apart by clashes, this program would in all probability lead to his final decision to return to Italy.[40] According to Bruno, the way to pursue his goal was to bring the world together under a single ethical and philosophical religion, free from dogmas and therefore from heresies, but fundamentally Catholic. In fact Bruno preferred the Roman confession, albeit subject to a profound reform. Just as his first accuser, the patrician Giovanni Mocenigo, would later testify before the Venetian Holy Office:

> He showed designs of wanting to be the author of a new sect under the name of a new philosophy [...] I heard him say that the procedure that the Church uses now is not the one used by the apostles, because they, with their preaching and examples of good lives converted the people, who now do not want to be Catholic because you have to endure punishment and penalties, because force is used and not love, and that this world could not endure like this, because there was nothing if not ignorance and no religion was good; that he liked Catholicism more than the others, but that it was still in need of great regulation, and that it was not well this way, and that soon the world would see a general reform of itself, because it was impossible for so much corruption to last, and that he hoped for great things from the King of Navarre, and that he wanted to hurry and expose his works, and take credit for this path, because when it was time he wanted to be a captain (*capitano*).[41]

Bruno ardently hoped that Henry of Bourbon would help him achieve his goal of general world reform. In fact, the suspicion of Navarrism was one of the fundamental elements of his indictment, and could have plausibly motivated Santa Severina's early interest in the case. But we will return to that at the appropriate moment.

The unstable situation he encountered upon returning to Paris continuously risked descending into violence, as demonstrated by Henry III's cruel death in 1589, and convinced Bruno to abandon French territory. Since he had fled Rome he had only traveled north, perhaps following the footsteps of other Italians who had seduced the courts of the Valois and the Tudors before him, or perhaps to explore political regimes and cultural ambiences he considered more liberal and creative than those of the Mediterranean or Germany.

His forays eastward seemed to confirm these apprehensions. In the summer of 1586 he stopped in Mainz, Wiesbaden, and then Marburg, a Protestant city where he enrolled in the prestigious *Studium*, perhaps to benefit from the protection Wilhelm of Hessen granted to astronomical research. However, he was nevertheless forbidden from giving public readings. Perhaps the rector of the University, a Lutheran, had become suspicious after reading the strange phrase *Theologiae Doctor Romanensis* which Bruno had appended to his name when he registered.[42]

He left Hessen, still headed east, but religious conflict seemed to follow him. He explained his next moves to the inquisitors in these words:

> I went to Wittenberg in Saxony; where I found two factions, one of philosophers, who were Calvinists, and the other of theologians, who were Lutherans. And among these was a doctor called Alberigo Gentile, from le Marche, who I had known in England, a professor of law, who favored me and introduced me to read a lesson from the *Organo* of Aristotle; which I read along with other lessons of philosophy for two years. During that time, the son, who was a Calvinist [Cristian I of Saxony], succeed his father, who was a Lutheran [Augustus I], as Duke, and began favoring the part contrary to those who favored me; at which point I left and went to Prague, and stayed six months.[43]

Terms which a few decades earlier had the flavor of an insult – such as Calvinist[44] – had by now become definitions of a religious rift that has remained irreversible to this day.

While at Wittenberg Bruno's publications followed one after another, with the in-depth study of the Aristotelian-Lullian program contained in the books of the so-called *Lampades* trilogy. However, the whirl of confessional divisions denied him the serenity needed to conduct his research. Not even the guarantees of freedom of teaching contained in the peace of Augusta of 1555 helped him to settle down in what had been Luther's university. In fact, religious disagreements led him to abandon the position found for him by the great jurist Alberico Gentili, a founder of international law and former instructor at Oxford. On March 8, 1588 Bruno declaimed a farewell *Oratio valedictoria* to colleagues and university students. It is a sometimes moving text, which recapitulated his history of exile and exposed his weariness with wandering a continent worn down by hate:

> I became, among the others, attracted by the desire to visit the house of knowledge, eager to contemplate the Palladium, where I am not ashamed to have endured poverty, the malevolence and hatred of my own, the curses, the ingratitude of those to whom I wanted to be good

> and would be useful, the effects of an extreme inhumanity and the most sordid avarice; and the rebukes, the slander, the wrongs, even the wickedness of those who owe me love, service, honor. Nor am I ashamed to have experienced the derision and contempt of the ignoble and foolish, people who, while they are actually beasts, in the image and likeness of men, for their way of life and fortune, pride themselves on reckless ignorance. What I do not regret is having incurred effort, pain, exile: because with effort I profited, suffering I gained experience, living as an exile I learned: because in brief hardship I found a long quiet, in mild suffering immense joy, in a narrow exile a wide open homeland.[45]

It is highly probable that the exile began to formulate the project of returning to his country of origin the year of his fortieth birthday. It was a design that was becoming increasingly clear, and it was far from being a simple, nostalgic trip to the homeland. A man like Bruno, tempered by experience, aware of himself and his mission, could not fail to think of something larger and more impressive for Italy and the world: something which would put an end to the human and spiritual catastrophe of his time, making him the messenger and architect of a new civilization.

But the moment to activate this plan had not yet arrived. Bruno had no guarantee that he could escape any negative repercussions from returning to an Italy where the Inquisition was tirelessly at work. The journey had to continue, in the direction of the continent's highest political authority: the Habsburg Emperor, Rudolf II. Bruno's next stop had to be Prague.

In 1588, the Bohemian city of 60,000, to which the Emperor had transferred his capital from Vienna, was the home of experimental philosophy. The Emperor protected natural philosophers, magicians, astronomers and alchemists, and was a researcher himself, attracted by occultism and wisdom literature [Pan-sapientialism]. His court, which had moved to the heart of Bohemia five years earlier, and his reputation could not help but entice Bruno, who was attracted by the novelty like a moth to light, although he was warned about the charlatanistic and credulous streaks among some of the visionaries who populated the Habsburg entourage. The jeers and sarcasm aimed at dealers in "arcana" and "mysteries" that are scattered among Bruno's previous works[46] kept him away from the seductions of Prague's occultism and Rudolph's obsession with prognostications – a passion which led the Emperor, again in 1599, to employ prestigious astronomers like Tycho Bache and Johannes Kepler primarily to write horoscopes.

It is significant that the only work Bruno published while in Prague was a philosophical-mathematical treatise: *Articuli centum et sexaginta adversus huius tempestatis mathematicos atque philosophos*, an argument for a purely mechanical concept of nature, with which he perhaps hoped to draw the Emperor on to less irrational terrain, even if strewn with hermetic implications. In the dedication of the work the author does not fail to address the Emperor with an intense profession of faith in tolerance and mutual love between all people as well as a prayer for lasting peace in Europe.[47]

The next three years saw Bruno pass from Prague to Helmstedt, where he studied the magical and esoteric-religious traditions he had cultivated for years but to which he had not yet dedicated himself systematically. He composed, among other things, three texts that were destined to remain unpublished until 1891: the *De Magia*, *Theses de magia*, and *De magia mathematica*. These works, perhaps preparatory material for a unified work of synthesis meant to illustrate his vision of magical practice in connection with religious and civil practice, were for obvious reasons kept secret from the Venetian and Roman inquisitors.

Here we are in the decisive phase of a specific formation in Bruno's work, based on his refusal, perhaps unique among the great philosophers of the Renaissance, to read the ancient magical and hermetic doctrines in light of their Christian reception. A famous historiographical tradition that stems from the work of Eugenio Garin (1909–2004) and Frances Yates (1899–1981) argues that for Bruno hermetic thought was essentially a recollection of Egyptian culture, seen as original wisdom compared to Christian culture, and considered superior to it. "Before this philosophy, which suits our mind, existed," Bruno wrote in *Cena delle ceneri*, "there was that of the Chaldeans, the Egyptians, the magicians, the Orphics, Pythagoreans and others of ancient memory." In *De magia*, the crisis in the world that Bruno meant to counter with his political and religious reforms was configured as a crisis of language, which once again referred back to the superiority of ancient Egyptian wisdom. This was expressed – in Bruno's vision – in images, rather than letters of the alphabet:

> They [the Egyptians] had at their disposal, to name individual things, specific images derived from things in nature, or around them: such inscriptions and such denominations were used by the Egyptians to converse with the gods in the execution of wondrous effects. But when Theuth [the mythological discoverer of the alphabet] or someone else invented letters such as we now employ in other kinds of activity, an extremely serious loss resulted, for memory as well as for divine science and magic.[48]

Bruno had long cultivated the study of the memory arts and the wise use of magic, with a view to the implementation of his mission as a hermetic magician and philosopher. It was a program that aimed at unifying the world under the religion of which he spoke in the dedication of the *Articoli centum et sexaginta* to Rudolf II: an intellectual and deist religion based on the philanthropic idea of reciprocal love. It was an idea in turn both magical and hermetic, a universal bond which in Bruno's vision bound together the forces of nature: "which reconciles the contrary, and unifies the multiple in one."[49]

Tensions and religious conflict also marked Bruno's sojourn in Helmstedt. Though he enjoyed the support of the Lutheran Duke Julius of Brunswick-Lüneburg, who died in May 1589, and to whom he dedicated an *Oratio consolatoria*, Bruno was publicly excommunicated by the leading

Pastor and Superintendent of the Lutheran Church, who accused him of Calvinist tendencies.[50] After the events in Geneva, Bruno had collided directly with the other protestant faith. This episode must have in some way contributed to the formulation of his project to return to the confessional area of Europe which by now had proclaimed itself Catholic.

July 1590 finds Giordano Bruno in Frankfurt. In the city of printing and the international book trade, he personally cut the typefaces for the printing of the three poems *De minimo*, *De monade*, and *De immense*. In the presentation of these he claimed, among other things, the existence of an "infinite universe" and of "infinite particular worlds similar to this Earth [...] hence this indirectly means a challenge to the truth according to faith."[51] He moved on to Zurich in the winter of that same year, and then returned to Frankfurt, where he delivered another text on memory techniques, *De imaginum, signorum ed idearum compositione* to the presses.

In the months he spent on the banks of the River Main Bruno deepened his study of magic, and finally made up his mind to return to Italy and settle within the borders of the Venetian Republic. He would later confess to the inquisitors of the Serenissima that this choice had been based on a contingent, almost random element:

> While I was in Frankfurt last year, I received two letters from mister Giovanni Mocenigo, a Venetian gentleman, in which he invited me to come to Venice, wishing, according to what he wrote to me, for me to teach him the art of memory and invention, promising to treat me well, and that I would be happy with him.[52]

In fact, we know from the trial papers that Bruno did go to live at the so-called *Ca' Vecchia* in the Venetian parish of San Samuele, which belonged to the powerful patrician Mocenigo family.

In Frankfurt Bruno had become acquainted with two Italian book-sellers, Giovan Battista Ciotti and Giacomo Brictano, who had flattered him with talk of the growing success of his work in Italy. Ciotti in particular was in touch with other Italians of heterodox tendencies, among them Jacopo Castelvetro and members of Andrea Morosini's Venetian "circle": this was a sort of informal academy that was also frequented by Paolo Sarpi, to whom Bruno was introduced once he had returned to Italy. In 1599 Ciotti would be fined by the Inquisition for trafficking prohibited books with Germany.[53]

It was actually Ciotti – as he would testify during Bruno's trial – who had put Bruno in contact with Mocenigo. Mocenigo had purchased a copy of *De minimo* from him in Frankfurt and was dazzled by it,

> This Giordano came to this city, so far as I know, because one day signor Zuane Mocenigo, a Venetian gentleman, buying a book published by the said Giordano entitled *De minimo, magno et mensura*, asked me

> if I knew him, and if I knew where he was at the moment. I told him yes, and that I had seen him in Frankfurt and believed he was still there.
>
> And the said signor Mocenigo – continues Ciotti's testimony – rejoined: 'I would like him to come to Venice to teach me the secrets of memory and the others he professes, as can be seen in this book of his'; and to this I replied: 'I believe that if he is sought for, he will come'.[54]

It seems clear that the familiarity between Ciotti and Bruno was not simply based upon the professional proximity between an author and a book-seller, but rather on a common political and spiritual sentiment that both were very careful not to reveal to the Inquisitors. The very certainty with which the book-seller responded to the Venetian aristocrat that the philosopher, "if sought for, he will come," seems to suggest that the two had openly discussed Bruno's ambition to return to Italy. It is also certain that Mocenigo himself shared – in whole or in part – those same ideal perspectives: it is certainly not by chance that he had Ciotti print, in three parts between 1592 and 1596, a collection of epistles by the Paduan writer Giovan Battista Leoni. A supporter of the party of Navarre, Leoni was in Venice at the time of Bruno's arrest, and had dealings with Mocenigo following the developments of the French civil war. In 1595, he would hail as a "most holy decree"[55] Clement VIII's pardon of Henry of Navarre, which definitively legitimized his accession to the throne of France as King Henry IV.

Return to Italy: A Grand Project

It is very likely that Bruno's decision to cross back over the Alps heading south was influenced by considerations that he could not confess to the Holy Office.

August of 1590 saw the death of Pope Sixtus V, a former Franciscan monk and inquisitor. In France, Henry of Navarre's victory over the Catholic League and its Spanish and papal allies was imminent. These two elements might well have rekindled Bruno's hope that the groundwork had finally been laid for the launch of a continental political-religious reform, in the preparation of which he meant to play a primary role. After the death of Sixtus V there were three very brief pontificates, all unfavorable to the Bourbon (Urban VII, Gregory XIV, and Innocent IX). But for Bruno, the very rapidity of these transitions that were hostile to the party of Navarre could have been cause for confident expectation; the expectation that a pope would arrive who was able to decipher French and European events with eyes more favorable to his own political side. And that pope seemed to be Clement VIII, who was elected towards the end of January 1592, when the philosopher was already settled in Venice.

However, just as it appeared that the general conditions making it possible for him to intervene in the political scene had finally come about, Bruno found himself marginalized by no less than four Churches: the Roman Church, which he had abandoned with his apostasy from the Dominican Order; the English Church, with which he had polemicized both verbally and in writing; the Calvinist Church, with which he had precariously reconciled in Geneva with an act of abjuration; and finally the Lutheran Church, from which he had been banished at Helmstedt. This last event had drastically limited his spaces for employment in numerous German universities and courts.

Faced with these obstacles, the prospect of a return to the Roman Catholic fold could have seemed to Bruno to be the least challenging option. On the theological level he had never tired of reiterating his preference for the Catholic Church.[56] The contacts and the patronage available to him in Italy, even through the Venetian patrician, could possibly help him, albeit after a trial, to return to the Dominican Order and find an academic or court post somewhere. In the end, the sphere of Roman power and the papal Curia may have seemed to him – after what had been for various reasons a disappointing experience at the imperial Court – to be the ideal place to finally embark on his program of religious reform.

Who had Giordano Bruno become in the long years of travel, readings, discussions, writing, and teaching; in over a decade of daily life among sovereigns and intellectuals, aristocrats and courtiers, magicians, book-sellers, alchemists and clergymen, crossing borders, sides and factions? Who did the Venetian Inquisitors face when they prepared to question Bruno after arresting and imprisoning him at the end of May 1592? Was he a prisoner like all the others, or was he the bearer of something unique?

Before trying to answer these questions, we need to formulate a methodological assumption which is perhaps disappointing, but which is obligatory for history. We shall do so by recalling the words of one of the most important architects of the revival of contemporary scholarship on Bruno, Frances Yates: "Bruno's mind works along lines that are extremely difficult for a modern person to fully grasp."[57] This means, among other things, that we cannot hope to fully understand the thinking and assumptions that informed the philosopher's practical decisions over the course of his life and during the trial. Based on the knowledge we have from his works, from his biography, and from the *modus operandi* of the Inquisition at the time, though, we can still try to formulate some plausible hypotheses.

First of all, Giordano Bruno had been a traveler. This element is not as banal as it may appear, since for centuries ecclesiastics regarded individuals and merchandise that circulated widely with suspicion: *qui multu peregrinantur, raro sanctificantur* still appears in the 15th century *De imitatione Christi*, the most popular among the devotional texts of medieval Christianity. During the 1500s the Holy Office tried to subject the foreign travel of Italian merchants and intellectuals to increasing surveillance. Between the 1580s and 1590s the forms of control established by the judges of faith and the Catholic bishops over Catholics who traveled or resided beyond the Alps became more severe, especially in areas where Protestantism prevailed. In the summer of 1596, Clement VIII would formally prohibit Catholics who were living permanently outside Italy from living in cities where the Roman rite was not permitted, and began to require certification of access to the sacraments for all those who were settled abroad.

For years the Congregation of the Holy Office had warned the secular governments of the peninsula that Italian merchants, traveling *more hereticale* in various Germanic territories, could be a cause of "infection" in their cities.[58] Rome ended up deciding which individuals could go to locations where Reformed religion predominated, based on documentation of the reasons for the trip along with attestations of the applicant's orthodoxy which were drawn up by the inquisitors. If a "commoner" asked the local judge of faith for permission to "be able to go to Geneva to recover many thousands of *scudi*, inherited on the death of a Catholic relative who had business in France," as for example happened in Venice in 1598, the cardinals could approve his request once they had received "the report that he [the inquisitor] made of his great goodness and Piety." Often, as was the case in the example under consideration, the Congregation required the local inquisitor to secure the consent of the bishop as well.[59]

So, it is no coincidence that Bruno's first two depositions before the Venetian judges of faith were focused almost exclusively on his travels and acquaintances beyond the Alps. Nor is the fact that as they gathered Bruno's testimony, the Venetian Inquisitors repeatedly stated that it was difficult for them to trust the statements of one who had escaped from his own Order and had lived for so long in the lands of heresy.[60]

In the second place, Bruno was a renegade friar. It was a profile that was not at all uncommon in 16th century society. The Council of Trent had addressed the question, forbidding monasteries and convents of other Orders from welcoming them, and the friars themselves from living *extra claustra*. The inquisitors themselves did not dwell too long on Bruno's profile as a Dominican apostate. Even the patrician Giovanni Mocenigo, who had denounced him to the Holy Office mentioned the fact mainly because he thought that his disappointing teacher of the magical arts had actually escaped a real Inquisitorial trial in the past: "he told me of having had other times at Rome quarrels with the Inquisition over some one hundred and thirty articles, and that he had fled."[61] Once it was ascertained – as we will discuss later – that this earlier trial did not exist, the Venetian judges of faith set the question aside. However, the Roman Congregation sensed that this ambiguity could be exploited to secure the prisoner's extradition from the Republic. An effort based on a substantial falsification which, as we shall see, was successful.

In the third place, Bruno had become a natural philosopher. Since the beginning of the 16th century, the Roman church had tried to restrict the spaces for intellectual research around naturalistic knowledge. The canons of Lateran V (1512–1517) required philosophers to privilege the truth of the

Christian religion in both research and teaching whenever it was in conflict with ideas or concepts deriving from other cognitive methods. After the compilation of the first Indexes of prohibited books, the suspicion grew further. In 1578, Giambattista Della Porta, one of the founders of the Accademia dei Lincei, was tried for necromancy, tortured and dismissed with prejudice (*assolto con formula dubitativa*). His work, *Magia naturalis* (1558), was banned in various Indexes, while in 1592 the Italian translation of his *De humana physiognomia* (1586) was prohibited, the correction of which was ordered in 1596. Francesco Patrizi's *Nova de universis philosophia* was also first condemned in 1592, a work that aimed at renewing cosmological doctrines by means of platonic philosophy in a way that was not altogether different from what Bruno tried to do. This took place despite the fact that Patrizi had been called to teach in Rome at the request of Cardinal Cinzio Aldobrandini, nephew of Pope Clement VIII.[62]

An even more tragic fate was suffered in the same years by Francesco Pucci, a figure we shall examine more closely, whose life story is comparable to Bruno's. After having traveled between Lyon, Paris, London, Krakow and Prague cultivating heterodox religious ideas, Pucci was disillusioned by his political and intellectual experiences. He tried to rehabilitate himself with the Roman Church, dedicating the manuscript *De regno Christi* to Cardinal Roberto Bellarmino, who also sent a copy to the pope. However, all his works were prohibited in 1594, and after his arrest he was tried in Rome by the Congregation of the Holy Office. Rejecting abjuration, he was condemned to death; he reconciled *in extremis* with a sacramental confession, and was thus spared – as was the custom in such cases – the horror of being burned alive. He was instead beheaded, and then his corpse burned in July 1597.[63]

In short, Giordano Bruno was a political reformer. He had interpreted Henry of Navarre's success in France as the signal of the dawn of a general reform of his times; a general political-religious transformation not only of France, but of the whole world, induced by reaching an overall level of corruption in civilization that he believed could descend no lower. He was sure that he could play a fundamental role in the context of that renewal, by virtue of his intense scientific activities in the 1580s and his own personal relationships. In this sense, Venice might constitute an excellent point of departure, as there was an aristocracy active in the city that was culturally open to Europe, and oriented similarly to leading French political thinkers.[64]

However, the theoretical arsenal that supported Bruno's ambition of *reformatio mundi* made him a very different figure from the prototypical *politique* of his era, Jean Bodin, the author of *Le six livres de la République*. This was also true because Bruno's anti-Aristotelian thought was radically permeated by Neoplatonism and magic. The debate between those who consider Bruno a precursor of modern science and those who instead emphasize the centrality of the magical and pre-rational dimension in his work and his life remains open – and is probably destined to remain so.[65] But there is no disagreement about the fact that throughout Bruno's entire life the philosophical dimension inescapably intertwined with the political and practical dimensions. In this regard, it is rather curious that until now there has not been a serious effort at a completely political reading of Bruno's behavior and his decisions during his inquisitorial trial, up to his decision to go to the stake. It is as if his arrest by the Holy Office had suddenly canceled the accused's capacity to think and to act in the terms that he himself had programmatically set down in over a decade of meditation and writing. But this is another subject to which we must return later.

Politics, philosophy, action: when Bruno returned to Italy, these three categories had been reduced to one. From the years in London when he wrote *Cena de le ceneri,* until the moment of his arrest he thought of himself as a kind of Mercury, sent by the gods to bring light after centuries of darkness. In his belief system even magic was not pure theory, nor was the magician simply a sage: he was someone who possessed the capacity to act, doing admirable things.[66] Bruno had determined his own existential profile and historical role, taking inspiration from the hermetic tradition, which led him to predict a great destiny for himself.[67] Giovanni Mocenigo, who knew him well and indeed may have shared his political orientations, said "He showed designs of wanting to make himself the author of a new sect, in the name of a new philosophy" at the beginning of his first denunciation to the Inquisition. The Venetian nobleman went on to say "He says he wants to work on divinatory arts and that he wants to make the whole world follow his footsteps." Friar Francesco Graziano, a fellow prisoner with Bruno in Venice, would later testify that when he had been in the prisons of la Serenissima Bruno had "professed [...] to lead a new sect, and said that in Germany they call themselves Giordanisti."[68]

In the years of his more recent research on the phenomenon of magic the philosopher had in particular investigated those fundamental "constraints" capable of harnessing the work of the wise as well as the simple, yet at the same time of opening up exceptional possibilities for action and the exercise of power for the magician. In his books on magic, and especially in *De vinculis in genere*, Bruno tirelessly investigates the systematic links between magic and politics, and considers the problem of consent: the magician and the politician both require techniques to convince and persuade; there are parallels between the techniques of magic and politics; one can – and must – formulate a universal theory of the links between politics and magic:

> [...] he who must bind must possess a universal theory of things, to be able to capture Man, who is, in a manner of speaking, the epilogue of all things. In the human species it is indeed possible to glimpse the nature of all other things, especially proportionally and numerically [...] Each man, then, randomly comes into differences in use, customs, purpose, inclination, temperament, age [...] these are the people who

> assume various roles in the civil administration (*in reipublicae administrationem*), where they use themselves as means or instruments, thus posing the question of binding them to themselves. It does not appear, in sum, that there is any reality that escapes a reflection on civil relations (*a civili speculation*) from this perspective.[69]

The man imprisoned by the inquisitors in May 1592 intended to carry out a program of political and religious reform of continental scope built on these theoretical foundations. A program aimed at bringing the world to a purified and unified creed, and establishing peace in a Europe reduced to the homogeneity of a philosophical religion, without heresies or dogmas. In carrying out this plan he also intended to implement the knowledge of magic he had so avidly studied and professed. Bruno meant to draw the power necessary to gain dominion over reality and the world from his philosophy of nature and his faith in ancient wisdom, bending consciences to his will, and inducing matter to perform miracles.[70]

At the same time, Bruno was not possessed: he was aware of the limits of his fate and of the power of circumstances to curtail his ability to have an impact on his times. The prisoner delivered to the judges of faith by Giovanni Mocenigo was a "tense person, almost split, between two antagonistic poles"[71]: perched between great self-awareness and a sufficient knowledge of the power relationships in play at that precise historical moment. It was a tension that would be fully transfused into the trial, in the crescendo of a struggle carried on until the final moment.

Notes

1 *Processo*, 149.
2 M. Ciliberto, *Giordano Bruno*, cit. p. 3.
3 A. Foa, *Giordano Bruno*, cit., pp. 23 ff.
4 What follows is based, unless otherwise indicated, on the reference biography by Saverio Ricci, *Giordano Bruno nell'Europa del Cinquecento*, Rome, Salerno editrice, 2000. For a general reconstruction of Bruno the Anglophone reader can begin with Ingrid D. Rowland, *Giordano Bruno: Philosopher/Heretic*, Chicago, IL, University of Chicago Press, 2008.
5 *Processo*, 156.
6 S. Ricci, *Giordano Bruno nell'Europa del Cinquecento*, cit., p. 55.
7 Ivi, p. 65.
8 Ivi, pp. 75–76.
9 *Processo*, 190. The first work was a popular paraphrase of the lyric to the Virgin attributed to Bernardo di Chiaravalle; the second was the *Vite* by Domenico Cavalca, a Dominican who lived between the 13th and 14th century, reprinted many times in the 16th century (S. Ricci, *Giordano Bruno nell'Europa del Cinquecento*, cit., p. 89).
10 S. Ricci, *Giordano Bruno nell'Europa del Cinquecento*, cit., p. 86.
11 The episode is not considered plausible by some commentators and possible by others: see ivi, p. 95.
12 He will be the author of apologetic writings and a lecturer in philosophy in various monasteries of central Italy: ivi, pp. 102–103.

13 *Processo*, 191.
14 *Ibidem.*
15 Cited by S. Ricci, *Giordano Bruno nell'Europa del Cinquecento*, cit., pp. 87–88.
16 *Processo*, 191.
17 S. Ricci, *Giordano Bruno nell'Europa del Cinquecento*, cit., p. 111.
18 The hypothesis is argued ivi, pp. 116–117.
19 *Processo*, 160.
20 *Ibidem.*
21 S. Ricci, *Giordano Bruno nell'Europa del Cinquecento*, cit., pp. 134–135 and 378.
22 A. Foa, *Giordano Bruno*, cit., p. 38.
23 S. Ricci, *Giordano Bruno nell'Europa del Cinquecento*, cit., p. 378.
24 *Processo*, 161.
25 The obligatory reference is to the classic work by Frances A. Yates, *The Art of Memory*, London, Routledge and Kegan Paul, 1966.
26 *Processo*, 161–162.
27 M. Ciliberto, *Giordano Bruno*, cit., p. 15.
28 S. Ricci, *Giordano Bruno nell'Europa del Cinquecento*, cit., pp. 152–177.
29 *Processo*, 162.
30 On the influence exerted on Bruno's work and existential decisions by the writings attributed to the legendary figure of Hermes Trismegistos, here I cite only the classic study by Frances A. Yates, *Giordano Bruno and the Hermetic Tradition*, Chicago, IL, University of Chicago Press, 1964.
31 S. Ricci, *Giordano Bruno nell'Europa del Cinquecento*, cit., pp. 178–184.
32 M. Ciliberto, *Giordano Bruno*, cit., pp. 40–41 and 51–52.
33 Ivi, p. 149.
34 Cited in ivi, p. 150.
35 S. Ricci, *Giordano Bruno nell'Europa del Cinquecento*, cit., pp. 301–331.
36 M. Ciliberto, *Giordano Bruno*, cit., p. 167.
37 S. Ricci, *Giordano Bruno nell'Europa del Cinquecento*, cit., p. 331. For the sake of brevity we will not expand upon the hypothesis (notoriously formulated by John Bossy in *Giordano Bruno and the Embassy Affair*, New Haven, CT and London, Yale University Press, 1991) according to which Bruno served as a spy in the French Embassy for Queen Elizabeth and her Secretary of State Francis Walsingham while he was in England. An evaluation of Bossy's work is provided by Simon Ditchfield in the introduction to *Christianity and Community in the West: Essays for John Bossy*, edited by Simon Ditchfield, Aldershot, Routledge, 2001, pp. xv–xxix.
38 *Processo*, 162.
39 A. Foa, *Giordano Bruno*, cit., pp. 75–76.
40 This line of interpretation was originally advanced by Antonio Corsano in *Il pensiero di Giordano Bruno nel suo svolgimento storico*, Florence, Sansoni, 1940. It was successively taken up by Eugenio Garin and Luigi Firpo, and was recently re-proposed by Anna Foa in *Giordano Bruno*, cit., pp. 73 ff.
41 *Processo*, 247–248.
42 S. Ricci, *Giordano Bruno nell'Europa del Cinquecento*, cit., p. 397.
43 *Processo*, 162.
44 On the original insulting meaning of the term, see Diarmaid MacCulloch, *Reformation: Europe's House Divided 1490-1700*, London, Allen Lane, 2003, p. 22 of the Italian edn.
45 Cited by Nuccio Ordine, *Introduzione a Giordano Bruno*, in *Opere italiane*, volume I, Turin, UTET, 2002, pp. 9–190, p. 187.
46 S. Ricci, *Giordano Bruno nell'Europa del Cinquecento*, cit., p. 419.
47 Ivi, p. 422.
48 Cited by M. Ciliberto, *Giordano Bruno*, cit., p. 151.

49 A. Foa, *Giordano Bruno*, cit., pp. 85–86, from which I draw the citations.
50 S. Ricci, *Giordano Bruno nell'Europa del Cinquecento*, cit., p. 431.
51 M. Ciliberto, *Giordano Bruno*, cit., p. 217.
52 *Processo*, 154–155.
53 S. Ricci, *Giordano Bruno nell'Europa del Cinquecento*, cit., p. 461.
54 *Processo*, 150.
55 S. Ricci, *Giordano Bruno nell'Europa del Cinquecento*, cit., pp. 460 and 482.
56 M. Ciliberto, *Giordano Bruno*, cit., p. 260.
57 This statement has been, among others, proposed by Paolo Rossi as a "provisional point of encounter" among the different interpretive traditions of Bruno's thought (*Il tempo dei maghi. Rinascimento e modernità*, Milan, Cortina, 2006, pp. 101–102).
58 The papal letter, renewed many times in the following years, was regularly forwarded to inquisitors stationed in the principle commercial cities of Italy. For Venice, see for example Biblioteca Apostolica Vaticana (from here on BAV), Vat. Lat. 10945, fol. 124*r*, invii da Roma, 13 dicembre 1598 and 12 maggio 1606:

> The Holiness of Our Signoria has again made a perpetual law that Italian merchants and businessmen living outside Italy may not reside in cities, lands or places where there is a prohibition and ban on the free and public exercise, and use of the Catholic religion, of a church, a priest, the mass, and other divine offices and holy sacraments. Here attached I send you a printed summary."

On the problem of "heretical infection," see Rita Mazzei, *Convivenza religiosa e mercatura nell'Europa del Cinquecento. Il caso degli italiani a Norimberga*, in *La formazione storica della alterità. Studi di storia della tolleranza nell'età moderna offerti a Antonio Rotondò*, edited by Henry Méchoulan, Richard H. Popkin, Giuseppe Ricuperati, Luisa Simonutti, 3 vols, Florence, Olschki, 2001, volume 1, pp. 395–428, p. 403.
59 BAV, Vat. Lat. 10945, fol. 124*r*, Roma, 24 gennaio 1598.
60 See, for example, the question formulated by the judges during the seventh hearing of July 30 in *Processo*, doc. 16, p. 196: "*Ei dictum*: l'apostasia de tanti anni vi rende molto suspetto della santa fede ,"[...]," "And they said: the apostasy of many years makes you highly suspect to the holy faith [...]."
61 Ivi, 144.
62 Andrea Del Col, *L'Inquisizione in Italia dal XII al XXI secolo*, Milan, Mondadori, 2006, pp. 542–544.
63 Giorgio Caravale, *Il profeta disarmato. L'eresia di Francesco Pucci nell'Europa del Cinquecento*, Bologna, Il Mulino, 2011.
64 M. Ciliberto, *Giordano Bruno*, cit., pp. 262–263.
65 For an initial summary of the two positions, see P. Rossi, *Il tempo dei maghi*, cit., especially pp. 79–102.
66 Ivi, p. 60.
67 M. Ciliberto, *Giordano Bruno*, cit., p. 263 and *passim*.
68 *Processo*, 144 and 250.
69 M. Ciliberto, *Giordano Bruno*, cit., pp. 248–249 (also for the text cited).
70 Taking up almost to the letter the analysis of Luigi Firpo in *Processo*, 11; see also A. Foa, *Giordano Bruno*, cit., p. 83.
71 Michele Ciliberto, *Giordano Bruno: dalla «nova filosofia» alla* reformatio mundi, in *Le filosofie del Rinascimento* edited by Cesare Vasoli, Milan, Bruno Mondadori, 2002, pp. 534–551, p. 538.

References

John Bossy, *Giordano Bruno and the Embassy Affair*, New Haven, CT and London, Yale University Press, 1991.

Giorgio Caravale, *Il profeta disarmato. L'eresia di Francesco Pucci nell'Europa del Cinquecento*, Bologna, Il Mulino, 2011.

Christianity and Community in the West: Essays for John Bossy, edited by Simon Ditchfield, Aldershot, Routledge, 2001.

Michele Ciliberto, *Giordano Bruno: dalla «nova filosofia» alla* reformatio mundi, in *Le filosofie del Rinascimento*, edited by Cesare Vasoli, Milan, Bruno Mondadori, 2002, pp. 534–551.

Antonio Corsano, *Il pensiero di Giordano Bruno nel suo svolgimento storico*, Florence, Sansoni, 1940.

Andrea Del Col, *L'Inquisizione in Italia dal XII al XXI secolo*, Milan, Mondadori, 2006.

Diarmaid MacCulloch, *Reformation: Europe's House Divided 1490-1700*, London, Allen Lane, 2003.

Rita Mazzei, *Convivenza religiosa e mercatura nell'Europa del Cinquecento. Il caso degli italiani a Norimberga*, in *La formazione storica della alterità. Studi di storia della tolleranza nell'età moderna offerti a Antonio Rotondò*, edited by Henry Méchoulan, Richard H. Popkin, Giuseppe Ricuperati, Luisa Simonutti, 3 vols, Florence, Olschki, 2001, volume 1, pp. 395–428.

Nuccio Ordine, *Introduzione a Giordano Bruno*, in *Opere italiane*, volume I, Turin, UTET, 2002, pp. 9–190.

Saverio Ricci, *Giordano Bruno nell'Europa del Cinquecento*, Rome, Salerno editrice, 2000.

Paolo Rossi, *Il tempo dei maghi. Rinascimento e modernità*, Milan, Cortina, 2006.

Ingrid D. Rowland, *Giordano Bruno: Philosopher/Heretic*, Chicago, IL, University of Chicago Press, 2008.

Frances A. Yates, *Giordano Bruno and the Hermetic Tradition*, Chicago, IL, University of Chicago Press, 1964.

Frances A. Yates, *The Art of Memory*, London, Routledge and Kegan Paul, 1966.

2 The Circle Closes

> I will tell the truth: many times have I been threatened that I would be made to come to this Holy Office, and I always thought it a joke, because I am ready to account for myself.

These were the first words spoken by Giordano Bruno when, after his arrest, he was brought before the inquisitors of Venice to be interrogated on May 26, 1592.[1] Certainly the prisoner could not have imagined that it would be the opening of a battle between him and the judges that would last for almost eight years, concluding only with his death at the stake.

The statement that opens Bruno's first deposition before the Inquisition has become justifiably famous, because it seems to signify the philosopher's desire to confront the tribunal on the level of truth.[2] However, it is curious that until now these words have not been interpreted from a more strictly procedural point of view. "I will tell the truth: many times have I been threatened that I would be made to come to this Holy Office" constitutes an official denunciation of the intimidation of which, we can infer, Bruno had been a victim while within the borders of the Serenissima. "This Holy Office" is certainly meant here in its literal sense, in the most classic bureaucratic-notarial cadence well known to scholars of Inquisition trials: it means the Tribunal of the Faith of Venice.

Someone, therefore, had previously threatened to haul the accused before the Venetian judges of the faith. Who? Why? Strangely, the inquisitorial tribunal of the Serenissima did not bother to ask these questions, which could have shed light – as the inquisitors always tried to do – on networks of heretical relations and collusion. The tribunal's silence is an anomaly – the first in a long series.

A Man in Danger

Giordano Bruno, who was just over 40 years old at the time of his return to Italy, was an intellectual known in the major courts of Europe. Now returned from lengthy wanderings, for over a decade he had lived, conversed,

DOI: 10.4324/9781003026082-4

taught, and published weighty volumes between Switzerland, France, England, and the lands of the Holy Roman Emperor. At the end of the summer of 1591 he had decided to return to Italy and settle in the Republic of Venice, within whose borders he took up residence in the month of October.[3]

La Serenissima boasted a long tradition of resistance to interference by the ecclesiastical authorities. This fact, along with the prestige and independence of the University of Padua – which had been the only university to reject the law issued by Pius IV in 1564 that required graduating students to recite the Catholic oath of faith – could have appeared to Bruno as reason enough to feel he was protected. From there he could imagine sounding out the mood of the papal Curia, moving to begin implementing the program of political and religious pacification which he had meditated upon for so long. The Republic was among the very first European powers to recognize, as early as 1589, the legitimacy of the still excommunicated Henry of Navarre on the throne of France. Venice had not even waited for the new abjuration by the king of Calvinism, which happened in 1593 and was branded by most as opportunistic. The Bourbon's second return to Catholicism would soon earn him fame for having spoken the famous phrase, now become an aphorism: "Paris is well worth a mass."

When Bruno returned to Italy he did not immediately settle at the Mocenigo family's home of *Ca' Vecchia* in Venice, where he would be arrested. For several weeks he moved between Venice and Padua, surely happy to have rediscovered the brilliance of the Venetian skies, to finally speak a language understandable to most, to measure a new living space and see new possibilities for work and study. The news of his return south of the Alps spread quickly among friends, students, and acquaintances, many of whom wondered at the fact that the philosopher had decided to return to a territory that was so dangerous for him. In a letter sent from Bologna in January 1592, the humanist Valent Havekenthal, alias Acidalius, wrote to an old German student of Bruno's in Padua expressing his alarm:

> It is really true? How could he dare to return to a country from which, by his own confession, he was exiled by force? I am astonished: I still don't believe it, though I have heard it from trustworthy people.[4]

The concerns and the shock of his friends were more than legitimate. In the Lagoon city Giordano Bruno's political and philosophical sympathies for France and Navarrism were evident, and shared by his aristocratic host Giovanni Mocenigo, as well as by the booksellers the philosopher associated with and the circles to which he was invited. His reputation for questionable orthodoxy could not help but accompany him on his return to the peninsula, along with the titles of his books: already well known to Venetian printers of the time, these titles indicated interests in mnemonic techniques, magic, and religion. Bruno had moreover been in contact with Calvinist, Anglican and Lutheran kings, courts, and centers of study; this doubtlessly contributed to making him an object of curiosity, but also of suspicion. It soon became known that he had resumed working with the Nuremberg noble Hieronymus Besler in Padua, brother of the famous botanist Basilius, who Bruno had met in Wittenberg and who in the past had helped him to compose studies on magic, some of which remain in manuscript form at Helmstedt. In the capital of the Venetian mainland the two re-elaborated and transcribed, among other things, another of Bruno's works on magic, the *De vinculis*, this too destined to remain in manuscript form for three centuries.

It is, however, very likely that Bruno was induced to return to Italy in part by the news, communicated to him by Besler himself while the maestro was still in Frankfurt, that the chair of mathematics at the prestigious University of Padua had become vacant. Besler had already become procurator of the German students of that *Studium* and could therefore have helped him and welcomed him in the city.[5] But Bruno was unable take the chair to which he had perhaps aspired, which shortly afterwards would be occupied by Galileo Galilei. The Pisan mathematician was given the chair in September 1592, a few months after Bruno's arrest in Venice.

The reputation for liberality and tolerance enjoyed by the authorities of the Republic of Venice and the University of Padua itself probably led the philosopher to let his guard down and to vent, in those months spent between the autumn of 1591 and the spring of 1592, the bitterness and frustrations which had accompanied him during his long years of exile. It is not difficult to imagine him, in the months when he was commuting between Venice and Padua, where he stayed at an inn composing mathematical works, breaking into provocative outbursts. At the Padua *Studium* he read for "certain German scholars"[6]; in Venice he attended, as Mocenigo would state, "an academy of Signor Andrea Moresini [...] where many gentlemen practice, who had chanced to hear him say a few things of his own." As Bruno himself admitted to the inquisitors, in Venice he had addressed thorny questions such as adultery or sodomy "in company"; he discussed issues regarding the Trinity "with certain priests" "in a pharmacy or bookstore"; "spoke with many gentlemen of philosophical things," as well as, according to what he said, to "censure" the religions "of Germany or England."[7]

The recently repatriated exile underestimated the scrupulous attention with which Rome now controlled the life of those Venetian lands, situated between an Italy now subjugated to the Inquisition and a Europe considered to be heretical and schismatic. The patriarch Lorenzo Priuli, who sat on the Venetian inquisitorial tribunal, had been ambassador to Paris at the court of Henry III in 1583, at the time Bruno lived there. It is probable that he had heard him speak and had kept an eye on him.[8] But it is also possible that the loquacious philosopher attracted the hostility of those he was closer to ideologically, that is, Venetian pro-Navarre circles. These groups may well have felt exposed by the nonchalance with which Bruno publicized their political and intellectual sympathies; and induced, for this reason, to betray him.

In Venice, therefore, Bruno quickly found himself in serious danger. His past could not be erased with the swipe of a sponge, and the present was only reviving it. The meticulous Bruno barely tried to hide his personal intellectual inclinations, too often falling victim to his taste for controversy and provocation. This was a quality which had certainly been appreciated in the days of heated Renaissance disputations, but had now become dangerous in the fog of the Counter-Reformation.

The story of Florentine philosopher Francesco Pucci's tragic end offers an example of the relentless determination with which the Holy Office could pursue an intellectual dissenter in those years. His story, as has been noted, has many characteristics in common with that of Giordano Bruno. Pucci had also stayed in France, England, Switzerland, Central and Eastern Europe between the 1570s and 1580s. There he developed Navarran sympathies and actually tried to meet King Henry IV in 1591 to present the ruler his proposal for a universal council of political and religious pacification.[9] Pucci also returned to Italy in the winter of 1592 because of the hopes he placed in Clement VIII, to whom he had sent a letter from Amsterdam that year and dedicated the volume *De Christi servatoris efficacitate*. In this book the Tuscan philosopher had developed an inclusive idea of the Kingdom of God, in many aspects comparable to the program of confessional tolerance formulated by Bruno.

Pucci had come to the attention and suspicions of the Inquisition in 1589. While he too, like Bruno a few months earlier, stayed at the court of Rudolf II, the apostolic nuncio (the pope's diplomatic representative) in Prague, Alfonso Visconti, had reported his heretical acquaintances to Rome. At the time the Curia responded to Visconti by ordering him to "do whatever it takes to secure his person [or, to arrest Pucci], then we will examine his doctrine." But a month earlier the papal secretary had written to the apostolic nuncio at Cologne recommending to him: "if [Pucci] allows himself to be seen in Cologne you will have to work with the Elector [i.e. the archbishop who governed the Electorate of Cologne] to have him arrest Pucci, so that Pucci's merits can be better examined."[10]

Rome's orders to the nuncio demonstrate, among other things, the ease with which they could move against heretics who were considered particularly dangerous. Pucci, like Bruno, was the protagonist of long travels in foreign lands, in territories and at courts that were religiously suspect: this element was sufficient for the judges of the faith to take a dim view of the defendant and order his arrest even before a formal inquisitorial trial had begun. This action was normally taken – as we will see just ahead – after a denunciation and a careful evaluation of the evidence against the accused.

Francesco Pucci, like Giordano Bruno, was formally questioned at the Holy Office only several years later, once he arrived in Italy. In fact, it was the inquisitor of Florence that called attention to the heterodoxy of his books, sending a manuscript copy of *De regno Christi* to Rome in 1592, along with the information that Pucci had lived "*ad haereticos*." Once again it was the cardinal of Santa Severina, Giulio Antonio Santori, who received the package in Rome. The documentation in our possession confirms that the Holy Office knew nothing of the attempts to capture the philosopher in Prague. This in turn confirms that the correspondence between the Secretary of State and the nuncios envisaged arresting Pucci without any dossier against him having been opened by the Roman Inquisition.[11]

Francesco Pucci would have been led to Campo de' Fiori to be burned alive at the stake on the morning of May 29, 1597 if he had not at the last moment declared himself willing to repent. Thus he was brought back to the prison, where he remained until July 5, when he was decapitated before being burned: this was the "merciful" fate reserved for prisoners who had been sentenced to death but were willing to confess and receive communion, thus reconciling with the Catholic faith *in extremis*. A letter written by the prisoner to his compatriot Filippo Della Luna, and sent a few days before his death has survived. In this letter Pucci reaffirms his desperate allegiance to the ideas for which he had been condemned. This was a very dangerous document because it proved the insincerity of his reconciliation, which had clearly been faked to avoid the immense suffering of being burned alive. Fortunately for the wretched Pucci the missive, intercepted by the inquisitor of Florence and then hastily sent to Rome, reached the pope after the decapitation had already taken place.[12]

All of this proves that in the beginning of the year 1592, Giordano Bruno, as he wound his way through the *calli* of Venice provoking booksellers and priests, nobles and shopkeepers, was in very serious danger. Something terrible was about to be done against a man with a history much like his own. And it was something that could also happen to him.

Stories of Conclaves

Centuries of "Vaticanology" literature, though often tainted by conspiratorial and disparaging predilections, have accustomed us to seeing the Roman Curia as a body that is anything but monolithic and united. The papal court of the late 16th century was by no means different from these later characterizations, divided as it was by conflicts and by political and personal rivalries. In the same months that Bruno decided upon and carried out his plans to return to Italy, the internal balances of power in Rome were rapidly changing.

The years 1590 and 1591 had seen the succession of four popes to the throne of Peter: the austere Sixtus V, an inquisitor and Franciscan, who died at the end of August 1590; Urban VII, Gregory XIV, and Innocent IX followed in rapid and disconcerting succession. At the end of January 1592 Cardinal Ippolito Aldobrandini was finally elected; he took the name of Pope Clement VIII Aldobrandini, and was destined to reign until 1605. The new pope raised great hopes among intellectuals and philosophers. Francesco Pucci and Giordano Bruno praised him. Francesco Patrizi was called as early as 1592 to teach at the prestigious *Studium Urbis*, the pope's Roman University. At the time Clement VIII did not appear to be overly concerned by the fact that Patrizi's *Nova de universis philosophia* had been subject to heavy censorship by the Holy Office a year earlier.

The book contained Latin translations of the *Corpus Hermeticum*, the *Oracula caldaica* and a polemical text against Aristotelianism. He claimed that Platonic philosophy was the only one that could save the nucleus of Augustine's thought, along with those of the other most important Church Fathers, against Aristotle's atheist philosophy, which according to Patrizi had withered Christian thought and religion.[13] This was hardly an original theoretical argument. It had already been attempted by Marsilio Ficino, in common with whose thought Bruno, also steeped in Hermeticism and Platonism, agreed that they had a role to play, albeit with important divergences. For Patrizi the recovery of the most ancient wisdom served to demonstrate its perfect harmony with Christian truth, while Bruno criticized Judeo-Christianity's philosophical becoming at its root, considering it a retrograde step with regard to preceding civilizations. With his always sharp tongue, the caustic Bruno had even defined the unfortunate Patrizi, in the third dialogue, *De la causa*, as "another excrement of Italian pedantry, who has smeared many notebooks [with ink]," accusing him of not having achieved any significant innovation in his books.[14]

Despite these differences, Patrizi's promotion to Rome was praised by Bruno, who saw in it the beginning of a new Roman season of intellectual tolerance in which he could participate. "When Patrizi went to Rome, he said that he hoped that the pope would receive him in his grace," his accuser Giovanni Mocenigo would reveal to the inquisitors, "because he did not offend anyone by believing in his own way."[15]

These yearnings for freedom, however, would be smothered in the cruelest fashion. Both Bruno and Pucci were sent to the stake under Clement VIII; Patrizi himself died in 1597, embittered and defeated by the definitive condemnation of *Nova de universis philosophia* and by the inclusion of the work in the Index of prohibited books in 1596. Between 1599 and 1602 Tommaso Campanella was also brought to trial. He came out alive, albeit sentenced to life in prison, only by faking insanity during an inhumane session of rope torture lasting 36 continuous hours between June 4 and 5, 1601.[16]

What was happening? How is it possible that the expectations and hopes of these men of such high intellectual caliber, all very well versed in politics and the faith, could end up so quickly and tragically disappointed? Who was Pope Clement VIII really, and what role did he play in these events? These are questions to which it is difficult to give a single response. We will address them gradually, over the course of the book, trying not to lose sight of our main interest: the story of the trial of Giordano Bruno.

Born at Fano, in the Marches, to a lawyer of modest means from Florence who was forced into exile because of his anti-Medici sentiments, Ippolito Aldobrandini studied law at Padua, Perugia and Bologna. He then embraced an ecclesiastical career. The decisive turning point of his life took place in 1585 when Pope Sixtus V decided, among the very first acts of his pontificate, to make him a cardinal.[17] In the space of a few months the Auditor of Rota thus reached the top of the Curia hierarchy. An opportunity to contend with the international problems of his time materialized three years later, when the same pope named him as legate *a latere* in Poland. The death of King Stefano Báthory in 1586 had inspired various aspirants to advance their candidacy to that elected throne. The two men who could seriously aspire to the office were the hereditary prince of Sweden, Sigismondo Vasa, and the Archduke Maximilian of Habsburg. They quickly took up arms. However, thanks to the mediation of the legate Aldobrandini, after laborious negotiations that involved Emperor Rudolph II they reached an accord in March 1589 that placed the Scandinavian prince on the throne.

After the success of his first legateship and his return to Rome, where he was publicly praised by the pope for the brilliant outcome of the mission, Aldobrandini was considered for the legateship in France, where the political and social situation had badly deteriorated in the wake of the assassination of Henry III. However, Ippolito's candidacy was derailed by opposition from the King of Spain, Philip II, who wanted a cardinal that was closer to his court for this mission.

In the conclave the followed the death of Sixtus V the name of Aldobrandini appeared on the short list of possible popes. Once again it was the King of Spain that stood in his way, believing that he was secretly supported by the Grand Duke of Tuscany, whose pro-French – and therefore anti-Spanish – sentiments were well known. Given the decisive influence that the "Catholic King" Philip II exercised over the cardinals gathered in conclave, they ended up electing the pro-Hapsburg Cardinal Giovanni Battista Castagna, who took the name Urban VII. The situation had not changed significantly at the conclave which followed soon after and elected Gregory XIV. However, in August 1591. Aldobrandini was called by the pope to the Congregation of cardinals and charged with studying the problem of the investiture of the papal fiefdom of Ferrara, where Duke Alfonso II d'Este had no direct descendants. The cardinal from the Marche was a fierce supporter of the transfer of the fiefdom to the Papal States, under the terms specified by the bull *De non infeudandis* issued by Pius V. This, in fact, is what took place in 1598, after the death of Alfonso, and under the papacy of the man who, in the meantime, had become Clement VIII.

The third pope, elected in 1590, died after a brief illness, and the conclave that gathered in October 1591 opened the reign of Innocent IX, which lasted only until December 30. For the fourth time in less than a year and a half, the problem of papal succession presented itself again.

The power relationships within the Sacred College had in the meantime remained substantially unchanged. Among Philip II's candidates, the one who seemed to have the best chance of success on the eve of the conclave was Santa Severina himself, who could also count on the support of the Venetian and Florentine cardinals. However, the outcome of the conclave remained uncertain, because Santori, a harsh and uncompromising inquisitor, had made many enemies over the long years of life in the Curia. Santori had been called to Rome by Pius V over a quarter of a century earlier, after having managed various heresy trials in the Kingdom of Naples. Nominated a consultor of the Congregation of the Holy Office and elevated to the dignity of cardinal, in the decades that followed he acquired extraordinary experience as an inquisitor. "In matters of the Holy Office," reports a contemporary source, "he gained the reputation of an oracle, and for that especially he was introduced to the pontiff Pius, too often abusing of his holy zeal."[18] He led, or took important roles in, the most spectacular heresy trials of the late 16th century, among which were those of Bartolomé Carranza, the counselor and confessor of Charles V and Philip II, and the Florentine protonotary Pietro Carnesecchi, sent to his death in 1567. In 1585, as we have seen, he contributed to the drafting of the bull *Ab immensa* with which Sixtus V excommunicated Henry of Navarre, who then became the King of France as Henry IV.

When the conclave gathered on the morning of January 11, 1592, Cardinal Lodovico Madruzzo – who led the Spanish faction – tried to proceed to the election of Santa Severina by acclamation, something which would have avoided a dangerous vote count. The procedure was described by the treatises that organized the conclaves in this way:

> [he rises] to seat the cardinal over the altar and then the cardinals one by one come forward and bow deeply to him. To similar adorations, as soon as it is published that the required number of cardinals is agreed for the said election, all the others (almost like a stampede) will be wont to concur, each not wanting to be noticed, to be the last or to not go along out of good will.[19]

However, when the time came to proceed in this fashion, a group of 16 cardinals left the Pauline chapel, where the election was celebrated, retreating to the Sistine Chapel. This simple act undermined the possibility of carrying on with election of the pope by acclamation. The only possibility left open for electing Santori was with a regular ballot. The count reveals that, in the secrecy of the ballot box, four cardinals who had promised their support had denied him their votes.

In the following days there were repeated efforts to elect Santori, always unsuccessful. The Spanish faction wasn't able to coalesce around a decisive candidate. In these conditions the conclave threatened to drag out indefinitely, with the risk for Philip II that a cardinal who was against him would prevail. Thus some felt that the time had come to consider Aldobrandini's candidacy, which in the meantime had gradually collected an increasing number of votes. The agreement reached between Madruzzo and Peretti, nephew of Sixtus V, allowed Clement VIII to be unanimously elected on the cold afternoon of January 30, 1592.

The new pontiff was not yet 56 years old, an age considered young for a pope. Of greater than average height, with a large and sturdy body – if you leave out the collar that was so commonly worn among prelates and priests of the time – that imposes itself under the velvet *mozzetta* painted in portraits, Clement VIII was a monarch who was aware of his responsibilities and intimately understood pontifical dignity. He also demonstrated sincere piety: every morning he celebrated mass and every evening he confessed; during the day he willingly retreated to meditation and prayer in his chapel, and he subjected himself to strict fasts every Friday. He astonished Rome by following processions wearing no shoes, and climbing the Santa Scala on his knees and barefoot.

He soon earned a reputation as a tireless worker. By virtue of his legal training, he also loved to involve himself personally in all of the Curia's affairs, to the extent that in 1598 the Venetian ambassador Giovanni Dolfin wrote that the pope "wants to know all, read all and order all."[20] His personality and jurist's mentality led him to analyze the tiniest details of issues, to study their precedents and to consider possible solutions at length. In short, Clement VIII was a pope who defied the stereotype of the frivolous and dissolute Renaissance pontiff: inquisitorial rigors and models of behavior that were slowly established in the Curia in the second half of the 16th century had by now expelled such men from the leadership of the Roman Church.

The new pope and his supporters had, *in extremis*, snatched the election to the papal throne from Giulio Antonio Santori, the cardinal of Santa Severina. It was a burning humiliation for Santori, made even worse because it happened just as he had already entered the Pauline Chapel, having been notified of his immanent acclamation, and his cell had already been subjected to the ritual sacking that normally came before election. Santori was so embittered by his defeat that, on the very same day of his failed ascent to the pontificate, he abandoned the writing of his autobiography, which he had designed to glorify his career as an inquisitor become pope. It remained a manuscript and incomplete.[21]

Aldobrandini's political and intellectual sensibilities were a long way from Santa Severina's temperament. From a Florentine family and trained in Bologna and Padua, the new pope and his family cultivated conspicuous philosophical interests; Santori, a Neapolitan in origin and studies, had by the time he was 20 written theological treatises in which he expounded Catholic doctrine, examined the controversies between the reformed world and the Orthodox Church, and declared the need to combat heresy in all its forms and at all costs. Santa Severina had predicted that Clement VIII would sooner or later accept the abjuration of the Navarre and bless the coronation of Henry IV as king of France. He was, however, determined to fight to delay that moment for as long as possible. The Neapolitan cardinal's power, authority and centrality in the political balances of the Curia, won thanks also to a tireless interweaving of relationships and positioning in the highest ranks of all the major Congregations, made him, to use the words of historian Maria Teresa Fattori, an "'autonomous' center of initiative and action."[22] And he intended to use all of his influence to prevent the presence of a heretic on the throne of France.

The Roman Curia was divided. On the one hand the pro-Spanish faction, led by Santori and well represented in the Holy Office, moved in concert with Iberian diplomacy and considered Henry of Navarre a relapsed heretic. The new King of France was thus technically subject to a death sentence. This prevented Rome from recognizing the legitimacy of his succession to the throne France, even after the new abjuration. The other faction in the Curia, supported by the diplomats of Venice and Florence, had quickly moved to convince the pope to rehabilitate the Bourbon, recognizing his legitimate succession to the throne of France because he had officially returned to Catholicism. The Spain of Philip II, in turn, threatened a schism with Rome in the event that the Holy See opened negotiations with the Navarran diplomacy, announcing their intention to mobilize the troops stationed at Naples against the Papal States.[23]

This was what was happening in the Curia while Giordano Bruno was wrapping himself in a web of increasingly dangerous contacts and statements. As we will see ahead, Santa Severina's interest in Bruno was immediate, and was certainly also motivated by Santori's suspicion of practitioners of the Renaissance type of *philosophia naturalis*; in the same years, in fact, the cardinal oversaw the censoring of books by Francesco Patrizi, Giovanni Battista Della Porta and Bernardino Telesio, in addition to trying Francesco Pucci, and later Bruno and Campanella. But, during those months Santa Severina was also vigorously active in the dismantling of the dense network of Navarran informants that crossed contemporary Italy.[24] In 1591 he captured the erudite Francesco Maria Vialardi from Vercelli, who was accused of clandestine Navarran activities, and had him sent to Rome where he entered the inquisitorial prisons on May 6, 1592.[25] A contemporary of Bruno's, Nicola Antonio Stigliola, a mathematician from Nola, was also arrested in Naples and extradited to Rome, where he submitted to a trial led by Santori for charges similar to those levied at Bruno. Suspected of Navarran sympathies, he was released in 1597 for lack of evidence, nevertheless permanently losing his prestigious position as cartographer for the Kingdom of Naples.[26]

As Santori had predicted, in September 1595 Clement VIII granted absolution to Henry IV. A tense ceremony of reconciliation was held in Saint Peter's; a huge crowd filled the plaza, but the king deserted them, only sending representatives to Rome. To achieve this result, the pope had acted with realism to the end: he bypassed the consistory – the opinions of individual cardinals were instead heard by the pope in private audience – and resolved the thorny issue with a ceremony, and not through the issuance of a formal act of rehabilitation of the King of France, which he considered incompatible with his position as the recognized legitimate sovereign of a growing number of monarchs and governments. The hardline anti-Navarre faction of the Roman Curia, led by Santori, once again emerged defeated.[27]

The reconciliation of Henry IV was the key political event of Clement VIII's papacy. One can well imagine the extent to which that conclusion, exacerbated by the legal instruments adopted to reach it and the compromises which the papacy agreed to abide by, infuriated the cardinal inquisitors, *in primis* Santa Severina. Santori had not only seen his tiara taken by Aldobrandini, but had failed to prevent the Bourbon's absolution. The presence of a heretic on the throne of France, bearing the title of "Most Christian King," a title which had been attributed to those monarchs since the Middle Ages for their support of the Church of Rome and help in the defeat of heterodoxy, was for him an intolerable event – displeasing to the King of Spain, and abhorred by God himself.

And God would be avenged for it.

Notes

1 *Processo*, 154.
2 It was, among other things, placed on the back cover of Giordano Bruno, *Un'autobiografia*, edited by Michele Ciliberto, Rome, Castelvecchi, 2013.
3 Regarding Bruno in Venice, see Gino Benzoni, *Venezia come sfondo*, in *Giordano Bruno. Destino e verità*, edited by Daniele Goldoni, Luigi Ruggiu, Venice, Marsilio, 2002, pp. 89–166.
4 S. Ricci, *Giordano Bruno nell'Europa del Cinquecento*, cit., p. 463.
5 Ivi, p. 460.
6 *Processo*, 153; deposition of the bookseller Giacomo Brictano, who with his colleague Giovan Battista Ciotti demonstrates that they at least know of the volumes listed here with the titles *De minimo, magno et mensura, Li heroici furori, Dell'infinito universo et mondi, Cantus Circaeus, De memoria* e *De lampade combinatoria* (ivi, 149–154).
7 Ivi, 171, 181 and 197.
8 See Domenico Berti, *Vita di Giordano Bruno da Nola*, Florence, Turin, and Milan, Paravia, 1868, p. 256, note 2. Bruno was in Paris from 1581 to the spring of 1583 (see S. Ricci, *Giordano Bruno nell'Europa del Cinquecento*, cit., pp. 142–178); Lorenzo Priuli obtained the ambassadorship in May 1579 and remained in Paris until June 1583, when he was sent to Rome to Pope Gregory XIII (see *Le relazioni degli ambasciatori veneti al Senato durante il secolo decimosesto*, edited by Eugenio Alberi, volume X, series II, tome IV, Florence, Società editrice fiorentina, 1857, pp. 291–292). "He loves the arts and sciences," Priuli wrote of Henry III in 1582, "and he mainly delights in poetry and eloquence, in which he succeeds quite admirably" (S. Ricci, *Giordano Bruno nell'Europa del Cinquecento*, cit., p. 121).
9 G. Caravale, *Il profeta disarmato*, cit.
10 See Diego Quaglioni, *«Ex his quae deponet iudicetur». L'autodifesa di Bruno*, in «Bruniana & Campanelliana», 2000, n. VI, pp. 299–319, 299–300.
11 Luigi Firpo, *Processo e morte di Francesco Pucci*, in «Rivista di filosofia," 1949, n. XL, pp. 371–405.
12 *Ibidem.*
13 Maria Muccillo, *La dissoluzione del paradigma aristotelico*, in *Le filosofie del Rinascimento*, cit., pp. 506–533, 518–522.
14 S. Ricci, *Giordano Bruno nell'Europa del Cinquecento*, cit., p. 282.
15 *Processo*, 249.

16 See Luigi Firpo, *I processi di Tommaso Campanella*, edited by Eugenio Canone, Rome, Salerno editrice, 1998.
17 Where not otherwise indicated I am referring to Agostino Borromeo, *Clemente VIII, papa*, in *Dizionario biografico degli italiani*, cit., volume XXVI, 1982, *ad vocem*.
18 See Massimo Firpo, *Inquisizione romana e Controriforma. Studi sul cardinal Giovanni Morone (1509-1580) e il suo processo d'eresia*, Brescia, Morcelliana, 2005, p. 416, note 54.
19 Günther Wassilowsky, *Dall'«adorazione» allo scrutinio segreto. Teologia e micropolitica nel cerimoniale del conclave riformato da Gregorio XV (1621-22)*, in «Dimensioni e problemi della ricerca storica», 2007, n. 1, pp. 37–56, note 32.
20 Cited by A. Borromeo, *Clemente VIII, papa*, cit.
21 See Saverio Ricci, *Il sommo inquisitore. Giulio Antonio Santori tra autobiografia e storia (1532-1602)*, Rome, Salerno editrice, 2002, pp. 373 ff.
22 Maria Teresa Fattori, *Clemente VIII e il Sacro collegio 1592-1605. Meccanismi istituzionali ed accentramento di governo*, Stuttgart, Anton Hiersemann, 2004, p. 347.
23 Ivi, pp. 284 ff. and the entry by Laura Fedi, *Clemente VIII*, in *Giordano Bruno. Parole, concetti, immagini*, scientific direction by Michele Ciliberto, Pisa, Edizioni della Normale, 2014, *ad vocem*.
24 S. Ricci, *Il sommo inquisitore*, cit., pp. 406 ff.
25 Luigi Firpo, *In margine al processo di Giordano Bruno. Francesco Maria Vialardi*, in «Rivista storica italiana," 1956, n. LXVIII, pp. 325–364.
26 See Saverio Ricci, *Nicola Antonio Stigliola. Enciclopedista e linceo. Con l'edizione del trattato* Delle apparenze celesti, edited and with an essay by Andrea Cuna, Rome, Accademia nazionale dei Lincei, 1996.
27 S. Ricci, *Il sommo inquisitore*, cit., p. 334. For a broader historical framework see Maria Antonietta Visceglia, *Politica internazionale, fazioni e partiti nella Curia romana del tardo Cinquecento*, in Rivista storica italiana," 2015, n. 3, pp. 721–769, and Miles Pattenden, *The Roman Curia*, in *A Companion to Early Modern Rome, 1492–1692*, edited Simon Ditchfield, Pamela M. Jones, Barbara Wisch, Leiden and Boston, MA, Brill, 2019, pp. 44–59.

References

Gino Benzoni, *Venezia come sfondo*, in *Giordano Bruno. Destino e verità*, edited by Daniele Goldoni, Luigi Ruggiu, Venice, Marsilio, 2002, pp. 89–166.

Domenico Berti, *Vita di Giordano Bruno da Nola*, Florence, Turin, and Milan, Paravia, 1868.

Agostino Borromeo, *Clemente VIII, papa*, in *Dizionario biografico degli italiani*, cit., volume XXVI, 1982.

Giordano Bruno, *Un'autobiografia*, edited by Michele Ciliberto, Rome, Castelvecchi, 2013.

Maria Teresa Fattori, *Clemente VIII e il Sacro collegio 1592-1605. Meccanismi istituzionali ed accentramento di governo*, Stuttgart, Anton Hiersemann, 2004.

Laura Fedi, *Clemente VIII*, in *Giordano Bruno. Parole, concetti, immagini*, scientific direction by Michele Ciliberto, Pisa, Edizioni della Normale, 2014, *ad vocem*.

Luigi Firpo, *Processo e morte di Francesco Pucci*, in «Rivista di filosofia», 1949, n. XL, pp. 371–405.

Luigi Firpo, *In margine al processo di Giordano Bruno. Francesco Maria Vialardi*, in «Rivista storica italiana», 1956, n. LXVIII, pp. 325–364.

Luigi Firpo, *I processi di Tommaso Campanella*, edited by Eugenio Canone, Rome, Salerno editrice, 1998.

Massimo Firpo, *Inquisizione romana e Controriforma. Studi sul cardinal Giovanni Morone (1509-1580) e il suo processo d'eresia*, Brescia, Morcelliana, 2005.

Le relazioni degli ambasciatori veneti al Senato durante il secolo decimosesto, edited by Eugenio Alberi, volume X, series II, tome IV, Florence, Società editrice fiorentina, 1857.

Maria Muccillo, *La dissoluzione del paradigma aristotelico*, in *Le filosofie del Rinascimento*, cit., pp. 506–533.

Miles Pattenden, *The Roman Curia*, in *A Companion to Early Modern Rome, 1492–1692*, edited by Simon Ditchfield, Pamela M. Jones, Barbara Wisch, Leiden and Boston, MA, Brill, 2019, pp. 44–59.

Diego Quaglioni, *«Ex his quae deponet iudicetur». L'autodifesa di Bruno*, in «Bruniana & Campanelliana», 2000, n. VI, pp. 299–319.

Saverio Ricci, *Nicola Antonio Stigliola. Enciclopedista e linceo. Con l'edizione del trattato Delle apparenze celesti*, edited and with an essay by Andrea Cuna, Rome, Accademia nazionale dei Lincei, 1996.

Saverio Ricci, *Il sommo inquisitore. Giulio Antonio Santori tra autobiografia e storia (1532-1602)*, Rome, Salerno editrice, 2002.

Maria Antonietta Visceglia, *Politica internazionale, fazioni e partiti nella Curia romana del tardo Cinquecento*, in «Rivista storica italiana», 2015, n. 3, pp. 721–769.

Günther Wassilowsky, *Dall'«adorazione» allo scrutinio segreto. Teologia e micropolitica nel cerimoniale del conclave riformato da Gregorio XV (1621-22)*, in «Dimensioni e problemi della ricerca storica», 2007, n. 1, pp. 37–56.

3 Return to the Past

When we imagine the inquisitors, influenced as we are by novels, cinema, and television, we think of obscure, cloistered theologians who suddenly appear from the halls of the monasteries to imprison, interrogate, torture, and cruelly punish their victims; destined to then return to a life of erudition, in the expectation of starting another trial.

The reality, especially in what historians call the early modern era (roughly from the late 1400s to the early years of the 1800s) was far different. Every trial conducted by the Holy Office involved an organizational machine made up of laymen and ecclesiastics who were anything but isolated from the world in which they lived: on the contrary, they were immersed in the economic and social life of the age.[1] To be fully comprehensible, therefore, their work must be placed within a broader historical framework. Naturally this is also true for the tribunals of the faith that conducted the trial of Giordano Bruno.

To understand what happened during the long and dramatic proceeding that led the most important Italian philosopher of the Renaissance to his death, we must now take several steps back in time. We must try to grasp the nature of the Inquisition as it was in the early modern era, and what normally happened in a trial *in causis fidei*: "in matters of faith."

Who Is a Christian?

The roots of every inquisitorial trial spring from a very remote past. It is important to remember this to understand how these religious courts, the tribunals of the faith, played such a decisive role in history, and what legitimized their actions in the eyes of our forebears.

We must journey back to the heart of the Roman Empire in the 4th century AD. This was the moment that saw the establishment of relations among the institutions that now belong respectively to either the Church or the State. These two entities, whose functions are considered clearly distinct today, were not that way at all for more than 1,000 years of Western European history. Indeed they were so tightly bound together that for men and women of the time it would have been inconceivable to think of them as

DOI: 10.4324/9781003026082-5

separate. Only with the French Revolution did State and Church, as these terms are intended today, begin to slowly configure themselves as two distinct spheres, splitting their roles in legal organization, in political life and in Western culture.

Emperor Constantine's famous conversion to Christianity in 312 AD lies at the origin of the whole story. According to the ancient biographers, who he directed, the conversion occurred on the eve of the battle of Milvian Bridge, at the gates of Rome, when the emperor decisively defeated Maxentius, thus becoming the leader of the western part of the Roman Empire. Shortly after this event – which was crucial for world history – the circular known as "the Edict of Milan" was issued, the result of an agreement between Constantine and Licinius, respectively the Emperors of the West and East. The Edict recognized "freedom of worship" for all religions; this officially put an end to the persecution of Christians, and at the same time inaugurated a policy of support for the Christian church, for which Imperial legislation became increasingly favorable, until it finally became the state church of the Empire with the Edict of Theodosius in 380. New churches were built in the major cities of the Empire – beginning with Rome – while Roman laws began to be inspired by Christian principles. Divorce became more difficult; adulterers and homosexuals were punished severely; rules favoring widows, orphans, prisoners, and slaves were introduced. Crucifixion was abolished, and the sale and prostitution of children was prohibited.[2]

In this way the Christian church slowly came to be under the patronage of the Emperors. When the final clash between East and West occurred in 324, Constantine besieged Byzantium, driving out Licinius, who died shortly thereafter. Constantine, who had now become the sole Augustus, or leader of the Roman Empire, continued his work. At that point, this meant giving the Christian Church a new legal Statute, economic privileges, among which was access to the imperial food supplies, as well as a series of new functions to be carried out in the framework of the public systems. The *Corpus Christianorum* thus became an autonomous legal entity that could – among other things – receive donations and bequests, which were then controlled by the crucial figures of this epochal transformation: the bishops.

Formerly simple "overseers"- according to the meaning of the Greek term *episkopos* – of individual Christian communities, after Constantine the bishops became economic, political and legal authority figures. The theory of episcopal succession elaborated toward the end of the 2nd century by Irenaeus, bishop of Lyon, became established. He called bishops the visible successors of St. Peter; those to whom Jesus had entrusted his Church and delegated the power to "bind" (with baptism) and "release" believers from the life of the Christian community, excluding those guilty of serious offenses. The bishops thus began to confess Christians publicly to determine what penance should be assigned to those who committed the more serious types of sins, which – as happens when legal justice is founded on religious principles – at the same time became a crime.

The Roman Emperors' desire to protect the unity of the Christian Church created the need to establish who was a Christian. In 325, Constantine called together the first ecumenical council in Nicea for the purpose of settling the doctrinal controversies which were beginning to threaten the unity of the Christian Church. Seated in the center of the meeting hall on a golden throne, richly adorned with all the symbols of royal dignity and surrounded on all sides by more than 250 bishops, the Emperor did not intervene directly in the theological discussions at Nicea, but he did his utmost to promote a solution that guaranteed unity. A conclusion was found in the affirmation of the "consubstantiation" of the Son with the Father, which then entered the formula of the Nicene Creed. Only Arius and two Egyptian bishops who supported him – proponents of so-called Arianism – refused to endorse the formula and were exiled by the Emperor. The Council's decisions were transmitted to all of the bishops – whom Constantine exhorted to accept them or be exiled. In other words, they assumed full civil and penal effect.

The origins of the Inquisition, and of Giordano Bruno's trial itself, are rooted in this historical passage. This is the moment when, in the 4th century, the State began to guarantee the margins of orthodoxy by law, and the bishops became public magistrates of the faith. Just as the Jews already did, Christians could now take advantage of a special jurisdiction. The bishops – also called Ordinaries of the Diocese – there were about 2,000 of them in this period[3] – set up courts that we can compare to today's *Shari'ah* Councils: often described as "courts" or "Islamic tribunals," these Councils currently operate in Great Britain (and elsewhere) in the shadow of civil law, and are solidly rooted in the local Muslim communities. It is in fact a parallel justice system, effectively competing with that of the State, and conforming to the dictates of Islamic law.[4]

As early as the Roman era the Episcopal tribunals already possessed a regime of penances that could last for years – even until the sinner's death. It was a truly punitive system whose purpose was to protect the community from crimes deemed to be more serious and, at the same time, to select candidates for admission to the ecclesiastical life from the growing masses of applicants. Excommunication was made the essence of this system. Literally, it is the power of a bishop to exclude the believer from the "communication" of the truth of faith, from the mediation of the word of God that came through reading and commenting on the Scriptures. Through the lens of religious justice, excommunication was a combination of two institutions which in modern penal systems are distinct: that of the summons to appear, which obliges the defendant to present himself before a court, along with the penalty of exclusion from the community and its privileges, and that of punishment, consisting of the exclusion itself pending their appearance. Someone who was excommunicated was therefore simultaneously punished and forced to appear before the bishop to be judged.

It is hard to overestimate the enormous power attributed to excommunication in ancient society. For example, in 390 AD Ambrose, the bishop of

Milan, at the culmination of a series of confrontations which had divided him from the Emperor Theodosius, wrote a secret letter to the Emperor, recently guilty of the appalling massacre of Thessalonica, enjoining him to submit to a severe penitential regime to pay for his sin. Theodosius was obliged to enter the Order of Penitents, publicly acknowledge his sin, and put aside his Imperial robes and adornments. He was reconciled in a solemn mass performed in the cathedral of Milan at Christmas, 390 AD. When, in later centuries, membership in the Christian church guaranteed the concession of what today we call civil rights – among which are the right to stipulate deeds, legal contracts, and marriage contracts – judicial excommunication represented a fearsome punishment, precisely because it automatically suspended those rights for secular courts as well.[5]

All of this reminds us how deep the interweaving of Church and politics, religion, and society had been since its origins, also and especially with regards to the terrain of tribunals of the faith. Though it would not be correct when discussing the Inquisition to superimpose the role of secular authorities with that of their ecclesiastic counterparts – even in Bruno's case we can see that their respective functions were distinct – what we have seen up to now reminds us that the fundamental moments in the history of religious justice coincided with episodes of profound political change.

The so-called Edict of Thessalonica, issued in Constantinople by Emperor Theodosius in February 380, was also formulated at a politically critical moment, when the very survival of the Empire was threatened by Nordic peoples, and the Romans had suffered the spectacular defeat of Adrianopolis at the hands of the Visigoths (378 AD). The reconciliation of religious identity was therefore experienced in the face of the grave threat that the State might disintegrate. The Edict established that the Christian Church, at that point catholic in the sense of a "universal" religious community, had become the sole Church of the Empire. The three ruling emperors: Theodosius of the East, Gratian of the West, and the latter's junior co-ruler Valentinian II proclaimed:

> All the peoples who are governed by the moderation of our clemency, it is our desire that they remain faithful to that religion which tradition affirms was transmitted to the Romans by the divine apostle Peter and, starting with him taught until the present day.[6]

This moment is at the heart of the historical and institutional development of the West. Christianity goes from being a "permitted" religion to becoming a State religion, in the traditional Roman model which integrated the two spheres – religion and state – and required believers to belong to the one Church recognized by the Empire.

With the end of the 4th century, the fight against heresy (from the Greek *hairesis*, "choice") was incorporated into the laws of the Roman Empire with explosive power. The heretic became a new type of criminal to be hunted down, isolated, and expelled from the religious and civic body. The Edict of Thessalonica defined all Christians who disagreed with the dogmas proclaimed at the council of Nicea as "mad and senseless," further declaring that "their conventicles could not be given the name of church."[7] Bishops opened new proceedings, based on Roman law, against those who embraced conceptions of faith judged to be erroneous because they had been condemned by the councils that accompanied the public affirmation of Christianity.

In late antiquity baptism became an obligatory ritual: a ceremony that sanctioned the indissoluble allegiance to the one Empire and its only Church. At that point baptism incorporated both a religious efficacy, since it defined a Christian, and civil power, because it created a subject. In the Middle Ages the sacrament of baptism thus became the basic requirement for Christians to be admitted to what we would today call citizenship. This condition could be suspended by judiciary excommunication, also suspending the civil rights it afforded. In countries such as Italy, where the Catholic Church remained the only obligatory Christian church until the French Revolution, baptism retained this power and this structure throughout the Old regime. It was an era, in fact, in which the registry of the civil state – at that time consisting of documents recording baptisms, marriages, and burials – was maintained and updated by parish priests.

The Church's Judiciary

Living as we do in an era and in a part of the world in which religion is confined to personal experience, and where its practice pertains to the sphere of individual liberties, it is difficult for us today to go back to the long centuries during which the Church had an organic and self-referential legal system: canon law, which is currently collected in the Code of Canon Law promulgated by Pope John Paul II in 1983. This normative system was born in the 12th century, when the Church began to build a variegated *Corpus* of ancient and contemporary rules, collected on the basis of a unified plan aimed at strengthening the centrality of the papacy. This happened while, in parallel, the law of the ancient Roman-Christian Empire, which was the basis for the political and identity building of Italian municipalities, was rediscovered in the Bologna *Studium*.

This concurrence led to the creation of a complex regulatory structure which Paolo Prodi has defined as "Roman-canonical-common-law."[8] This is not just a technical detail. Recognizing this means explaining how, in the West, the religious and the civic spheres were able to communicate for centuries: they spoke a common language, thanks to the common conceptual framework represented by the ancient Roman-Christian law. On the one hand, the Church – or, more precisely, the papacy – managed the laws governing souls; on the other, secular princes employed civil law "over bodies." These two spheres were not opposed but rather entwined, their concrete exercise being carried out in the ecclesiastical tribunals and the civil courts. The tribunals that prosecuted Giordano Bruno based their authority on Roman canonical common law, and they took advantage of it – as we will see – in obtaining the cooperation of the civil authorities of the Venetian Republic.

It is certainly no accident that that the tribunal of the Inquisition was also developed during the same historical period in which the *Corpus iuris canonici* was established. Thanks to the Inquisition, in fact, a long process of criminalization of the so-called "hidden" sins, sanctioned by canon law, is completed. These were sins that in preceding centuries had been confined to the individual conscience and therefore not subject to legal judgement.[9] In the Roman Empire, as we have seen, the problem for the Emperors and the bishops was actually that of penalizing behaviors that threatened the unity of the Christian communities, and which therefore manifested in public forms. Heresy itself was considered a concern because it provoked doctrinal disputes and could thus lead to schisms. The elimination of the distinction between sins and public crimes came about in the Middle Ages, when – for reasons we cannot expand upon here – the judges of the faith increasingly began to probe individual consciences and search for heresy lurking in their circles of personal and domestic relations. This was the last piece in the construction we have retraced, which resulted in the affirmation of the principle – central to the whole history of religious justice that followed – that any sin, even unspoken, had to be punished as disobedience to ecclesiastical authorities.

The birth of the Church's judiciary, understood as canon law, the formation of the Inquisition in the early modern sense, and the establishment of the hierocratic Roman State whose king was the pope are, therefore, three phenomena that must be considered as a whole in order to understand the events of the trial of Giordano Bruno.

It is very important to understand the interrelation between these three historical processes, which will also inoculate us against interpreting the sentence against Bruno, and for that matter those against Galileo Galilei and other contemporary philosophers and scientists, as being the result of the inquisitors' desire to judge the credibility of the defendant's theories. A persistent apologetic tradition continues to claim – completely in the abstract and without documentary references – that the Holy Office, during trials, judged the ideas stated by philosophers in comparison to what at the time was considered (though it is not clear by whom) to be the truth. The inquisitors, however, never did anything of the sort, and the Inquisition was certainly not created for this purpose. The judges of the faith who opened a criminal proceeding took their mandate from canon law to pursue the sin/crime of heresy, even where it was "hidden": or even where the sin was of mere intention and was not spoken of, much less written about. Heresy is canonically conceived of as breaking the baptismal promise, the breach of a contract, and therefore like perjury. Thus it came to be condemned *as such*, as the greatest social sin.[10] The instrument of this condemnation, even before the inquisitorial sentence, was excommunication. This in itself contains an element that is manifestly pre-rational, meaning it is carried out *ipso facto* or *latae sententiae*, or immediately, and as a sentence already pronounced. Excommunication, in the most serious cases, among which were cases of heresy, is based on the presumption that the legislative text promulgated by the bishop or the pope was made authoritative by God himself, who sees all, even what is "hidden" in the heart of a person. Thus it goes into effect from the very moment in which the penitent committed the sin/crime of heresy, even in a completely private form.

As further proof of this, it should be recalled that the Roman Inquisition, once it had issued a sentence, confiscated materials *a die commissi criminis*: or rather the assets owned by the criminal at the exact moment in which they committed heresy for the first time. That moment was established based on what emerged from the trial evidence, often from the statements – more or less coerced – of the defendant or from elements gathered through a direct relationship between the inquisitors and the confessors. This method of confiscation involved the recovery of assets which had previously been objects for sale, donation, or bequest, carried out by the Holy Office and the Chambers of the secular princes, who eventually participated in the division of the seized assets. In addition, everything that had since changed the makeup of the offender's assets *a die commissi criminis* was cancelled, including marriage contracts, grants of credit, lease agreements, and the stipulation of mortgages.[11]

"Agents of a Power That Intends to Dominate the World"

The Middle Ages set three bolts on the prison door that locked up heretics. The first was the formation of the hierocratic Roman State, with the pope as monarch; the second was the formation of a legal *Corpus* for the Church; the third was the advent of the tribunal of the Inquisition in the form then passed on to early modernity. To understand the significance of this decisive passage – with respect to the Bruno trial as well – we have to take a few more steps back.

The historical origin of the inquisitorial criminal trial is not clear. In the oldest forms of Roman law, trials were conducted with the system of *quaestiones*, and were therefore of the *accusatory type*: that is, it was up to the "private citizen" to set the trial in motion, carry out an investigation, provide evidence, and support his accusations. In the Imperial age, a more flexible procedure was established; judges began to take the initiative in prosecuting cases *ex officio* following a full investigation and after the denunciation from a private citizen, who at that point acted only as an informant. It was up to the judge to gather the evidence. The procedure concluded with the pronunciation of a verdict and determination of the sentence.[12]

Thus in the late Roman Empire the *inquisitio* became a method of gathering evidence through the direct intervention of the judge as an expression of the public interest in the repression of crime. This precedent will be constantly recalled by medieval legal science as the founding moment of the Inquisitorial trial.

We are in the era, between the 11th and 12th centuries, in which the papacy took on a new political centrality in the life of Christendom. This transformation was given a definitive direction by the work of popes like Gregory VII (1073–1085) and Innocent III (1198–1216) who established a precise design for the doctrinal and juridical supremacy of the bishop of Rome. These pontiffs not only claimed the superiority of the Roman Ordinary over the Emperor on the subject of the appointment and deposition of feudal princes and bishops, but also the power to govern all of Western Christianity. This was the premise, among other things, for a growing, albeit slow and difficult, process of hierarchization of the Latin Church: procedures for the election of the pope were permanently established; jurisdiction over bishops and over monasteries was concentrated in his hands; temporal rule was established over the territory which had become the Papal States; an efficient bureaucratic organization was developed in connection with the cardinals, who were gathered in a single college alongside the pope; a papal tribunal was created, the Roman Curia, equipped with differentiated governing bodies. It was the creation of a true supranational power structure, stable over time and based, at the legal and at the same time religious level, on the reorganization of canon law.

It was in this context that, in the 1230s, some inquisitors delegated by the Holy See began to act across a large part of Western Europe, tasked with the job of combatting "heretical depravity" by encouraging the actions of the bishops or opening new proceedings. It is at this point that the way was opened for the Inquisition to be understood as an institution founded on a precise plan for the repression of religious heterodoxy and on *ad hoc* measures. This therefore took place while the Roman Catholic Church established its grand hierocratic design for dominion over Christianity – or rather the world. The Inquisition was called upon to defend the reasons for the existence of the new papal monarchy, which identified itself with the entire political and social order. In the decree *Vergentis in senium* (1199), promulgated by Innocent III – who points to himself as a model for all civil powers – established that heresy is a *crimine di lesa maestà* – a crime of treason. This concluded a centuries' long evolution, simultaneously political, religious, and legal, upon which the Old Regime was founded.

Who, then, were the Inquisitors? As Grado Giovanni Merlo has observed, we must think of the judges of faith as "agents of a power that intends to dominate the world, and which finds in the defense of orthodoxy (...) one of its strongest elements of legitimization."[13] Pope Gregory VII had affirmed the new, fundamental principle: "whoever does not agree with the Roman Church, is not to be considered Catholic." This was put into action with the new organization of the Inquisition as *officium fidei* ("ecclesiastical function of the faith") or *inquisitio haereticae pravitatis* ("prosecution of heretical depravity"), operating by direct delegation of the pope, and through members of the new Mendicant Orders.[14] What made the Dominican and Franciscan friars especially suitable for the task of inquisitor was the fact that these new Orders had rules that promised obedience and deference to the papacy, the prime architect and central authority of the new tribunals of the faith. Moreover, the members of these Orders studied and taught in the schools of theology and law, thus preparing themselves in the two major disciplines required to prosecute a case of faith. The friars then lived in monasteries that were situated in urban centers, where heterodox ideas and texts arose more frequently. They were loved by the local residents for the simplicity of their customs and the way they embraced pauperism, so they were able to mix easily with the population and obtain the tips and accusations needed to identify, prosecute, and extirpate heresy as early as possible.

From the 1230s, inquisitors were appointed in Italy and France, in the kingdoms of Aragon and Navarre and elsewhere in the Empire. The heretical movements of dualistic or pauperistic-evangelical inspiration that emerged in the previous century, starting with the so-called "Cathars" or Albigensians and the Waldensians, had at that point drastically reduced in size, so this was not the priority that spurred the popes to create the new form of Inquisition. The real motivation was the need to consolidate the supremacy of Rome over Christianity and the Latin Church – to build a genuine system of orthodoxy that guaranteed the dominion of the popes over the world, for eternity.

Pope Paul III created the Congregation of the Sacred Roman and Universal Inquisition, or Holy Office in 1542. This was the tribunal that, in the decisive phase of the trial, "heard," or rather adjudicated the case and condemned Giordano Bruno to death. What was the purpose of its establishment? What were its powers? We must try to answer these questions briefly. Further ahead we will describe how this tribunal actually operated.

The first half of the 16th century witnessed a deepening religious and political rift in Europe. As is well known, this rift was opened in the German world by the 95 theses nailed to – or perhaps read before – the door of Wittenberg castle by Martin Luther in 1517. There were several elements concerning Luther that alarmed the popes and the papal Court in the 1520s and 1530s: the great success of his message, which fundamentally challenged the authority of the Church of Rome; his burning of the *Corpus iuris canonici* and of the papal bull *Exsurge Domine*, in which Leo X had decreed his condemnation in 1520; and his refusal to bow and retract his doctrinal stance in front of Emperor Charles V. The great revolt of German peasants of 1524–1525 made clear to all the potential social and political consequences of the faith proclaimed by Luther, who had not hesitated to entrust its protection to certain Princes, thus stimulating the birth of a powerful "Protestant" party in Germany.

In 1530, the day after the solemn coronation of Charles V in Bologna by Clement VII, the presentation of the Lutheran *confessio* at the Diet of

Augsburg, and the severe imperial edict ordering dissidents to yield dissolved any hope for a political solution to the religious conflict. Menacing war clouds were gathering in the skies over Germany, and the battle of words seemed to be passing to one of weapons. From the beginning, however, it was actually Rome, fiercely adverse towards any doctrinal compromise, and still very far from any authentic prospect of renewal, that pushed in this direction. This despite the warning of the tragic sack of 1527, which had seen the Papal States occupied by foreign troops, and the city of Rome devastated by German mercenaries who had been enlisted by the Habsburg Emperor in pursuit of his war with the kingdom of France, an ally of the papacy.[15]

In the first half of the 16th century, the doctrines that sprang from Luther's protest also spread widely in Italy, taking on peculiar connotations and intertwining with other religious movements and cultural legacies. In particular, during the years that were the backdrop to the opening of the Council of Trent (1545–1563), the Spanish exile Juan de Valdés introduced a spiritual teaching on the peninsula which, while not attributable to Protestant Reform, directed anxieties and demands for renewal which had spread both at the popular level and at the top of the social hierarchies, among scholars and aristocrats, bishops and cardinals. Well aware of the extremely serious risks that this season of renewal meant for the stability and the temporal and spiritual power of the Roman Church, the most hardline component of the Curia stressed the need for central coordination of the activities of the local inquisitors scattered throughout the territories. At that point the local inquisitors still operated as individual judges of the faith, without any central coordination, following the model established in the Middle Ages.

Centuries-old continental political and religious balances were in play, and their disruption threatened to forever undo the spiritual and ecclesial unity of the West. It was the political necessity of confronting this emergency – and not, as has sometimes been suggested, the abstract "mentality" of the time – that in June 1542 prompted a faction of hardline cardinals to promote the creation of a genuine Dicastery of the Papal States. It was the first Dicastery created in the history of the State, and the only one to have the pope himself as its leader. Its primary aim was to reduce the risk of prelates who had been contaminated by the Lutheran disease from penetrating the leadership of Latin Christianity. If necessary, it would also exhibit documents in conclave that had been secretly collected by the cardinal inquisitors in order to demonstrate the inadmissibility of one or more colleagues by declaring them to be heretics. This is what happened in the elections that would lead Julius III in 1550 and Paul IV in 1555 to the papal throne, when, as mentioned previously, the candidacies of Reginald Pole and Giovanni Morone were undermined in precisely this way.

The new "Supreme" Congregation of the Roman Holy Office was set up as a central and supranational tribunal, composed of six or more cardinals who were empowered to bypass the sovereignty of the States of the Italian peninsula, impeach government authorities, princes, and even the highest ecclesiastical leadership, and to direct local tribunals, monopolizing the repression of heresy in Italy. Even the very prestigious Cardinal Giovanni Morone was confined by the Supreme Inquisitors in Castel Sant'Angelo from 1557 to 1559. He was released only after the death of his bitter enemy, Pope Paul IV Carafa. The new pope, Pius IV, later sent Morone to Trent to preside over the Council as his Legate and bring it to a close. In the mid-1500s even the Diocese Ordinaries were subject to judgement by the Holy Office, such as the bishop of Limassol on Cyprus, Andrea Centanni; or the bishop of Bergamo, Vittore Soranzo; the bishop of Cava dei Tirreni, Giovanni Tommaso Sanfelice; the Ordinary of Otranto, Pietro Antonio di Capua; and the bishop of Cheronissos, Giovanni Francesco Verdura. Prominent prelates were prosecuted as well, such as the apostolic protonotary Pietro Carnesecchi, who was sentenced to death in 1567.[16]

Although its jurisdiction covered all of Christianity, the Congregation of the Holy Office operated almost exclusively within the continental Italian peninsula. Sicily and Sardinia were under the authority of the Spanish Inquisition, established in 1478 against the backdrop of the *Reconquista* (Reconquest) of the Iberian peninsula from Islam and the unification of the territory under the "Catholic Monarchs," Isabella of Castile and Ferdinand of Aragon. In 1492 the two rulers expelled Jews who refused baptism from their lands, thus creating a new intolerant Iberian identity, legitimized by the use of the instruments of the justice of the faith against religious minorities and heretics.[17] The Spanish State Inquisition was followed by the Portuguese Inquisition in 1536, and the last to arrive, the papal Inquisition. The latter's mission continues to this day through the Congregation for the Doctrine of the Faith, which Vatican law also designates as a tribunal that "judges crimes against the faith" and "the most serious crimes committed against morality and in the celebration of the sacraments."[18]

In the second half of the century other Roman Congregations were established, among which were the Congregation of the Council (1564), the Congregation of the Index (1572), and the Congregation of Bishops (1573). With the apostolic constitution *Immensa aeterni Dei* of 1588, Pope Sixtus V reorganized the Congregations and created new ones, making them the backbone of papal government. It was a fully realized system of ministries, endowed with their own bureaucracy, a system which made the Roman Curia a prototype of government organization for contemporary and future European States. The Holy Office always remained the first and most important among the others, an instrument to facilitate the pope's control over the Sacred College. The commission of cardinal inquisitors had at that point defeated Reform and achieved supremacy, visually represented by the solemn palazzo which had been its home from the 1560s.

This prominent building, rebuilt by Pius V on the south side of Saint Peter's Basilica, was where Giordano Bruno would remain imprisoned for over six years. At that moment the power of the Holy Office was at its apogee, during the secretariat of Giulio Antonio Santori, cardinal and Supreme Inquisitor from the year 1586 until 1602.

Notes

1 I tried to demonstrate this point in Germano Maifreda, *The Business of the Roman Inquisition*, New York and London, Routledge, 2017.

2 For an initial bibliographical orientation refer to Charles Freeman, *A New History of Early Christianity*, New Haven, CT and London, Yale University Press, 2009; on the Italian area see especially Giovanni Filoramo, *La croce e il potere. I cristiani da martiri a persecutori*, Rome and Bari, Laterza, 2011, pp. 104 ff. and 130–131.

3 Ivi, p. 175.

4 Russell Sandberg, Sharon Thompson, *The Sharia Law Debate: The Missing Family Law Context*, in «Law and Justice», 2016, n. 177, pp. 181–192.

5 Elena Brambilla, *La giustizia intollerante. Inquisizione e tribunali confessional in Europa (secoli IV-XVIII)*, Rome, Carocci, 2006, p. 53.

6 G. Filoramo, *La croce e il potere*, cit., p. 261.

7 *Ibidem.*

8 Paolo Prodi, *Una storia della giustizia. Dal pluralismo dei fori al moderno dualismo tra coscienza e diritto*, Bologna, Il Mulino, 2000, p. 66.

9 Jacques Chiffoleau, *Introduction. De la nécessité du secret dans la construction de l'espace (et du sujet) politique*, in *La necessità del segreto: Indagini sullo spazio politico nell'Italia medievale ed oltre*, edited by Jacques Chiffoleau, Etienne Hubert, Roberta Mucciarelli, Rome, Viella, 2018, pp. 9–67.

10 P. Prodi, *Una storia della giustizia*, cit., pp. 96–97; Heikki Pihlajamäki, Mia Korpiola, *Medieval Canon Law: The Origins of Modern Criminal Law*, in *The Oxford Handbook of Criminal Law*, edied by Markus D. Dubber, Tatjana Hörnle, Oxford, Oxford University Press, 2014, pp. 201–214.

11 G. Maifreda, *The Business of the Roman Inquisition*, cit. I cannot elaborate here on the relationship between sacramental confession and inquisitorial investigations: refer to the now classic volume by Elena Brambilla, *Alle origini del Sant'Uffizio. Penitenza, confessione e giustizia spirituale dal Medioevo al XVI secolo*, Bologna, Il Mulino, 2000.

12 Mario Sbriccoli, *Storia del diritto penale e della giustizia. Scritti editi e inediti (1972–2007)*, Milan, Giuffrè, 2009.

13 Grado Giovanni Merlo, *Inquisitori e inquisizione nel Medioevo*, Bologna, Il Mulino, 2008, p. 20, also for the information that follows. For a long term view one can now see *A Companion to Heresy Inquisitions*, edited by Donald S. Prudlo, Leiden and Boston, MA, Brill, 2019.

14 It is therefore impossible to establish a precise moment for the foundation of the medieval Inquisition. One can think of a "polycentric origin" that joins the theoretical assumptions expressed in the pontifical bulls with legislative interventions, be they papal, imperial or civil, and practical arrangements in which the mendicant Orders participated: see Marina Benedetti, *Gregorio IX: l'inquisizione, i frati e gli eretici*, in *Gregorio IX e gli Ordini mendicanti. Atti del XXXVIII Convegno internazionale. Assisi, 7–9 ottobre 2010*, Spoleto, Fondazione Centro italiano di studi sull'Alto medioevo, 2011, pp. 293–323.

15 Massimo Firpo, *Juan de Valdés and the Italian Reformation*, Leiden and Boston, MA, Brill, 2016.

16 *Ibidem.*

17 Chris Lowney, *A Vanished World: Muslims, Christians, and Jews in Medieval Spain*, New York, Oxford University Press, 2006.

18 http://www.vatican.va/roman_curia/congregations/cfaith/index_it.htm.

References

Marina Benedetti, *Gregorio IX: l'inquisizione, i frati e gli eretici*, in *Gregorio IX e gli Ordini mendicanti. Atti del XXXVIII Convegno internazionale. Assisi, 7–9 ottobre 2010*, Spoleto, Fondazione Centro italiano di studi sull'Alto medioevo, 2011, pp. 293–323.

Elena Brambilla, *Alle origini del Sant'Uffizio. Penitenza, confessione e giustizia spirituale dal Medioevo al XVI secolo*, Bologna, Il Mulino, 2000.

Elena Brambilla, *La giustizia intollerante. Inquisizione e tribunali confessional in Europa (secoli IV-XVIII)*, Rome, Carocci, 2006.

Jacques Chiffoleau, *Introduction. De la nécessité du secret dans la construction de l'espace (et du sujet) politique*, in *La necessità del segreto: Indagini sullo spazio politico nell'Italia medievale ed oltre*, edited by Jacques Chiffoleau, Etienne Hubert, Roberta Mucciarelli, Rome, Viella, 2018, pp. 9–67.

A Companion to Heresy Inquisitions, edited by Donald S. Prudlo, Leiden and Boston, MA, Brill, 2019.

Giovanni Filoramo, *La croce e il potere. I cristiani da martiri a persecutori*, Rome and Bari, Laterza, 2011

Massimo Firpo, *Juan de Valdés and the Italian Reformation*, Leiden and Boston, MA, Brill, 2016.

Charles Freeman, *A New History of Early Christianity*, New Haven, CT and London, Yale University Press, 2009.

Chris Lowney, *A Vanished World: Muslims, Christians, and Jews in Medieval Spain*, New York, Oxford University Press, 2006.

Germano Maifreda, *The Business of the Roman Inquisition*, New York and London, Routledge, 2017.

Grado Giovanni Merlo, *Inquisitori e inquisizione nel Medioevo*, Bologna, Il Mulino, 2008.

Heikki Pihlajamäki, Mia Korpiola, *Medieval Canon Law: The Origins of Modern Criminal Law*, in *The Oxford Handbook of Criminal Law*, edited by Markus D. Dubber, Tatjana Hörnle, Oxford, Oxford University Press, 2014, pp. 201–214.

Paolo Prodi, *Una storia della giustizia. Dal pluralismo dei fori al moderno dualismo tra coscienza e diritto*, Bologna, Il Mulino, 2000.

Russell Sandberg, Sharon Thompson, *The Sharia Law Debate: The Missing Family Law Context*, in «Law and Justice», 2016, n. 177, pp. 181–192.

Mario Sbriccoli, *Storia del diritto penale e della giustizia. Scritti editi e inediti (1972–2007)*, Milan, Giuffrè, 2009.

4 The Machine of the Inquisition

The Inquisition was a politico-religious court or tribunal established to overcome any other state or particularistic jurisdiction in the Catholic world, in order to repress forms of dissent that could threaten the stability and the mission of the Church of Rome. Consequently, as Elena Brambilla has observed, its procedures were

> completely different from those of the criminal courts to which they have [also] been compared, because they did not aim to absolve or punish but to convert, that is, to *compel abjuration*: like all totalitarian censors, they are not instruments of justice, but of ideological propaganda of truth and confessional unity.[1]

This interpretation also explains why the justices of the faith succeeded in creating space for themselves in almost all the peninsular Italian states. Secular rulers saw the spread of heresy and other deviant behaviors – such as belonging to ethno-linguistically and religiously separate groups such as Jews and Waldensians; the practice of sanctioned sexual orientations; exercising the right of divorce (seen by the Catholic Church as bigamy); or magical and esoteric practices – as a serious threat to the stability of society and to the prevailing power structures. Thus there was a common bond of intent between the territorial States and the Church of Rome. The activities of the "courts of conscience" were also considered by both princes and republics as the most effective means of rooting out dissent. Meanwhile, they provided the Roman Curia with the hegemony that it maintained in Italy until the threshold of the modern era.[2]

But how was an Inquisitorial trial for a case of faith conducted? Was the Holy Office, as a tenacious apologetic reading seems inclined to believe, really a criminal court meant to protect civil liberties, and thus essentially indistinguishable from secular courts? Or was it moved by the blind and instrumental irrationality of the torturer painted by proponents of the black legend?[3]

DOI: 10.4324/9781003026082-6

The Eradication of Heresy

In the second half of the 16th century an imposing inquisitorial machine was functioning, driven by the cardinals of the Congregation of the Holy Office, who usually met twice a week, at least once in the presence of the pope. A constellation of tribunals revolved around them, called local or peripheral, some of which were traceable to tribunals established in the Middle Ages, and some created *ex novo*. Among these was that of Venice, the city where Giordano Bruno was arrested on May 23, 1592.

The capital of the Serenissima had seen the activity of individual inquisitors delegated by popes since the Middle Ages. By the Early Modern era, however, the powerful Republic of Venice had succeeded in imposing significant compromises on the Holy See. First of all, in Venice itself the most powerful judge of the faith was not the inquisitor, but the apostolic nuncio, who was the pope's diplomatic representative. Beside him, along with the official inquisitor – who was usually a Dominican (but was sometimes a Franciscan, as in the case of Sixtus V before he became pope, though he was so assiduous in his duties that the Republic demanded his recall) – was the Venetian patriarch's Vicar-General, Ordinary of the Venetian Diocese, or the patriarch himself. Furthermore, starting in 1547 the authorities of the Serenissima required the Holy Office to accept the permanent presence of three "sages of heresy" (*savi all'eresia*), senior judges charged with controlling and containing the actions of the ecclesiastical inquisitors. This meant, among other things, that death sentences pronounced by the Venetian Inquisition were not all actually carried out by the secular authorities, but were also formulated in terms which departed from the dictates of canon law.[4]

The presence of the civil magistrate in the Venetian inquisitorial tribunal is an aspect worth careful evaluation. The secular official nominated by the Venetian Republic shifted the balance of power within the judging tribunal, generally in favor of the Patriarch. In fact, the latter was usually a Venetian patrician, from the same social background as the civil magistrate. Consequently, it was the Venetian inquisitor who lost importance: as a simple mendicant friar, often not Venetian, he was forced to submit to the guidelines established by the other judges of the tribunal.[5] As will be better explained ahead, however, this aspect has been strangely overlooked by scholars of Bruno's trial, who have disregarded the patriarch's role in the conduct of the trial and also, in all probability, incorrectly identified the physical location of Bruno's imprisonment in Venice.

By virtue of its economic and political power and its republican form of government, Venice was therefore able to put limits on the operation of the Roman tribunals of the faith. This situation, however, was an exception. The norm in the second half of the 16th century was much different. The Congregation of the Holy Office was in a position of absolute supremacy with respect to the other Roman magistracies and the local inquisitorial tribunals, which increasingly depended upon its directives. The Holy Office intervened directly in the more important or delicate trials, often moving the proceedings to Rome. The cardinals normally pressured state governments to extradite the accused. This happened above all in places like Venice, where the presence of deputized laymen on the tribunal threatened to limit the discretion of the judges of faith and the effective application of canonical norms. So it was with Bruno as well; after a few months on trial in Venice, he was extradited to Rome and imprisoned there, while the trial was taken over by the supreme inquisitor.

Thanks to the strict application of the inquisitors, in the second half of the 1500s the outbreaks of heresy scattered across Italy had been substantially eliminated, starting with the reformed evangelical doctrines of Erasmus or Luther. In the meantime a string of papal dispositions placed new subjects under the jurisdiction of the Inquisition. In addition to heretics, apostates, and other "criminals"[6] suspected of practicing magic and demonic witchcraft, the Holy Office would also be concerned with blasphemers, sodomites, bigamists, so-called "judaizers," astrologists, and simonists (or simoniacs). Other behaviors were also placed under the purview of the Inquisition; laymen who celebrated mass without being ordained, people who simulated sanctity, people who consumed forbidden foods, those who believed in and spread popular superstitions, and confessors who solicited sexual favors from a penitent during the sacrament. Over the course of the early modern period, intolerance towards Jews and Waldensians worsened, and there began to be investigations and trials brought against members of the Greek Orthodox community. Books were subjected to ever-increasing inspection, and to expurgation or even total prohibition by the Congregation of the Index, created in 1572. Even after that date, however, the Holy Office continued to play a dominant role in censorship activity.[7]

The tribunals of the Inquisition also began to prosecute philosophers accused of opposing or denying the truth of the Catholic faith, which the Roman Church believed could be found in the Scriptures, Conciliar Decrees, and in the written and unwritten traditions and the authority of the Holy See and of the Church Fathers. We have already referred to the legal basis for that prosecution, which dates from 1513 and was formalized by a decree of Lateran V, promulgated by Leo X as the papal bull *Apostolici regiminis.* This bull required philosophers, during their lectures and disquisitions on hypotheses of the eternity of the world and the mortality of the individual soul, to use every means to demonstrate the truth of the Christian religion, which of course had to emerge as predominant in both oral and written lessons.

Given that the discourse of natural philosophy had for centuries taken place in a climate of relative freedom from investigation, this provision was a fundamental break with what had gone before. It established the principle – full of dangerous consequences – that there could not be two truths, one philosophical and one theological, that could be freely enunciated and supported in parallel. From that moment on, research and instruction on some of the central themes of philosophical inquiry, especially in the developing natural sciences, had to take into account a theology which had hardened as it emerged from the Middle Ages, as well as the scholastic elaborations of the religious Orders.[8] This turning point offered a powerful legal basis for the set of accusations brought against Giordano Bruno, as well as those made against Galileo Galilei a few decades later.

Acknowledging the unquestionably repressive efficiency of the 16th century Inquisition does not imply the assumption that the machine always worked flawlessly, or that it was spared from the internal contradictions, opacity, and power struggles that are typical of every human institution. In particular, it must be noted that the Holy Office sometimes pursued initiatives autonomously, even when it came to papal policy. Because it maintained this proud independence from the orientations of the popes, it was able to influence the Roman Church's lines of government and pervade them with its own ideology.[9]

The very origins of the Congregation of the Holy Office are rooted in a lengthy conflict which had divided the factions of cardinals, in a disagreement over the strategy to employ concerning the Lutheran threat. These conflicts were often bitter, moved by personal pride, the strenuous defense of the reasons for orthodoxy, factional rivalries, or straightforward disagreements. The definitive failure in 1541 of the Colloquy of religions with the Protestants held in Ratisbon had been received with relief – if not, indeed, been provoked – by the hardline wing of the Sacred College. The apostolic legate Gasparo Contarini, advocate of an irenic policy towards the Protestants that was shared by the nuncio, Giovanni Morone, was repudiated. The next step was the decision by Paul III (1534–1549) to coordinate the repression of the Reformation in Italy through a commission of cardinals with a majority of hardliners, to be led by the cardinal who founded the Theatine Regular Clerics: the Neapolitan aristocrat Gian Pietro Carafa.

In the years that followed it became normal practice to gather documents and accusatory testimony against personal adversaries, or enemies of what the cardinal-inquisitors considered to be the authentic faith; as did launching investigations and trials without the knowledge or even in open defiance of the pope. Having become pontiff with the name of Paul IV (1555–1559), Carafa introduced a fundamental discontinuity in the history of the modern Inquisition. His election definitively eliminated the last spaces for dialogue within the Holy College between the hardline and conciliatory factions regarding the Protestant world. With Paul IV, Massimo Firpo has observed, the "process of the affirmation of the Roman Inquisition as the supreme normative, theological, pastoral, legal and political authority for the leadership of the Church" was thus irreversibly established. The Congregation of the Holy Office, "much more than the [Tridentine] council chambers," became the place where the Church posed "the conditions for a

Counter-Reformation destined to go on for centuries, and in many ways to last until today."[10]

The internal conflict in the Roman Curia did not recede with the creation of the Holy Office. The same relations between the popes and the cardinals of the Holy Office sometimes resulted in bitter clashes, stemming from differences between the political and religious directions of the popes and those of the inquisitors. For example, Pope Julius III (1550–1555), troubled by the enormous power the new Dicastery was acquiring in the Curia, as well as in Italian and international political life, attempted to bring it back under pontifical control. He accordingly issued decrees limiting the cardinal Inquisitors' discretion by preventing them from judging other cardinals and bishops without his personal authorization. He furthermore personally guaranteed the orthodoxy of the two cardinals who had most exposed themselves in the context of the German Colloquy on religion or by joining the circle of "Spirituals," Reginald Pole and Giovanni Morone: two figures of high intellectual and diplomatic stature, who he considered suited for conducting a policy of religious conciliation in Europe. Julius III also made sure to resolve other legal issues involving high-ranking prelates outside the tribunals, prompting the resentment of the future Pope Carafa.[11]

Pope Pius IV (1559–1565) also opposed a cardinal Inquisitor, Michele Ghislieri, who would later become pope as Pius V. The pontiff, who rehabilitated Morone, was determined to find reconciliation *in extremis* with the Protestants on the crucial terrain of communion *sub utraque specie* and the abolition of the obligation of ecclesiastic celibacy in Germany. This forced him to face the attacks of the hardline faction, headed by Ghislieri, who was determined to overrule him: the pope reacted by depriving Ghislieri of his powers of control over the Inquisition. These events involved Giulio Antonio Santori, who at the time was an inquisitor in the Kingdom of Napoli, and vicar of the Neapolitan archbishop, who himself was summoned to Rome to answer for the crime of treason. Accused by Pius IV of having withheld information about a conspiracy against his person, Santori was let go thanks to protection from Ghislieri, to whom he was linked by strong commonality of purpose and by a providential vision of the workings of the Inquisition and the role of the Church in history.

Elected pope as Pius V, Ghislieri would nominate Santori to be archbishop of Santa Severina, calling him to Rome permanently as a consultor of the Holy Office. The cardinal's red berretta was placed on his head in 1570.[12] This marked the beginning of Santori's unstoppable rise to the leadership of the Roman Inquisition, which was under Santa Severina's leadership at the time of Giordano Bruno's arrest in Venice in May 1592. At that moment, as we have seen, a bitter conflict was also unfolding in Rome between the new pontiff, Clement VIII Aldobrandini (1592–1605), and the Holy Office, which was firmly opposed to the reconciliation of the King of France, Henry IV.

The Law and Discretion

The Middle Ages bequeathed a rich production of inquisitorial manuals to the 1500s. These were manuscripts written by the judges themselves – or by theologians, or jurists – who recorded for posterity the procedures they followed for opening, managing, and "hearing" (or really discussing the evidence and reaching a sentence) a trial for a case of faith. Among these texts two works from the 14th century assumed particular authority: the *Directorium inquisitorium* by Inquisitor General of Aragon Nicholas Eymerich (c.1316–1399), upon which the Spanish jurist Francisco Peña (c.1540–1612) wrote an authoritative commentary in the late 16th century, and the *De haereticis* by Zanchino Ugolini, co-auditor of the Franciscan inquisitors in Romagna, which was printed in Rome in 1568 by order of Pius V.[13] The procedures illustrated by these manuals, along with the large *Corpus* of canon law solemnly promulgated by Gregory XIII in 1580 and reprinted two years later, constitute the normative basis for the work of the inquisitors, including those who prosecuted Giordano Bruno between 1592 and 1600.

Thanks to research conducted in the last two decades, and the opening of the historic Archive of the Congregation for the Doctrine of the Faith, today we possess a rich harvest of information regarding the *modus operandi* of the Holy Office. As I mentioned in the Introduction, prior to the recent renewal of studies of the Inquisition, historians put perhaps too much faith in the overall transparency and procedural consistency of the Roman tribunals of faith. Today, this view is hard to reconcile not only with what we know of the Holy Office operation, but also with the well-known fluidity of judicial procedures in the Old Regime, based on the broad discretion of the judge (*arbitrium*), superseded across Europe only with the French Revolution, modern codifications, and the legal positivism of the 19th–20th centuries.[14] Before those historic turning points, the framework of canonical norms and medieval procedures that constituted the backbone of the *officium fidei* could also be perceived as a cumbersome obstacle. The way to overcome this obstacle was through the discretion of judges who were animated by a providential vision of their office, engaged in the achievement of goals to which they subscribed unconditionally, and imbued with the belief that their mission would endure until the end of days. The emerge of the *Ius Commune* – a plethora of juridical commentary, interpretation, and elaboration dating from the late medieval and the early modern period[15] – had recreated a cultural and legal horizon that was quite far from what we know today, in whose context concrete procedural "exceptions" could be used by judges to redefine rules and general legal principles.

These elements point us in an important direction. To try and understand what happened in the final years of Giordano Bruno's life – something which will never be completely possible – we cannot assume that every event in the trial left traces in the surviving documentation, even where the documents appear complete to us. Nor is it possible to hypothesize that the inquisitors made decisions by applying the current "laws" as a judge would today; or that they blindly respected procedures of medieval origin, which also had never had true canonical dignity, and had never been organized in codices comparable to those that were established between the 18th and 19th centuries.

Having said all this, it cannot be argued that the *arbitrium* of the ecclesiastic tribunals was total, and that some consistencies cannot be found in history.

Normally a trial for heresy was divided into five stages:

1 The tribunal established a proceeding after receiving a formal denunciation. Although the judges of the faith could also operate on the basis of simple information about criminal facts – public reputation, being caught in the act of committing the offence, official reports, reporting of crimes by private individuals – this last practice was mostly abandoned over the course of the modern era and was specifically recommended against by authoritative manuals, among which was the widely used *Sacro arsenale*.[16]
2 The information phase followed, meant to verify the basis of the accusations and, eventually, proceed to the arrest of the offender. The tribunal could call for the interrogation of witnesses and the defendant himself, and could order the use of torture. The depositions of the witnesses and the defendant were recorded by a notary. In the meantime the trial moved on to the collection of evidence, including through searches, the objects of which included books and other writings.
3 The defendant was given the opportunity to defend himself with the drafting of a defense brief. Copies of the trial documents were also made available to him, though they did not show the names of the accusers. In the most complex cases, the tribunal could order the drafting of a *Sommario* (Summary) of the trial to facilitate the work of the judges. Meanwhile, the repetition of the witness interrogations took place, with the purpose of exposing contradictions and unmasking slanderers.
4 The trial moved to the "hearing" of the case (*expeditio causae*), where over the course of one or more sessions the tribunal decided on a verdict.
5 Finally, during a session that was often public, the judges read a sentence that reviewed the elements that had emerged in the trial and communicated the verdict. The condemned was normally required to recite an abjuration in public that listed and "detested" the errors he had committed.

If the crime of heresy was demonstrated and formally confessed, the trial proceeded to an *abiura de formali*, recorded by the notary, and the imposition of corporal penalties – confinement and forced labor, normally on the papal galleys – along with pecuniary or spiritual penalties like fines, fasts, pilgrimages, abstinence, physical mortification, alms, regular participation in divine offices, and frequent sacramental confessions. The death penalty was normally called for in cases where the offender persistently refused abjuration (thus being judged "unrepentant"). Execution was also the penalty for those found guilty in a second trial for the same crime as the first (thus being "relapsed"). In the frequent cases where the accusation of heresy was not entirely proven or formally confessed but the judges remained suspicious, they ordered abjurations and sentences that were milder (*de vehementi* or *de levi suspicione*). The most fortunate cases could hope to end in absolution "for lack of evidence," which was called a canonic purgation, or with a simple admonition. Aristocrats, prelates, and other notables would normally abjure in secret.

Inquisitorial trials were usually begun and conducted in the local tribunals distributed throughout the territory of the peninsula, excluding Sardinia and Sicily where the Spanish Inquisition operated.[17] The only Italian State in which the Inquisition did not operate was the Republic of Lucca: a territory in which a secular *Offizio sopra la religione* operated from 1545 and was endowed with authority over issues of religious orthodoxy. An important decree of the Congregation of the Holy Office in 1581 ordered the inquisitors to only send to Rome the final sentences of the trials conducted in the outlying tribunals. An exception, however, was made for those disputes that were considered to be more problematic, defined by the decree as *arduis causis*: "difficult cases." For these, the Supreme Inquisitor had to be alerted immediately. For example, the Venetian inquisitor, friar Gabriele da Saluzzo, immediately listed the Giordano Bruno case among the "difficult," promptly informing the Roman authorities of the arrest that had been carried out and the trial in progress.[18]

However, trials could be initiated directly by the Roman Congregation, or at times it would assume control of cases after they had been started by an inquisitor in a peripheral tribunal, as happened with the trial against Giordano Bruno. In this situation the trials were normally conducted by the so-called officials of the Holy Office, among who the figures of the Assessor and the Commissioner were of particular importance. The first was responsible for presenting outstanding cases in the meetings of the cardinals and taking note of their decisions. The Commissioner instead had the task of interrogating witnesses and defendants, as well as that of writing up the lists of clauses that the condemned had to abjure. This was a delicate and prestigious assignment, the satisfactory execution of which was often the prelude to a promotion in an ecclesiastical career. In Rome, public prosecution was finally given to the Tax Procurator, who participated in the compilation of the judicial dossiers. Only once the trial had been started by the Commissioner and the Tax Procurator did the cardinal inquisitors take charge of it, possibly assisted by theologians as consultants and qualifiers. Their role was that of "hearing" the trial, discussing the evidence that had emerged, in the presence of the pope, who was the head of the Congregation. The cardinals thus proceeded to judgement and imposed their sentence.

The inquisitorial process for judging matters of faith was actually a mixture of two forms of trial provided for by Roman law: the accusatory trial, established in the most ancient era, and the *inquisitio*, which appeared in the first centuries of the Empire. The first model could not begin without an accusation by a private citizen: the evidence had to be provided by the accuser, and the magistrate therefore participated in the judgement as a simple moderator and arbitrator between prosecution and defense, who fought on equal terms. The inquisitorial trial, however, did not require an accuser or an accusation, since the body for public prosecution proceeded ex officio, based on a wide variety of sources of information. Here the magistrate had complete freedom of *inquirere*, proceeding ex officio in the search for and gathering of evidence. Hence the judge played a dominant role, resulting in very significant disparities between the two parties in the case.[19] This was what happened in a trial for a case of faith, where the magistrate was an ecclesiastic who was inevitably on God's side: He whose "majesty," in terms of canon law, had been "injured" by the heresy.

Although some attempts have been made in this direction, at times with unspoken justificatory intentions, it is simply not possible to in any way compare the activity of the Inquisition and that of criminal courts past and present. This is for a number of reasons, which are important to keep in mind in order to understand what concretely took place during a trial for a case of faith.

The inquisitors' activity began in a very different way from that normally followed by an ordinary criminal court. The Inquisition operated with a methodical secrecy[20] that allowed the judges to work without communicating the names of the accusers to the defendant until the end of the opening interrogation phase of the trial; the charges were also not made known to the accused until the interrogation – which sometimes included torture. In fact, the right of the accused to be informed of the accusation and the names of the accusers was at the center of many conflicts with and revolts against the inquisitors.[21] The operational secrecy of the inquisitors created a climate of spying and suspicion that encouraged pre-emptive self-denunciation. These were the so-called "spontaneous appearances," which almost always involved self-incrimination driven by the fear of being accused by others or by pressure from confessors. The latter, unable to absolve penitents who were guilty of the sin/crime of heresy, encouraged them to present themselves to the inquisitor or bishop; the penalty for not doing so being their inclusion on the list of the unconfessed and the consequent risk of being prosecuted in an ordinary inquisitorial trial. It should be recalled that Lateran IV (1215) had required the obligation of annual confession at Easter. In many places, however, this was observed only after the Council of Trent.[22]

For those who were guilty, then, the danger of being denounced by others created a kind of precautionary psychological mechanism, which drove victims to pre-emptively appear before the inquisitors "spontaneously" and report themselves. This gave the judges the opportunity to gather a wealth of information about them and their protectors and accomplices that had no equal in the ordinary criminal courts. Furthermore, the crimes that the inquisitors prosecuted did not require damage to a third party: they were victimless crimes, involving behaviors that today are almost entirely decriminalized or even protected by individual guarantees, such as freedom of speech or of sexual orientation.[23] From this point of view, the Holy Office is therefore closer to the political courts of modern totalitarian regimes, instituted to persecute dissenting opinions and discourage their very formation through secrecy, fear and spying, than to ordinary criminal courts.

In general, the phrase "procedural consistency" cannot be legitimately used in reference to an inquisitorial trial. In the first place this is because there was no genuine codified inquisitorial procedure, and the judge's *arbitrium* was the true compass that guided his work. In addition, the actual procedural phase, from the denunciation to the end of the opening interrogation, was completely secret. Accusers and accusations were normally unknown to the offender, even if maintaining anonymity in practice was difficult: we know cases such as that of a Niccolò Cid, incarcerated in Milan between 1565 and 1571, who corrupted his jailers and came to know everything that was being testified in the courtroom against him.[24] Confession and repentance were rewarded with being excused from the penalty of burning at the stake, which instead was called for in cases of obstinate silence and refusal to abjure. The prospect of this horrifying fate was almost always enough to guarantee the offender's confession to the judges of the faith as soon as the end of the opening interrogation phase. At that point any effort to appoint an attorney was totally useless, because the full proof of the confession left nothing to hope for other than clemency from the tribunal. If this was his first trial, the defendant who confessed his guilt – regardless of his actual guilt – could save his life. However, this irremediably invalidated the correctness of the sentence, undermining the consistency between offender's motivation for confessing and what was actually committed.[25]

Moreover, it makes no sense to weigh the intensity of inquisitorial repression by counting burnings at the stake, nor to evaluate its "cruelty" by comparing the latter to the number of death sentences imposed by the secular criminal courts. The legal instruments available to these two types of courts were completely different, because they had different goals. The Holy Office's priority was not to absolve, nor was it to punish: it aimed to convert, forcing the offenders to abjure, testify against themselves, renounce their own ideas, and betray their own consciences and accomplices. The task of the Inquisition was to propagandize a truth of faith with the goal of guaranteeing confessional unity, both by preventing the formation of dissent and by preventing its spread.

In order to establish how effective the Inquisition was with respect to its goals, it would be necessary to count the people who were unable, by law or from fear of disgrace, to cultivate, communicate, but also – and above all – to *conceive* heterodox ideas. Such a survey is almost impossible to carry out with the tools of historical research.

Notes

1 E. Brambilla, *La giustizia intollerante*, cit., p. 131.
2 A. Prosperi, *Tribunali della coscienza*, cit.
3 Regarding the opposition between the "black" legend and the "white" legend in historiography on the Roman Inquisition, see Adriano Prosperi, *L'Inquisizione nella storia: I caratteri originali di una controversia secolare*, now in Id., *L'Inquisizione romana. Letture e ricerche*, Rome, Edizioni di storia e letteratura, 2003, pp. 69–96.
4 A. Del Col, *L'Inquisizione in Italia*, cit., p. 359.
5 See Elena Bonora, *L'Archivio dell'Inquisizione e gli studi storici*, cit., pp. 981–982.
6 This term is used in the sense of "*parte in causa*," typical in Roman law.
7 Gigliola Fragnito, *L'applicazione dell'indice dei libri proibiti di Clemente VIII*, in «Archivio storico italiano», 2001, n. CLIX, pp. 107–149.
8 Adriano Prosperi, *Dare l'anima. Storia di un infanticidio*, Turin, Einaudi, 2005, pp. 229–230.
9 E. Bonora, *L'Archivio dell'Inquisizione e gli studi storici*, cit., p. 997.
10 Massimo Firpo, *Da inquisitori a pontefici. Il Sant'Uffizio romano e la svolta del 1552*, in «Rivista storica italiana», 2010, n. CCXXII, pp. 911–950, 949–950.
11 M. Firpo, *Juan de Valdés and the Italian Reformation*, cit.; M. Firpo, G. Maifreda, *L'eretico che salvò la Chiesa*, cit.
12 Elena Bonora, *Morone e Pio IV*, in *Il cardinale Giovanni Morone e l'ultima fase del concilio di Trento*, edited by Massimo Firpo, Ottavia Niccoli, Bologna, Il Mulino, 2010, pp. 21–52, p. 44. On the ideological and political continuity between Santori and his predecessors, see M. Firpo, *Inquisizione romana e Controriforma*, cit., pp. 15, 53 and 399 ff.
13 See Andrea Errera, *Processus in causa fidei. L'evoluzione dei manuali inquisitoriali nei secoli XVI-XVIII e il manuale inedito di un inquisitore perugino*, Bologna, Monduzzi, 2000.
14 See initially Mirjan Damaška, *Evaluation of Evidence: Pre-Modern and Modern Approaches*, Cambridge, Cambridge University Press, 2019, esp. at pp. 116–126.
15 See Tamar Herzog, *A Short History of European Law: The Last Two and a Half Millennia*, Cambridge, MA, Harvard University Press, 2018, pp. 75–92.
16 An. [Eliseo Masini], *Sacro arsenale overo Prattica dell'Officio della santa Inquisitione*, Genua, appresso Giuseppe Pavoni, 1621.
17 A recent analysis of the inquisitorial collaborations in Rome, the correspondence between the center and its peripheries, as well as the actions of these sub-central tribunals, is *The Roman Inquisition: Centre Versus Peripheries*, edited by Christopher F. Black, Katherine Aron-Beller, Leiden and Boston, MA, Brill, 2018.
18 Giovanni Aquilecchia, *Schede bruniane 1950-1991*, Manziana, Istituto italiano per gli studi filosofici-Vecchiarelli, 1993, pp. 151–152.
19 Bernardo Santalucia, *«Accusatio» e «inquisitio» nel processo penale romano di età imperiale*, in «Seminarios complutenses de Derecho romano», 2002, n. XIV, pp. 179–194.
20 J. Chiffoleau, *Introduction. De la nécessité du secret*, cit.
21 E. Brambilla, *La giustizia intollerante*, cit., p. 130.
22 Ead, *Alle origini del Sant'Uffizio*, cit.
23 Joel Feinberg, *Harmless Wrongdoing*, in Id., *The Moral Limits of the Criminal Law*, volume IV, Oxford and New York, Oxford University Press, 1988, pp. 28–33.
24 J. Tedeschi, *The Prosecution of Heresy*, cit., p. 178.
25 E. Brambilla, *La giustizia intollerante*, cit., p. 131.

References

Giovanni Aquilecchia, *Schede bruniane 1950-1991*, Manziana, Istituto italiano per gli studi filosofici-Vecchiarelli, 1993.

Elena Bonora, *Morone e Pio IV*, in *Il cardinale Giovanni Morone e l'ultima fase del concilio di Trento*, edited by Massimo Firpo, Ottavia Niccoli, Bologna, Il Mulino, 2010, pp. 21–52.

Andrea Errera, *Processus in causa fidei. L'evoluzione dei manuali inquisitoriali nei secoli XVI-XVIII e il manuale inedito di un inquisitore perugino*, Bologna, Monduzzi, 2000.

Joel Feinberg, *Harmless Wrongdoing*, in Id., *The Moral Limits of the Criminal Law*, volume IV, Oxford and New York, Oxford University Press, 1988, pp. 28–33.

Massimo Firpo, *Da inquisitori a pontefici. Il Sant'Uffizio romano e la svolta del 1552*, in «Rivista storica italiana», 2010, n. CCXXII, pp. 911–950, 949–950.

Gigliola Fragnito, *L'applicazione dell'indice dei libri proibiti di Clemente VIII*, in «Archivio storico italiano», 2001, n. CLIX, pp. 107–149.

Tamar Herzog, *A Short History of European Law: The Last Two and a Half Millennia*, Cambridge, MA, Harvard University Press, 2018.

An. [Eliseo Masini], *Sacro arsenale overo Prattica dell'Officio della santa Inquisitione*, Genua, Appresso Giuseppe Pavoni, 1621.

Thomas F. Mayer, *The Roman Inquisition: A Papal Bureaucracy and Its Laws in the Age of Galileo*, Philadelphia, University of Pennsylvania Press, 2013.

Adriano Prosperi, *L'Inquisizione romana. Letture e ricerche*, Rome, Edizioni di storia e letteratura, 2003.

Adriano Prosperi, *Dare l'anima. Storia di un infanticidio*, Turin, Einaudi, 2005.

The Roman Inquisition: Centre Versus Peripheries, edited by Christopher F. Black, Katherine Aron-Beller, Leiden and Boston, MA, Brill, 2018.

Bernardo Santalucia, *«Accusatio» e «inquisitio» nel processo penale romano di età imperiale*, in «Seminarios complutenses de Derecho romano», 2002, n. XIV, pp. 179–194.

Part 2

"Many Times Have I Been Threatened That I Would be Made to Come to This Holy Office"

5 The End in the Beginning

> I Zuane Mocenigo, son of the most illustrious sir Marco Antonio denounce to Your Most Reverend Holiness out of obligation to my conscience, and by order of my confessor, to have heard Giordano Bruno Nolano say, at times that he has discoursed with me in my home: that it is a great blasphemy that Catholics say that bread is transubstantiated into flesh; that he is an enemy of the Mass; that he likes no religion; that Christ was a villain, and that since he was engaged in reprehensible work of deceiving the people, he could well have predicted that he would be crucified; that there is no distinction of people in God and that this was an imperfection in God; that the world is eternal, and that there are infinite worlds, and that God continuously makes them infinite, because he says that he wants as many as he can; that Christ only seemed to perform miracles and was a magician, and also the apostles, and that he had been given the spirit to do much, and more than them.[1]

Giovanni Mocenigo's first denunciation of Giordano Bruno opens with these words. Written "from home" on May 23, 1592, it was promptly dispatched to the inquisitor of Venice, friar Giovan Gabriele da Saluzzo. Immediately that same evening, "at the 3rd hour of night" – or rather three hours after sunset – the philosopher was taken from the nobleman's palazzo "in contrà de San Samuel"[2] and brought to the inquisitorial prisons.

The flood of accusations in the letter itself went on at length, and in the following days two more charges were added, again from Mocenigo's hand, written and sent to the tribunal on May 25 and 29. The Venetian gentleman's attack was so virulent, and so much hate came through this hail of accusations that the zealous Mocenigo ended up exposing himself as motivated by personal hostility towards Bruno. Moreover, Mocenigo was a sole witness. This element, combined with the clear enmity harbored by this just over 30-year-old scion of an illustrious family,[3] made his testimony almost unusable in a trial setting.

Bruno himself sensed that the overwhelming hatred in the accusations was an element to be seized upon quickly for his defense. He would mention it in his first deposition:

> When I was in Frankfurt last year, I received two letters from signor Giovanni Mocenigo, a Venetian gentleman, in which he invited me to

DOI: 10.4324/9781003026082-8

> come to Venice, wishing, according to what he wrote to me, for me to instruct him in the art of memory and invention, promising to treat me well, and that I would be happy with him; and so I went, it will be 7 or 8 months ago. I taught him various terms pertinent to these two sciences, at first staying elsewhere, and eventually in his home; and it seeming to me that I had done and taught him enough, and what I was obliged to, with respect to the things he had sought, I thus deliberated returning to Frankfurt to print certain works of mine, asking his permission last Thursday for me to leave. He, hearing this, and doubting that I wanted to leave his house right away to teach other people the same sciences which I had taught to him and others, that to go to Frankfurt, according to what he said to me, he in turn would quickly stop me; and I still insisting that I wanted to leave, he first began to complain that I did not teach him what I had promised, and then he threatened me, saying that if I did not want to stay of my own good will, that he would find a way to make me stay.[4]

We will never know what happened in that palazzo in the *sestiere* of San Marco during the first weeks of May 1592, but we do know that the events that took place in mid-Spring on the lagoon were a prelude to the arrest and long trial which would lead the philosopher to die at the stake.[5] Certainly the aristocrat's malice was motivated by personal disagreements. A plausible hypothesis, albeit never considered by scholars, is that the hostility was emotional in nature. The bitter resentment that appears in the denunciation, which is difficult to explain in political or religious terms, could have been provoked by an intense affection nurtured by the Venetian nobleman and not reciprocated, or brusquely rebuffed by the Neapolitan friar. Both of them, as we know, harbored the same hope in the reign of Henry IV, the ruler of Navarre who taken over the throne of France. It may also be taken for granted that Mocenigo had known about – or perhaps shared – Bruno's religious heterodoxy for some time. "Zuane" had read some of Bruno's books and discussed his work with Venetian booksellers, who had a broad picture of it; the same booksellers who acted as intermediaries for him in Frankfurt, when the nobleman had wanted at all costs for Bruno to move into his home at San Samuele to teach him the art of memory.

In any case, Mocenigo was clearly a hostile accuser, in addition to being the only one: *unus testis, nullus testis*, goes a legal adage from the high Middle Ages. The sources of this ancient rule of guarantee (called "negative legal proof") were identified in the Biblical story of Susanna, the events of which were accordingly frequently represented in 16th century paintings.[6] What's more, the philosopher Bruno was not officially known to the Holy Office, neither in Venice nor – as we shall see – in Rome. Despite this, the inquisitors hurriedly arrested the suspect just hours after having received a denunciation from a single and obviously hostile witness. Why?

An Illegitimate Arrest?

Giordano Bruno had just gone to bed in his room in *Ca' Vecchia* when a tumult of footsteps suddenly shattered the peace of that Friday night. The master of the house burst into the bedroom with a faithful servant and some *gondolieri* who roughly seized the philosopher, dragged him into the corridor, and pushed him until they locked him up on the upper floor.

> The said signor Giovanni seeing that I persisted in my resolve to depart, and that I had already organized my things and taken care of sending my goods to Frankfurt, came when I was in bed, under the pretext of wanting to talk to me; and after he entered, his servant, called Bortolo, entered with five or six others, if I remember well, who were according to my belief and judgement, gondoliers for those who lived nearby. And they lifted me off the bed and took me up one floor; and they locked me on the said floor, this signor Giovanni saying that, if I wanted to stay and teach him the terms of memorizing words and those of geometry, that he had sought from me at first, that he would free me; otherwise something unfortunate would happen to me.[7]

In vain Bruno responded to his now former student that to him it "seemed that I had taught him enough and more than what I should have, and that I did not deserve to be treated in that manner." The gentleman left him locked in the room for the whole night, while he wrote a denunciation to the Holy Office, the *incipit* of which we read at the beginning of the chapter, accusing the philosopher of serious crimes prosecutable by the Inquisition.[8]

Bruno also spent the next convulsive day at palazzo Mocenigo. "A captain came accompanied by certain men who I did not know," Bruno would later declare;

> and I was led by them to the bottom of the house into a ground level storage room, where they left me until the night, when another captain came with his ministers, and they took me to the prisons of this Holy Office.[9]

So, Giordano Bruno was taken to the prisons of the Venetian Inquisition the evening of May 23. Three days later, the captain of the prisons certified the arrest in bureaucratic language:

> I detained Giordano Bruno da Nola, who I found in a home in contrà de San Samuel, which is the residence of the most illustrious sir Zuane Mocenigo, and I incarcerated him in the prisons of the Holy Office; and in doing this I carried out the order of this holy Tribunal.[10]

From that moment on the prisoner would never again know freedom.

It is essential to precisely follow the opening phases of the dramatic trial that led to the death of Giordano Bruno. The sudden arrest, the equally immediate opening of the formal trial, and the procedural shortcuts revealed by the first trial documents from the Venetian judges of the faith are elements that converge to form evidence that is difficult to challenge; that is, that the decision to prosecute Bruno had formed very early in the minds of the Venetian inquisitors. Perhaps even before Mocenigo's denunciation.

The procedure in the medieval inquisitorial tribunals – as we read, for example, in the authoritative 14th century manual *Directorium inquisitorum*, the text of which was republished with exhaustive commentary by the canonist Francisco Peña in Rome in 1578 – established that pre-emptive imprisonment without prior examination of the evidence was admissible only in cases where there was clear risk of flight.[11] Opening an inquisitorial trial with the immediate arrest of the suspect after a single denunciation is a completely anomalous act. After the complaint was filed the judge normally launched a preliminary investigation to verify if the accuser was reliable and not hostile to the defendant. Following this the tribunal carefully considered the evidence gathered during the investigation, from both theological and legal points of view. In fact, during the 1500s the Congregation of the Holy Office intervened against those inquisitors who were too precipitate in arresting suspects several times, with Rome even ordering the halt of trials and freeing of prisoners who had been arrested without respecting their decrees.[12] A few decades after Bruno's death, the authoritative *Sacro arsenale*, the manual most commonly used by Italian tribunals of faith in the 17th and 18th centuries, would again prescribe that

> when imprisoning suspects the greatest prudence must be used, because even just imprisonment for the crime of heresy brings notable infamy to the prisoner. Which he will have done very well to consider himself, as well as the nature of the evidence, the quality of the witnesses, and the condition of the accused.[13]

Giovanni Mocenigo's first denunciation revolved around the suspicion that his teacher of mnemonics was preparing to leave for Frankfurt. This element might to some extent have legitimized the tribunal's forcing the procedure and proceeding with the immediate arrest of the suspect due to the risk of flight. However, here Mocenigo contradicts himself. The opening statement from the complaint of May 23 states, as we have seen, that the nobleman made the decision to lock up and denounce Bruno "by obligation of his conscience, and by order of his confessor." This would indicate that the decision had materialized over time as the result of an interior conflict, and not from the sudden need to prevent an escape.

At the same time, however, Mocenigo stated in the same letter that

> having noted all these things to account for them to Your Most Holy Father [the inquisitor], when he doubted that he could leave, as he said he wanted to, I locked him in a room requisitioned for him; and because I believe him to be possessed, I ask you to find a quick resolution for him.

He also added that he knew that Bruno "had at other times had conflicts with the Inquisition in Rome," a charge that theoretically put the philosopher in the very serious condition of a relapsed heretic, for whom the death penalty was mandatory.[14] All these reasons contribute to giving juridical legitimacy to the tribunal's decision to accelerate the arrest without a preliminary investigation, empowered by the social authority of an aristocratic plaintiff and his potential influence on the relevant government offices of the Serenissima.

Another revealing passage from Mocenigo's first complaint adds to the suspicion that when the Venetian judges had ordered Bruno's arrest they were acting on decisions already made, based on elements unknown to the prisoner, as well as to us. The passage proves that the patrician had already discussed Bruno with the Venetian inquisitor friar Gabriele da Saluzzo before producing the denunciation that spurred the arrest.

> I designed to learn from him, *as I told him myself*, not knowing he was a scoundrel as he is, having noted all these things to account for them to Your Most Holy Father, when he doubted that he could leave, as he said he wanted to, I closed him in a room [...].[15]

Given that is unthinkable that the aristocrat spoke with the inquisitor about his cumbersome guest if not to complain about him and accuse him, it seems clear that in the days or weeks preceding the arrest Father Gabriele – and through him other components of the local Holy Office – knew of Bruno's presence in Venice and about his heterodox profile.

After all, it is more than plausible that Mocenigo, having settled on the decision to accuse Bruno, began keeping a prudent distance from him, talking about him with his confessor before going to the judges of the faith. He knew well that he was in the very uncomfortable position of being the protector of a heretic, of an "advocate" who medieval canon law equated with the heretic himself. This may explain why it was impossible for Mocenigo's confessor to absolve the penitent in the usual way, and thus the need for him to go to the inquisitor and denounce Bruno. At that point the judge of the faith could have asked Mocenigo to present a written denunciation to assure the philosopher of receiving the Church's justice. They were within the borders of a Republic that had spared no criticism of or obstacles to the action of the ecclesiastical tribunals, therefore risking that if the arrest was delayed too long it could protect the offender and allow him to hide himself again, perhaps forever.

Another anomalous detail about what happened in Venice that May 23, 1592 is the fact that Bruno's arrest was carried out in the almost total absence of the precautions prescribed by contemporary jurisprudence and canon law. Bruno's incarceration took place without the completion of another document, one considered indispensable by contemporary jurists, even for cases of heresy: the citation. The top legal authorities of the age, who included Cesare Carena and Sebastiano Guazzini, agreed on the subject, affirming that the absence of a citation of the offender annulled the inquisitorial process. Likewise Sebastiano Vance, bishop of Orvieto, jurist and author of the fundamental *Tractatus de nullitatibus processuum ac sententiarum* which was printed in 1552 at Lyon, and had by that time already been published in Venice in five editions, explained that the citation was to be considered as a fundamental part of the defense, rooted in the *ius gentium* and in the Law of God. Its absence nullified the trial.[16]

The papers from the Venetian trial of Giordano Bruno, which also included a very brief report of the delivery and presentation of Mocenigo's denunciations, do not preserve any document of citation. Nor is it plausible that one was ever issued, given how quickly incarceration took place. According to the juridical parameters of the era and the sources available to date, Bruno's death sentence resulting from this trial should therefore be considered illegitimate.

A Flood of Accusations

It is not simple orienting oneself in the swirl of accusations unloaded upon Giordano Bruno's head by Giovanni Mocenigo in those final days of May. Nor is it easy to understand what hypothesis of crime these charges might have implied to the mind of an inquisitor at the end of the 16th century.

We begin by noting that major scholars are inclined to consider the very serious assertions contained in the Venetian nobleman's three denunciations to be substantially reliable. It is true that the angry student maliciously exaggerated the significance of some of his teacher's statements, and that in all probability Mocenigo's limited intellectual stature and resentment led him to crudely distort or twist some of Bruno's *boutades*. However, all of the Venetian's main charges are confirmed, not only by Bruno's declarations during the trial, but also by the contents of his works, though they are presented with greater philosophical depth and sophistication. Today, Bruno's books make it possible to find the heterodox opinions of which he was accused almost point by point: especially in *De immenso, De monade, Sigillum sigillorum e De vinculis*.[17]

However, the inquisitors could not, or did not want to undertake the work of systematically checking Bruno's books, the most compromising of which, moreover, had been printed abroad without enjoying wide circulation. Therefore not all of the charges that appear in Mocenigo's complaints will be proven in the trial. Bruno could still defend himself effectively and persuasively in his depositions, even benefitting from Mocenigo's oversimplifications, refuting the crudest accusations and insisting on the purely philosophical nature of his research.

At this point it should be noted that, because the documentation relating to the final phase of the trial is incomplete, we do not know which counts Bruno was actually charged with in the crucial moment of the trial: or rather during the "hearing," which took place in Rome in 1599. It is, however, certain – and proven by the surviving documentation – that the extreme accusations, which we will now mark in italics, were identified as such by the Roman bureaucracy when, in the following years, it transcribed and classified all of the denunciations received against Bruno and the witness interrogations.

The first complaint lodged by Mocenigo could on its own have allowed the inquisitors to identify at least ten charges.[18]

Stating – quoting the words written by the Venetian aristocrat – that "he likes no religion"; that he intended to promote a "new sect in the name of a new philosophy"; that the Catholic faith was full of "blasphemies"; that the friars, "all asses," should have their "revenue" taken away to prevent them from continuing to "foul the world [with their lies]"; that it could not be proven that "our faith is worthy of God," exposing Bruno to the accusation – as was noted when the trial moved to Rome – of *having opinions adverse to the Holy Faith* and to have given *speeches contrary to it and to its ministries.* The opinion "that there is no distinction of people in God" and the fact that this would have meant identifying an "imperfection in God" could have become the accusation of having *erroneous opinions on the Trinity, the divinity of Christ and the incarnation.* The charge of holding erroneous opinions *on Christ and on transubstantiation and the Holy Mass* could derive from charges of such statements as "that Christ was a villain" and that otherwise he would have foreseen his own death, which "he would flee as best he could"; that he was a "magician" and that his miracles were "obvious"; that "in saying the bread transubstantiates into flesh" one committed a "great blasphemy."

One of the best known charges against Bruno was that related to – as noted again by the Roman Holy Office – the *existence of multiple worlds and their eternity.* This came from Bruno's declaration "that the world is eternal, and that there are infinite worlds, and that God continuously makes them infinite, because he says he wants as many as he can." The belief *in metempsychosis and the transmigration of the human soul in beasts,* in addition to the accusation of practicing *divinatory and magical arts* could emerge from his having said "that souls created by work of nature pass from one animal to another; and that just as ugly, corrupted animals are born, men are also born so, when after the floods they return to be born," but also from having claimed "to want to work on the art of divination, and to make the whole world run behind him." Finally, the accusation *of not believing in the virginity of Mary* could instead come from Mocenigo's statement – added orally during the interrogations – that Bruno had said "that the Virgin could not have given birth."

In addition to these serious charges, the denunciation of May 23 contained at least three other accusations from which Bruno could clear himself rather easily: that of having been in error concerning *i Dottori della Chiesa* ("that Saint Thomas and all the Doctors did not know anything compared to him, and that he will clarify all the foremost theologians of the world, who would not know how to respond"), of having claimed *that sins are not punished* ("that there is no punishment of sins [...] and that not doing unto others that which we do not want done to us is enough to live well; and that this absorbs all the other sins") and *of having already been tried by the Inquisition.* The prisoner cleared himself of this last accusation by recounting – as we have seen in reviewing his life – particulars of the trials he had already gone through within the Order. Furthermore, communication from Rome, which we will discuss shortly, arrived in Venice almost immediately confirming that nothing against Bruno could be found in the central archives of the Holy Office. The other two accusations were dismissed during the proceeding when confronted with the arguments in defense of the accused, among which was the citation of the dialog *De la causa* and of a passage of *De l'infinito.*[19]

The second letter of accusation that Mocenigo sent to the inquisitors of Venice, dated May 25, contained little more than confirmation of the charges in the first, in particular those inherent to magical practices. However, the text of the letter is interesting for at least two reasons: first of all because it reports a vivid description of the reasons for the conflict between the two men that led up to the arrest; in the second place because it demonstrates how "Zuane" Mocenigo did not hesitate to reiterate to the inquisitor that his denunciations were motivated by personal hostility and by Bruno's arrogant persistence in wanting to leave the palazzo. The accuser was so certain of the inquisitors' understanding that he did not at all fear incriminating himself to the Inquisition as the host and supporter of a heretic.

> On that day, when I kept Iordano Bruno locked up, I asked him, if that which he had not wanted to teach me, since he had promised me on the strength of many courtesies and many gifts that I made for him, if it seemed to him that he could at least do this, so that I would not accuse him of the many foul words he has said to me [...] he did not respond otherwise, if not to ask me to let him go free: and that, although having prepared his things and told me that he wanted to leave, that he had done it not thinking of actually going through with it, but to curb my impatience to be taught, with which I afflicted him continually.[20]

It is true that in a brief passage at the closing of the letter, Mocenigo demonstrated his awareness of the need to justify the protection he had extended to Bruno:

> And since he has favored me with much charity to forgive me for my error in the delay of this accusation, thus I ask that he please excuse us before the Illustrious gentlemen [the other members of the tribunal] with the respect for my good intentions.[21]

But at the same time these expressions of gratitude ("he has favored me with much charity in forgiving me my error") show Mocenigo's certainty of having obtained the inquisitors' pardon, even before the interrogation of Bruno began, and therefore before the trial took shape. This is a further confirmation of the fact that the tribunal had very likely already been in negotiations with the nobleman and granted specific guarantees before Bruno's arrest.

Mocenigo's third and final denunciation of May 29 was markedly more political in nature. In addition to providing further details about the accusations already advanced, it revealed the hopes that Bruno had pinned on Henry of Navarre, and concluded by bringing a new charge: that of indulging in sins of the flesh. The *incipit* of this letter also proves that the dialogue between the gentleman and the friar inquisitor continued outside the trial. At that point Mocenigo had not yet been called by the tribunal to testify, but he wrote the following nevertheless:

> Because Your Most Holy Father has enjoined me that I would do well thinking on all that I have heard from Giordano Bruno, what he has done against our Catholic faith, I remembered hearing him say [...] that, since this Republic is reputed to be very wise, he could not help but condemn it for leaving the friars so wealthy: and that they should do as they had in France, that the income of the monasteries should go to the nobility, and the friars eat a little *prodo* [*sic*] [...]. In addition to this, he told me that he very much liked women and that he had not yet reached the number of those of Solomon; and that the Church committed a great sin in making a sin of that which serves nature so well, and which for him had the greatest merit.[22]

The gentleman's third and final complaint closed by addressing the following indication to the inquisitor: "I am again sending you a book by the aforementioned Giordano, where I have noted an evil passage, as you will be able to see, and you may consider it like the others."[23] Once again, it is difficult to resist the temptation to glimpse in the censorial zeal demonstrated by the aristocrat the possibility – already noted by a well-informed modern biographer of Bruno – "that someone better informed about Bruno stepped in to support [Mocenigo] with advice, 'tips', and documents to help him pin down Bruno before the Holy Office."[24]

In fact, Mocenigo attached several of Bruno's books and some handwritten notes to the three denunciations. The volumes were the *Cantus Circaeus* – to which the Venetian later returned in formulating the accusation of heresy against the pope, decoding a passage from it that had alluded to the pontiff "as the figure of a pig," the *De la causa*, the *De minimo,* and the *De la monade*. These were seized from Bruno's room by the master of the house, along with "some money, items, papers," the "worksheets" written for him – the materials used for his lessons in mnemonics – and "a booklet of spells" (perhaps the Parisian manuscript of *De' predicamenti di Dio* from 1582) which the patrician claimed to have "found among certain [...] written papers" belonging to the philosopher.[25] None of this material has come down to us.

The Many Reasons for a "*causa ardua*"

The sudden arrest of Giordano Bruno in Venice just a few hours after the receipt of the denunciation by Giovanni Mocenigo, a sole and hostile witness; the absence of a citation; the off-the-record agreements made between the accuser and the judges. These are elements which sketch the framework of a trial which, in the Venetian phase that unfolded between May 1592 and February 1593, was atypical compared to the ordinary actions of the Inquisition at the time.

To wit: a trial which was compromised *ab origine* by the desire of the judges to prosecute the suspect with quick efficiency. A suspect who was evidently of great interest to the inquisitors: perhaps because Mocenigo himself had convinced them, perhaps because they were informed of the danger he posed by other trustworthy people. After all, we cannot take it for granted that the threats that Bruno reports in the opening of his first brief – which we discussed at the beginning of Chapter 2 – had come from only Mocenigo. We have seen the indiscretion with which Bruno had moved between Padua and Venice in the preceding months, without hiding his interest in the most delicate subjects, instead discussing them passionately and provocatively. Anyone could have gone to the inquisitor: or better, anyone powerful enough to be able to confide his suspicions to a judge of the faith without officially appearing as a witness before the Inquisition. In the society of that time, where testifying in a tribunal of the faith was inherently considered to be a disgrace for a gentleman or gentlewoman, the publicity of a trial like Bruno's could tarnish the witnesses themselves. Mocenigo's political career was damaged, in fact, and despite his illustrious birth he never attained the highest government offices of the Republic.[26]

The judges acted with great speed after the philosopher's arrest. Bruno appeared before them just three days later, opening his first deposition with words that we are already familiar with: "I will tell the truth: many times have I been threatened that I would be made to come to this Holy Office, and I have always thought it a joke, because I am ready to account for myself," a complaint that the inquisitors left unanswered. In the meantime, the Venetian Inquisition moved with equal rapidity to guarantee the endorsement of the Roman Congregation. But something unclear weighs on this step as well.

In the second half of the 16th century, which saw the Roman Church react to the diffusion of the religious ideas of the Reformation, the explosion of trials for cases of faith provoked, among other things, an exponential growth in the trial documentation that the local tribunals sent to the Roman Dicastery. To put a stop to this flood of paper by making the peripheral tribunals autonomous, in 1581 the Congregation of the Holy Office released an important decree requiring the inquisitors to send to Rome, as a rule, only the final sentence of the trials conducted in their tribunals. An exception was made for the cases considered to be more problematic (defined by the decree as "*arduis causis*"); for these the Supreme Inquisitor had to be alerted and quickly receive the documentation.

The Venetian inquisitor Gabriele da Saluzzo counted the Bruno case among the "arduous," given that immediately after the philosopher's arrest he informed the Roman authorities about the trial that was underway.[27] Rome acknowledged receipt of the envelope on June 11, and replied that there was no trace in the archives of prior or pending charges against the accused, even hypothesizing that the prisoner had provided a false name.[28] Therefore Mocenigo had either lied or misrepresented Bruno's words where he had claimed that the philosopher had already been tried by the Holy Office.

In addition to seriously undermining the trustworthiness of the sole witness, Rome's response eliminated the possibility, which the Venetian judges had likely been counting on, of trying Bruno as a relapsed heretic. Instead, the accused was unknown in Rome, which had even suggested that the Venice judges should check his identity more thoroughly.

That June 11, 1592, when the officials of the Roman Congregation communicated to the Serenissima's inquisitors that they did not know of Bruno, the latter simultaneously wrote a report to Rome about the trial underway in Venice. In this document the philosopher is qualified as a suspect with a rather broad and vague definition, "*de et super heretica pravitate rebusque aliis*" ("for heretical depravity and other charges").[29] Less than 15 days after a denunciation brought by a sole and hostile witness, against a Dominican friar who they had never heard of, the Supreme Inquisition was therefore already convinced that the Bruno case should be placed under special supervision. This despite the fact that a first complete copy of the trial documentation was only sent to Rome two months later, in early August 1592, by Venetian inquisitor Gabriele da Saluzzo: according to procedure this is the only official document that could prompt the attention shown by the cardinals.[30]

Let's recap these steps. The Inquisition of Venice, shortly after having imprisoned Bruno, and already before gathering any proof of the accusations made by Mocenigo, a sole and hostile witness, wrote to Rome to inform them that a case had been opened in the Lagoon that, by all accounts, was considered "arduous." The cardinals of the Supreme Inquisition – for whom Bruno was, at the time, only an obscure apostate friar whose trial documentation was not even known – judged the case worthy of maximum attention.

Clearly there is more here than meets the eye.

First of all, it should be noted that if by early June 1592 Venice had already succeeded in convincing Rome that Giordano Bruno was a dangerous prisoner, this means that the Venetian judges were in fact aware of this before the start of the trial. Once again, this is evidence that the Venetian tribunal was holding cards in its deck that it did not reveal, and that in all probability will remain hidden forever.

In the second place, it is equally clear that the communication between the judges in Venice and Rome concerning the anomalous case of Bruno took place through verbal exchanges, correspondence that has not survived, and arguments unknown to us today; despite centuries of work digging deeply in the archives in search of documents regarding the life and death of the great philosopher.

This is confirmed by the quite surprising fact that, in the months here under consideration, there was actually a double channel of correspondence between the tribunal of Venice and the leaders of the Roman Inquisition. This is revealed by a note written by the cardinal of Santa Severina, Giulio Antonio Santori, on August 8, 1592; it reached Venice, having traveled the usual five days of postal service between the two cities, on August 13.

> It also seemed right to update you about the fact that the copy of the trial of fra' Giordano Bruno has already been received, but the letter has not yet been received, that he wrote had been sent by another route, in response to mine of the 25th past. We will therefore be waiting, and in the meantime send greetings.[31]

Why did the Venetian inquisitor, updating his superiors on the progress of the Giordano Bruno trial, use "another route"? Why would Gabriele da Saluzzo not have made use of the official channel of correspondence that efficiently connected him with the Congregation of the Holy Office, a channel suitable for sending highly confidential documents, such as the complete trial documentation of a philosopher who was known to be a heretic, perhaps a heresiarch, and a Navarran?

Maybe it is because official correspondence from Rome had to be carefully preserved, as letters written in Congregation were not simple operational suggestions but actual decrees that made jurisprudence, established precedents, and were meant to guide the actions of the local judges of the faith into the future.[32] We have other testimony of the destruction of compromising documents by the inquisitors, in some cases on orders from Rome. A few years later, for example, the Congregation wrote these words to friar Ignazio Pino da Cagli, who was the inquisitor of Aquileia and Concordia, and so working within the boundaries of the Serenissima:

> he will secretly burn the prohibited writings and books that had been presented to them warning not to impart this to anyone so as not to cause any impediment or any pointless noise, and so he will carry this out.[33]

By all indications the Venetian judges periodically transmitted top secret documentation to Santa Severina concerning the trial of Giordano Bruno, files which had to reach the capital through people and means of absolute trust – and then disappear without a trace.

Forever.

Notes

1 *Processo*, 143–144.
2 Ivi, 148.
3 Born in 1558 and died in 1623. See the entry by Laura Fedi in *Dizionario storico dell'Inquisizione*, directed by Adriano Prosperi, with the collaboration of Vincenzo Lavenia, John Tedeschi, 4 volumes, Pisa, Edizioni della Normale, 2010, which collects several entries by the same author involving the Bruno trial).
4 *Processo*, 155.
5 For general reconsiderations of the trial one can begin with Leen Spruit, *Giordano Bruno eretico: le imputazioni del processo nel contest storico-dottrinale*, in *Cosmología, teología y religión en la obra y en el proceso de Giordano Bruno, Actas del congreso celebrado en Barcelona 2-4 diciembre de 1999*, edited by Miguel A. Granada, Barcelona, Publicacions de la Universitat de Barcelona, 2001, pp. 111–128 and Id., *Una rilettura del processo di Giordano Bruno: procedure e aspetti giuridico-formali*, in *Giordano Bruno. Oltre il mito e le opposte passioni*, edited by Pasquale Giustiniani, Carmine Matarrazzo, Michele Miele, Domenico Sorrentino, Napoli, Biblioteca teologica napoletana, 2002, pp. 217–234. Along with I. Rowland, *Giordano Bruno*, cit., chapters 28–34 one may also consult the entry by L. Fedi, *Processo*, in *Giordano Bruno. Parole, concetti, immagini*, cit.
6 See the acute observations in Bruno Cavallone, *La borsa di Miss Flite. Storie e immagini del processo*, Milan, Adelphi, 2016, pp. 122 ff.
7 *Processo*, 155.
8 Ivi, 155–156.
9 Ivi, 156.
10 Ivi, 148.
11 Francesco Beretta, *Giordano Bruno e l'Inquisizione romana. Considerazioni sul processo*, in «Bruniana & Campanelliana», 2001, n. VII, pp. 15–49, pp. 31–32.
12 See for example the cases referred to by J. Tedeschi, *The Prosecution of Heresy*, cit., pp. 132–133.
13 E. Masini, *Sacro arsenale*, cit., p. 360.
14 *Processo*, 143–144.
15 Ivi, 144.
16 T.F. Mayer, *The Roman Inquisition*, cit., pp. 171 ff.; Antonio Montanari, *Sebastiano Vanzi vescovo e giurista*, in «Quaderni dell'Accademia Fanestre», 2011, n. 10, pp. 203–226.
17 *Processo*, 15; M. Ciliberto, *Giordano Bruno*, cit., p. 265; S. Ricci, *Giordano Bruno nell'Europa del Cinquecento*, cit., pp. 486–487; A. Foa, *Giordano Bruno*, cit., p. 45.
18 Here I follow *Processo*, 16–17 and notes.
19 Ivi, 17.
20 Ivi, 145–146.
21 Ivi, 147.
22 Ivi, 159.
23 *Ibidem*.
24 S. Ricci, *Giordano Bruno nell'Europa del Cinquecento*, cit., p. 492.
25 Ivi, p. 146; L. Fedi, *Mocenigo Giovanni*, entry in *Giordano Bruno. Parole, concetti, immagini*, cit.; S. Ricci, *Giordano Bruno nell'Europa del Cinquecento*, cit., p. 487.
26 L. Fedi, *Mocenigo Giovanni*, cit.
27 As is known Giovanni Aquilecchia: see now *Schede bruniane 1950-1991*, cit., pp. 151–152.
28 Leen Spruit, *Due documenti noti e due documenti sconosciuti sul processo di Bruno nell'Archivio del Sant'Uffizio*, in «Bruniana & Campanelliana», 1998, n. IV, pp. 469–473, p. 471.

29 *Ibidem.*
30 The timeframes have been reconstructed in detail by Carlo De Frede, *L'estradizione di Giordano Bruno da Venezia (agosto 1592-febbraio 1593)*, in «Archivio storico per le province napoletane», 1994, n. CXII, pp. 57–101, now in Id., *Religiosità e cultura nel Cinquecento italiano*, Bologna, Il Mulino, 1999, pp. 379–424.
31 Published by Giovanni Aquilecchia, *Un nuovo documento del processo di Giordano Bruno*, in «Giornale storico della letteratura italiana», 1959, n. CXXXVI, pp. 91–96, and incorporated in *Processo*, 200–201.
32 An example that insists on this is A. Del Col, *L'Inquisizione in Italia*, cit., pp. 759–760.
33 Letter of May 28, 1609, in Giuliana Ancona, *Autonomia giudiziaria e dipendenza amministrativa del Sant'Ufficio di Aquileia e Concordia all'epoca di fra Girolamo Asteo (1598-1608)*, in «Metodi e ricerche», 2006, n. 1, pp. 11–46.

References

Giuliana Ancona, *Autonomia giudiziaria e dipendenza amministrativa del Sant'Ufficio di Aquileia e Concordia all'epoca di fra Girolamo Asteo (1598-1608)*, in «Metodi e ricerche», 2006, n. 1, pp. 11–46.

Giovanni Aquilecchia, *Un nuovo documento del processo di Giordano Bruno*, in «Giornale storico della letteratura italiana», 1959, n. CXXXVI, pp. 91–96.

Francesco Beretta, *Giordano Bruno e l'Inquisizione romana. Considerazioni sul processo*, in «Bruniana & Campanelliana», 2001, n. VII, pp. 15–49.

Bruno Cavallone, *La borsa di Miss Flite. Storie e immagini del processo*, Milan, Adelphi, 2016.

Carlo De Frede, *Religiosità e cultura nel Cinquecento italiano*, Bologna, Il Mulino, 1999.

Dizionario storico dell'Inquisizione, directed by Adriano Prosperi, with the collaboration of Vincenzo Lavenia, John Tedeschi, 4 volumes, Pisa, Edizioni della Normale, 2010.

Laura Fedi, various entries in *Dizionario storico dell'Inquisizione*, cit.

Antonio Montanari, *Sebastiano Vanzi vescovo e giurista*, in «Quaderni dell'Accademia Fanestre», 2011, n. 10, pp. 203–226.

Leen Spruit, *Due documenti noti e due documenti sconosciuti sul processo di Bruno nell'Archivio del Sant'Uffizio*, in «Bruniana & Campanelliana», 1998, n. IV, pp. 469–473.

Leen Spruit, *Giordano Bruno eretico: le imputazioni del processo nel contest storico-dottrinale*, in *Cosmología, teología y religión en la obra y en el proceso de Giordano Bruno, Actas del congreso celebrado en Barcelona 2-4 diciembre de 1999*, edited by Miguel A. Granada, Barcelona, Publicacions de la Universitat de Barcelona, 2001, pp. 111–128.

Leen Spruit, *Una rilettura del processo di Giordano Bruno: procedure e aspetti giuridico-formali*, in *Giordano Bruno. Oltre il mito e le opposte passioni*, edited by Pasquale Giustiniani, Carmine Matarrazzo, Michele Miele, Domenico Sorrentino, Napoli, Biblioteca teologica napoletana, 2002, pp. 217–234.

6 The Stalemate

While letters and trial documentation were exchanged between Venice and Rome, the judges in Venice carried out the initial phase of the heresy trial. As we have seen, this meant interrogating witnesses and the offender himself, with the application of torture if considered appropriate by the tribunal. The depositions were recorded by a notary. In the meantime, evidence was collected, including books and manuscripts, some of which were also found through searches.

In the case of the Giordano Bruno trial, the information phase meant to verify the validity of Mocenigo's accusations had been completely passed over, and the philosopher had been formally arrested based solely on the nobleman's denunciation. Thus the inquisitors had to begin unraveling the tangle of testimony while the offender was already in jail. Or, better put, they had to simultaneously question the prisoner and the witnesses who – in Bruno's case – as we will now see, were uniformly in support of the accused.

This unexpected difficulty in gathering evidence that corroborated Mocenigo's accusations –made by a sole hostile witness and therefore almost unusable in the trial – must have surprised and perhaps irritated the tribunal of the Venetian Holy Office. As the procedure gradually unfolded, the inquisitors began to fear that something was not going as they had predicted.

The Parade of Witnesses

The tribunal that launched the trial against Giordano Bruno included the papal nuncio Ludovico Taverna and Patriarch of Venice Lorenzo Priuli, in addition to the inquisitor of Venice, the Dominican friar Gabriele da Saluzzo. Thus it included the three supreme ecclesiastical offices of the Republic. However, these were accompanied by a representative of the secular government, the patrician Alvise Foscari – which, as we have seen, constituted a rare privilege that had been stripped from the Serenissima government in preceding centuries. The "sage for heresy" sent by the Venetian authorities did not actually have an active role in the trial, and only listened to the depositions in silence.

DOI: 10.4324/9781003026082-9

The judges immediately began to examine the two witnesses called to the case by Giovanni Mocenigo in support of his accusations: the booksellers Giovan Battista Ciotti and Giacomo Brictano, personal acquaintances of Bruno from his time in Frankfurt who had imported some of his books to Venice. The booksellers, however, did not confirm Mocenigo's accusations. Ciotti, after having given the only physical description of Bruno to emerge during the trial ("a small man, [with a] thin [face], with a bit of black beard, around 40 years of age"), exonerated him, merely reporting some rumors.

> When I spoke and did business with the aforementioned Giordano here and at Frankfurt, as I said, he never came out and said something for which I could have doubted that he was a catholic and good Christian [...]. When I was at Frankfurt, I spoke with various scholars, who went to his lectures in that city while he was there and who have had acquaintance and conversation with him; about whom I was told, in short, that the said Giordano knew the art of memory and other secret forms of knowledge, but that he had never been seen to act on this knowledge with anyone; rather, that everyone who has had something to do with him for similar reasons remained dissatisfied, telling me "I don't know how he is in Venetia because here he is taken for a man who has no religion at all."[1]

Ciotti also put Bruno's accuser in a bad light, presenting him as a petty manipulator; aware of the philosopher's irreligiosity but determined to exploit his knowledge to the point of blackmailing him, threatening to refer him to the Inquisition. According to his statement, after having told Mocenigo what he had learned about Bruno in Frankfurt, the bookseller heard the patrician respond:

> I also have doubts about this one: but I want to see what I can get out of the things he promised me, so that all I have given him is not a complete loss, and then I want to turn him in to the censure of the Holy Office.[2]

However, not even this new element, which further detracted from the accuser's reliability, appeared to attract the attention of the inquisitors.

Giovan Battista Ciotti was called by the tribunal to testify a second and final time on June 23. Asked that day by the inquisitors if in the intervening time he had "recalled anything in particular," he provided an important detail: that Bruno, at the moment of the arrest,

> had made a book *Delle sette arti*; this being provided [or really finished], he wanted to make a book and bring it to present to His Holiness; but he did not tell me which book it was that he wanted, nor to what end he wanted to do so; he only said to me: 'I know that His Holiness delights in letters, and I want to make this book and go to present it to him'.[3]

This detail confirms Bruno's intention to implement the program of rapprochement with the Roman Curia and the pope, to develop and give form to the ideas he had elaborated in previous years.

The deposition of Ciotti's colleague, bookseller Giacomo Brictano, was more scathing. For him, Bruno – he had learned in Germany from the Father Superior of the Carmelite monastery of Frankfurt – "mostly occupied himself in writing and going about prophesying and fantasizing [like an astrologer would] about novelties." However, the accusations of irreligiosity advanced by Mocenigo against Bruno were toned down, invoking mitigating circumstances ("he read heretical doctors, because the whole city are heretics, universally speaking") and confirming Ciotti's statements. In addition, he reported rumors that alluded to Bruno's grand project. A program of religious unification and political pacification which the reckless philosopher had widely publicized during his years in Germany, making no secret of it even in conversations that took place in the monastery of the Frankfurt Carmelites:

> With me the aforementioned Giordano has not said, neither have I noticed anything that is not Christian; this is what the father Prior of the Carmelites of Frankfurt told me, when I asked him what kind of man was the said Giordano, that he had good ingenuity and letters, and that he was a universal man, but that he had no religion at all, as far as he believed, adding: "He says that he knows more than the Apostles knew, and that the spirit was enough for him, if he had wanted, to make it so the whole world would be one religion." Beyond this I don't know anything else about the said Giordano on account of things that concern the Holy Office.[4]

It is clear that repairing the sectarian clashes which had bloodied his era had become, during his years of long peregrinations, a true life project for Bruno. A sort of obsession, the realization of which he paid for personally, taking serious risks and being willing to pay an even higher price: the price of returning to Italy, his homeland, now under the control of the papal Inquisition.

The last two witnesses heard in the Venetian tribunal were the Dominican friar Domenico da Nocera and the nobleman Andrea Morosini.

Friar Domenico da Nocera was called on request of the accused. In one of his depositions, Bruno had indicated his superior as a favorable witness, because da Nocera would be able to attest to his desire to seek absolution from the pope and return to living the life of a cleric. The austere gentleman Andrea Morosini was instead cited by Mocenigo in the first denunciation because he was the owner of the "academy [...] where many gentlemen practice," previously attended by Bruno.

On May 31 Father Domenico met with the brother inquisitor and other friar advocates – among who were the Provincials of Venice and of

Terra Santa – in their oldest Venetian monastery, San Giovanni e Paolo (*San Zanipolo*), connected to the imposing medieval basilica. The church was considered to be the *pantheon* of the Serenissima, because of the many tombs of Doges – whose funerals were customarily held there – as well as of illustrious figures of the Serenissima that lay within. The General Chapter of the Dominicans had been held in the same sumptuous setting just a few days earlier, on May 17. This was a meeting of a true legislative assembly, which constituted, and constitutes, the supreme authority of the Order. The Master General was elected here, laws that regulated the life of the Dominicans were formulated, and disciplinary functions were carried out: the chapter judged and punished the friars, and had the power to interrogate the superiors of their offices.

For these reasons, the fact that the General Chapter of the Dominicans was being held in Venice could not help but attract the attention and reignite the hopes of friar Giordano da Nola. In fact, for the occasion he conceived a plan to get himself reaccepted to the Order by sounding out a superior from his Province of origin. So, on the day of Pentecost he approached the Father Regent of his old university, the Studio di San Domenico of Napoli, as he was exiting the sacristy of *San Zanipolo.*

Friar Domenico da Nocera related that strange meeting in the half-light of the basilica, protected by the gothic faces which soared overhead on enormous columns, to the inquisitors in these words:

> I saw a student give reverence to me, one whose face I did not know well; then as I considered it I realized that it was one of our friars in the province of Regno, a scholar, who was named friar Iordano da Nola. And so we retreated to a quiet place in the church, where he told me the reason for his departure from our province, and for having removed the habit [...]; he told me of many kings who he had walked with in regal courts, that he had done important things in literature, but that he had not always lived catholically.[5]

One can imagine the relief, and perhaps emotion, with which the apostate friar, after long years of exile, opened his heart to a superior from his homeland – an intellectual, but also a man expert in the things of life, whose words suggested the ability to listen without judgement. In the cool darkness of the basilica another piece of the complicated mosaic that Bruno intended to create was taking form: return to the Order, "quiet down" and go back to living "catholically." Not so much because of intimate conviction or spiritual necessity, but rather to reach an objective he considered more important and elevated; a plan to be pursued "with strong personal support." He freely opened up to his superior about this, just as he had already done with the Prior of the Carmelite monastery of Frankfurt:

> And I asked him what he did in Venice and how he lived, he told me that he had arrived in Venice a few days before and that on his own he

> had enough to live comfortably, and that he had resolved in his mind to seek quiet and to work on writing a book he had in mind, and then, with strong personal support, to present it to His Beatitude; and from him to obtain grace for what he had expressed to quiet his conscience; and to see at the end that he can stay in Rome, and here apply himself to literary work and show his virtue and perhaps from this gain the possibility of holding some classes at university.[6]

We will never know if it was only by coincidence that two apparently unrelated events both took place in Venice that second half of May 1592: the meeting of the General Chapter of the Dominicans, and the threatening accumulation of inquisitorial clouds over Giordano Bruno's head. If, in other words, the Venetian Holy Office might have been alarmed by Bruno's careless openness with his fellow brothers, who may have accepted the narration of his life and his projects with less understanding than that shown by Father Domenico da Nocera. In such cases the Orders normally tended to deal with cleaning their dirty laundry at home, opting for internal justice and turning to the work of the inquisitors only in extreme cases. But at that moment the Italian Regulars themselves began to feel the wind of the organizing and moralizing actions imposed by Pope Clement VIII, which we will try to understand later on.

Whatever really happened in the Venetian church of *San Zanipolo* during those days around Pentecost in 1592, it should be noted today that the deposition of friar Domenico da Nocera was an important moment in the trial of Giordano Bruno. This is not only – or not as much – for its informational content, which all told is fairly modest. In fact, the regent of the Neapolitan *Studium* penned a written deposition – therefore enjoying the privilege of not appearing as a witness before the Inquisition – after meeting with the inquisitor brother Gabriele da Saluzzo in the monastery of *San Zanipolo*, with other superiors of the preachers present, among who were the Provincial of Terrasanta and the Provincial of Venice. That episode was therefore the first alarm bell to ring within the Dominican Order regarding the Bruno case. Their leader, as we will see later, played an important role at the moment of the actual "hearing" of the trial, in the Rome of the year 1599.

The last witness heard by the inquisitors in the case against Bruno was the patrician Andrea Morosini. The literary and philosophical "*academia*" which he and his brother Nicolò created in their family residence of San Luca, at the head of a dirty alley that opened to the Canal Grande, was attended by the most important aristocrats, men of government and culture in the city: among others were Leonardo and Nicolò Donà, Nicolò Contarini, Giovan Francesco Sagredo, Antonio Querini, Galileo Galilei (after he took his chair at Padua), and the future consultor, friar Paolo Sarpi. Natural sciences, history, customs, as well as earthly and divine things were all debated.[7]

The heterodox veins of the discourses and initiatives promoted at the Morosini's "meeting" were well known in Venice, and certainly also to the

Venetian judges of the faith. The latter, out of respect and fear of the ancient lineage – which had already produced three Doges starting from the 12th century, as well as the first Catholic Patriarch of Constantinople – dared to summon Andrea, but declined to look into these heterodox attendees, all of whom were formally devoted but notoriously averse to the outcomes of the Tridentine and inquisitorial turn taken by the Roman Church in the decades of the second half of the 1500s.

Upset about having to testify before the Inquisition, and perhaps because of this, Andrea Morosini vigorously exculpated Bruno. He testified on June 23, in elegant and dry statements, facing the tribunal, assembled in full force for the occasion, without hesitation. The Patriarch and the papal nuncio, who were represented by vicars for other interrogations, were both present. The two highest ecclesiastical offices of the Republic were certainly not able to compete with Morosini's nobility. The Taverna family, from which the nuncio came, had been granted a duchy in Lombardia by Emperor Charles V little more than half a century earlier. The Priuli family, of which the bishop was a member, belonged to the group of less ancient Venetian Patricians, those of the "new houses," who came to power when the elite "old houses," to whom Morosini belonged, had already been established for centuries. The Doge Domenico Morosini had successfully fought the Normans of Roger II, forcing them to make peace with an increasingly wealthy and resplendent Venice, in the distant past of 1154.

Just a few sentences were enough, spoken in a tone that did not admit replies: "I have never been able to gather from his reasoning that he had any opinion against the faith," Morosoni testified in regard to Bruno; "and as far as I am concerned, I have always believed him to be a Catholic; and if I should have had the slightest suspicion to the contrary, I would never have allowed him to enter our home."[8]

The parade of witnesses had come to an end. Something was not going as predicted.

The Accused Takes the Floor

We must continue to move among the narrow alleys (*calli*) of Venice, in May and June of the year 1592. Almost all of the events that determined the fate of the inquisitorial trial of Giordano Bruno took place during those weeks: the denunciations, the arrest, the depositions of witnesses and the accused, the initiation of correspondence between Rome and Venice, the bright light of attention that Cardinal Santori wanted to shine on him. And finally, there was an event as mysterious as it was decisive: the entrance on the scene of an obscure Capuchin friar who would become Bruno's mortal enemy.

Now, let us rewind the images of the witnesses who filed before the Venetian inquisitorial tribunal in that early summer of 1592, and return to the days at the end of May, when, immediately after being arrested, Giordano Bruno was questioned by the inquisitors at length.

Bruno's torrential testimony before the inquisitorial tribunal of Venice was divided into seven hearings, which produced as many signed statements, called "*costituti*," on the days of May 26, May 30, June 2 (which had two separate hearings), June 3, June 4, and, finally, July 30, 1592. At the end of each interrogation the prisoner was returned to his cell.

In his works, Bruno had theorized the need to fake and conceal the truth, whenever conditions made it necessary.[9] The seriousness of the situation forced him to emphasize wherever possible the conformity of his thought and of his works with the dictates of Roman Catholicism, hiding or smoothing over the suspicious or openly heterodox elements of his life and declaring himself open to repentance. This was all to minimize the destructive effect of abjuration and benefit from a relatively mild sentence. It was a painful passage which would, however, have brought him back into the fold of the Roman Church, allowing him, once the penalty was served, to return with even greater vigor to developing his project for the political and religious pacification of Europe.

The duel between the tribunal and the defendant opened on these assumptions. In their first meeting with Bruno, the inquisitors immediately investigated the subject of his return from Frankfurt and his relations with Mocenigo. Evidently the tribunal considered this subject to be the top priority for its attention. Bruno was only asked for his name, who his parents were, and where he was born during the continuation of that first interrogation: all elements that we would normally expect to see addressed by the investigators in the first question. Clearly the judges of the faith – always careful to uncover accomplices, track down associates, and grasp the internal dynamics of heterodox groups – were more concerned with the circumstances of the Navarran intellectual's presence in Venice than with his actual identity.

Four days later, the second deposition featured a narration of Bruno's life, from his stay in Venice of 1576 until his return to the Lagoon in autumn 1591. Naturally the defendant omitted the thorniest aspects of his stay in Geneva and his adherence to Lutheranism at Helmstedt. We have already cited the passages from this interrogation in which Bruno acknowledged his relations with the principal tribunals of Europe, and revealed that it was his intention, upon returning to Italy, to appear before the pope. Bruno's second deposition was therefore configured as a soliloquy. The defendant shed light on the path his life had taken in the period most suspicious to the inquisitors: that of his interactions with sovereigns, diplomats, universities, and city authorities located in areas that had already long before converted to Protestantism. At the end of the monologue, the philosopher says that his desire to return to Italy had materialized in Frankfurt, in his desire to write a new book with which he would personally present before Clement VIII.

In this case it is also important to pay attention to the behavior of the inquisitors. At the end of Bruno's story, when the late hour made it necessary to adjourn the session, the tribunal felt it should ask the defendant one, and only one, question. The inquisitors had just learned, from the mouth of the prisoner himself, that he had worked in Lutheran universities and in the capital of Calvinism; that he had frequented the entourage of Protestant sovereigns and princes; that he had lived in places that had prevented him regular access to the sacraments, or which had required him to take part in reformed liturgical services. In spite of all these things, the inquisitors, in the waning hours of that second day of questioning, ventured to ask just one immediate question. It concerned the reasons that had lead Bruno to hypothesize that he would come into contact with the pontiff.

We don't have the text of this query, which was not – perhaps *pour cause* – transcribed by the notary. But Bruno's answer unequivocally reveals the content of the question: "I said, that I wanted to present myself at the feet of His Beatitude, with some of my approved works, having several others that I don't approve of."[10] Thus the Venetian Holy Office's first reaction to Bruno's complete life story consisted of wanting to investigate if there were any links between his political-religious profile and his desire to approach Clement VIII. Once again, it is as if the initiation of this trial was very closely connected to the dispute underway in Rome in those months between Santori and his followers with the Aldobrandini; between the pro-Spanish and the pro-French factions. This was – we must not forget this – only four months after the turbulent election of the pope, and the humiliating frustration this had caused for the cardinal of Santa Severina.

In the following interrogation, on June 2, the inquisitors went into an examination of Bruno's printed works. As we know, the judges were only slightly familiar with these works. Putting his hands forward, the philosopher described his books in these words:

> I have some of my works written by me and printed, which I do not approve of; because in these I spoke and discoursed too philosophically, dishonestly and not much like a good Christian; and in particular I know that in some of these works I taught and believed philosophically in things which should be attributed to the power, wisdom and kindness of God according to the Christian faith, basing my doctrine on sense and reason and not on faith. And as regards specifics, I refer to the writings, as now I don't remember a precise article or particular doctrine that I taught, but I will respond according to what I am asked and I will remember.[11]

With this declaration Bruno set up the line of defense that he held in the years to come, until the end of the trial. This defense hinged on the distinction between "law" and "truth," religious discourse and philosophical discourse which had already been presented in *Cena de le Ceneri*.[12] What's more, at that moment the defendant did not know which of his books were being examined by the inquisitors and, completely rationally, he waited for precise disputes over specific works or textual passages in order not to expose himself with careless self-incrimination.

In subsequent interrogations the Venetian judges focused on the details of the philosophical doctrine laid out in Bruno's books, working from a list of titles produced by the prisoner at the request of the tribunal. Regarding fundamental dogmas, the accused admitted to not having "understood" "in the terms of philosophy" how Christ was the Word incarnate; but to have "doubted it and believed with inconstant faith." He then confessed that the doubts about the Trinity were personal, "to myself," and therefore not exposed in his writings. Bruno also tried to demonstrate – counting on the fact that the judges did not know the works from his English period – that his philosophy was founded on a principle of transcendence which allowed it to be rooted in Catholic doctrine (defining "God" as "universal providence," understood as "spirit" that "in an ineffable way [...] is in everything and over everything"). He rejected the accusation of having denied the transubstantiation and the sacrifice of the Mass, from which he said that he had abstained only because his apostasy from the Dominican Order meant excommunication, and therefore exclusion from the sacraments until reconciliation.

With regard to the central point of the relationship between philosophy and the Catholic faith, in his depositions Bruno claimed to believe in the immortality of the personal soul according to the Catholic doctrine. He acknowledged, however, that he had believed the "opinion of Pythagoras" about the transmigration of the soul to be "likely." It was easier for him to demonstrate, with citations from his own works, that he had judged the Lutheran, the Calvinist, and the other non-Catholic confessions as formulated by "pedants" and not by "theologians." Claiming that he had defended the Catholic doctrine of "good works" while across the Alps, he also expressed his contempt for "reformed religion," which he defined as "badly deformed." "I read books by Melanthone, Luther, Calvin and other northern heretics, not ever to learn their doctrine nor make use of it, as I hold them to be more ignorant than me, but I read them out of curiosity,"[13] he added, probably telling the truth.

The defendant effectively deflected Mocenigo's accusation of having deplored the use of the Holy Office in the extirpation of heresy, admitting to having praised the "preaching, good lives, examples and miracles" of the apostles as opposed to the "force that can be applied today," but stating that he had not meant to criticize the "due punishments" against "obstinate" heretics.

The charges concerning the use of "magical arts," and through them the possibility of imitating the miracles of Christ and the apostles, prompted an indignant reaction from the philosopher, whose reaction is reported in the minutes:

> *Respondit extollendo ambas manus et dicendo* [He responds raising both his hands and saying] "What is this? Who was it who found these devilries? I have never said this thing, nor has such a thing ever crossed my imagination. O God, what is this? I would rather be dead than have this thing suggested about me."[14]

These were skilled defense techniques, but not unusual for anyone at the time who had some experience with ecclesiastical tribunals or had done some reading on the subject. The inquisitorial manual itself suggested that defense attorneys advise their clients to deny the most serious accusations, attribute them to the bad faith of the accusers, bring proof of their Catholic solidity, and state their willingness to recognize individual error and secondary faults. Perhaps Bruno had prepared some of these responses in the preceding years, foreseeing that something could go awry upon his return home, already practicing while he was abroad the "rhetoric of sincerity" which had become common knowledge in the Italy of the second half of the 16th century. It is recognizable today by its echoes in contemporaneous depositions by victims of the Inquisition. The already cited opening of Bruno's first deposition – "I will tell the truth" – is echoed, for example, in "I will always respond with the truth because I see [that] before you one must speak the truth"; a statement made before the inquisitor of Pisa in November 1582 by a hermit friar of Sant'Agostino, Valerio da Bologna.[15]

We can read in this same line of defense Bruno's willingness to acknowledge before the Inquisition of Venice that he had believed that fornication was a sin "so slight that it was close to venial sin"; his insistence on not having ever accepted the "rites" of non-Catholic nations, accompanied, however, by the admission of having listened to preaching by reformed ministers "out of curiosity"; his denial (which contradicted Mocenigo's denunciation) of having owned books on magic, along with his acknowledgement of having intended to study "judiciary astrology," or rather the art of horoscopes already prohibited by Sixtus V, "to see if it had any truth or conformity" but not to take advantage of it.

It was not as easy for him to gloss over the issue of the relations he had with heretic rulers and princes in foreign lands, which attracted peremptory questions from the tribunal. In particular, Bruno found himself in the thorny position of having to provide a response to a question about the statement "if speaking of the King of Navarre, he said in particular that he hoped for great things from him." The question was posed by a Holy Office that answered to the cardinal of Santa Severina, an open adversary of Henry of Bourbon, but which at the same time included pro-Navarre members of the Venetian government and the nuncio Taverna himself, a diplomatic representative of Clement VIII; a pontiff whose positions concerning the king of France could perhaps already be guessed, and in whom Bruno, as we have seen, placed his hopes of political and personal achievement.

After admitting to having "praised many heretics and also heretic princes" in his works, "but only for the moral virtues that they have" and not "as religious and pious," Bruno added that he had named Elizabeth I of England "diva," and acknowledging that he had erred. He continued:

> I do not know the King of Navarre nor his ministers, nor have I have ever seen him; and regarding me having spoken about him, I said I did

> not believe him to be a Calvinist nor a heretic if not for the needs of ruling, and that, if he did not profess heresies, he would have no followers; saying more, that I hoped that, with him peacefully attaining the throne of France, having confirmed the orders of the past King, that I would have had from him the favors that I had from the previous King regarding public lessons [...] When I praised the King of Navarre, I did not praise him because he was an adherent of heretics, but for the reason I just stated above, believing that he is not otherwise a heretic, but that he lives heretically from his desire to rule. And I do not believe these are the heresies of the Catholics.[16]

Bruno was certainly aware of the fact that at the time the Holy Office was hunting down Navarre's agents in Italy, and tried with these words to stave off the suspicion of being a crypto-Calvinist follower of the Bourbon. The solution of attributing the French King's religious positions to political Machiavellianism, on the other hand, was in all probability meant to pursue the favor of the Serenissima government and – eventually – the pope. This was also related to the very delicate problem of possible extradition to Rome, which was very rarely accepted by Venice for defendants charged by the Inquisition. Touching on the issue of Henry IV's religion in the way he did, Bruno may have hoped to win the benevolence of the Venetian civil magistrate, strengthening his chances of remaining safe within the borders of the Venetian Republic. These were ingenious calculations and expectations that were unfortunately disappointed by the facts.

During the last of the interrogations that took place between the end of May and the beginning of June 1592, the one on June 4 saw both parties put their cards on the table:

> *Ei dicentibus dominis*, [...] that, if you obstinately persist in denying a thing of which you are then convinced, pertinent to the Catholic faith and against the determination of the Holy Church, you should not wonder if the Holy Office proceeds against you with these terms of justice that should and can be used against the unrepentant who do not want to recognize the mercy of Lord God; and it is dear to this Holy Office to redirect with kindness and Christian charity those who find themselves in the darkness to the light, and off the straight path to the way of eternal life.
>
> *Respondit*: So God will pardon my sins, as I have spoken the truth in all the things that have been asked of me and that I have recalled; but for my greater contentment and satisfaction I will go on thinking more about my actions; and if anything was to come to my memory that I have done or said against the Christian and Catholic faith, I will say it freely; and so I protest that I have said what is just and true, and to say it for the future, and confide that I have never been convinced otherwise.[17]

That day the defendant listened to the reading of the minutes from the previous session and approved them, declaring that he had nothing to add or remove, save for a brief explanation regarding the *De sigillis*. Questioned about the existence of enemies or people with bad intentions toward him, he immediately mentioned the name of Giovanni Mocenigo, and explained the angry resentment of the young patrician over his dissatisfaction with the instruction he had received. It was another element that debunked, if not completely invalidated, the statements of his sole accuser.

The Investigation Languishes

The first month of intense activity in the Venetian trial of Giordano Bruno concluded on June 23, 1592. The accused had been questioned six times. All of the witnesses had been heard, and they had all lined up in defense of the prisoner. Mocenigo appeared to be a sole and hostile witness, completely insufficient as the basis for a serious accusation such as heresy. Bruno's most compromising books were unknown to the inquisitors, and his activities abroad could not be accounted for with direct evidence. At that point the judges of the faith in Venice found themselves in a stalemate.

The investigation languished. The Venetian inquisitors, as Luigi Firpo writes, were "disoriented and dissatisfied [...]. They certainly sensed the seriousness of the case, but were unable to ascertain clear legal proof of guilt beyond the suspect's reticent and evasive admissions."[18] Five weeks passed, waiting in vain for new evidence to emerge. Then, on July 30, 1592, they tried interrogating Bruno one last time.

The bias of some of the questions put to the accused that day once again demonstrates that the judges had formed less than charitable views, but that they still lacked the elements to bring the trial to completion. "It is necessary that you consider very well and recall your status," they threatened in the lagoon heat of those days,

> since for a long span of many years you were an apostate subject to censure, and practiced in the lands of heretics where you could easily be guilty in some articles and actions beyond those expressed in your other depositions.[19]

However, Bruno maintained his unshakeable confidence in himself and declared that he had already reported everything "in full."

We can see just how weak the prosecution's position was by the fact that during this interrogation the judges lied to the defendant to induce him to betray himself. In fact, they challenged him with a non-existent "deposition by someone," which allegedly proved that Bruno had been "teaching false doctrine." None of the witnesses had accused Bruno of having been a heresiarch. The accused firmly denied this: "I will not believe that anyone can be found who can say that I have taught false and heretical doctrine, nor do

I suspect that anyone else can say anything against me on the subject of the Holy faith."[20]

At the end of his last deposition in Venice, Giordano Bruno performed his famous theatrical proclamation of contrition. Prostrating himself before the inquisitors, he declared his repentance for all the errors he had committed and invoked the forgiveness of God and the Catholic Church.

> *Postquam genuflexus dixit*: I humbly ask forgiveness of the Lord God and of Your Illustrious Lords for all the errors I have committed; and I am here ready to carry out whatever is, in your prudence, deliberated and will be judged expedient for my soul.
>
> And I further plead, that they give me an excessive, rather than a public punishment, since the latter could redound some dishonor to the sacred habit of the religion which I wore: and if from the mercy of God and of Your Illustrious Lords I will be granted life, I promise to make significant reforms to my life, so I can pay for the scandal which I gave with equal edification.
>
> *Postquam sanctum Tribunal eidem iniunxit ut elevetur a terra prout pluries eidem iniunctum fuit* [He rose up from the ground after the Tribunal repeatedly invited him to do so].[21]

This was the first and the most expertly staged of a series of declarations of willingness to abjure that punctuated the trial of Giordano Bruno, during the years in Rome as well. These declarations followed one after the other until the tragic conclusion of the philosopher's life, when his voluntary burning at the stake implied their unexpected denial.

If Bruno had wanted to defend his positions with lucid and programmatic intellectual consistency, he would have declared himself unwilling to repent from the start of the Venetian phase of the trial, and would not have ended up surrendering as he did on July 30, 1592. The theatrical prostration acted out in front of the inquisitors that day clearly aimed to facilitate the procedure, avoid the suspicion of obstinacy in heresy, and promise quick achievement of the Holy Office's primary goal: to secure abjuration, the public and official renunciation of heterodox ideas.

There is no trace in the Venetian trial documentation of the philosopher wanting to present briefs to the tribunal. That desire would instead manifest in Rome, where Bruno could communicate directly with the leaders of Catholicism and the pope himself. If those writings had been conceived by the prisoner as a simple delaying tactic, they could have also been presented in Venice, where the accused remained imprisoned until mid-February 1593, with nothing else to do than await the judges' decisions.

Giordano Bruno, at the end of his questioning in Venice, showed that he had no intention of defending his philosophy with his life. He had done the same thing in Geneva, when in August 1579 he was brought before the Consistory and sentenced to tearing up the offending booklet with his own hands and acknowledging his wrongs, on pain of exclusion from the Calvinist Eucharistic supper and prison time.[22] It is clear that Bruno was trying to reach a much higher goal than intellectual martyrdom; he wanted to bring a more ambitious program to fruition. Pursuit of this objective made it necessary to reconcile with the Catholic Church, and to return, sooner or later, to moving undisturbed on the continental political scene. For Bruno, at that moment, dying at the stake as a martyr for free thought was not a desirable destination.

If the inquisitorial trial against Giordano Bruno had been "normal," the defendant's declaration of unconditional willingness to repent and abjure would have led to its conclusion. There were no previous charges of heresy against the accused; no evidence had been found against him, apart from a *testis singularis* whose reliability was tainted by clear enmity. Perhaps the inquisitors might have judged the sibylline titles of the books written by Bruno and cited by the booksellers Ciotti and Brictano to be suspicious. However, there is no record that the judges searched for these volumes, nor any evidence that the books had aroused the attention of the cardinal of Santa Severina, who in Pucci's case, as we have seen, had immediately reminded the judge in Florence of his obligation to carry out the "reconnaissance" of the text. Anyway, it would have to wait for almost three years, until on February 16, 1595 Clement VIII himself, as head of the Congregation of the Holy Office, asked the judges to procure the list of books written by Giordano Bruno in order to track them down in markets across Europe.[23]

If Bruno's had been a "normal" trial, his final gesture, that humble request for forgiveness from God and the Holy Office for the errors he committed, the declaration of willingness to do what he was commanded, begging for "an excessive, rather than a public, punishment, since the latter could redound some dishonor to the sacred habit of the religion which I wore" would have *ipso facto* exempted him from the death penalty. The trial would have ended.

However, all indications are that the trial of Giordano Bruno was not normal. Its incomprehensible opening, the compromising, albeit elusive profile of the defendant, the sudden and persistent attention of both the local and the Roman Inquisition, the indirect involvement of kings, queens and emperors in the context of a very delicate international situation, and its early setting in Venice contributed – contribute – to making this an atypical trial. This singularity is reflected symbolically by its duration: almost eight years of overwhelming confinement makes this case nearly unique in the history of the Holy Office. A quarter of a century earlier, Duke Francesco de' Medici – trying in vain to help the Florentine protonotary Pietro Carnesecchi, who was incarcerated in the Roman inquisitorial prisons between 1566 and 1567 and then sent to the scaffold – admonished his ambassador, thundering: "after nine months of imprisonment – which would have been enough to create a kingdom – it seems an impiety that a prince refuses to recommend one of his vassals."[24]

Notes

1 *Processo*, 151.
2 Ivi, 152.
3 Ivi, 195.
4 *Ibidem.*
5 Ivi, 165.
6 *Ibidem.*
7 See Vittorio Frajese, *Sarpi scettico. Stato e Chiesa a Venezia tra Cinque e Seicento*, Bologna, Il Mulino, 1994, p. 260; Gaetano Cozzi, *Paolo Sarpi tra Venezia e l'Europa*, Turin, Einaudi, 1978, pp. 137–142; Giuseppe Trebbi, *Morosini, Andrea*, in *Dizionario biografico degli italiani*, cit., vol. LXXII, 2012.
8 *Processo*, 194.
9 S. Ricci, *Giordano Bruno nell'Europa del Cinquecento*, cit., p. 476.
10 *Processo*, 164.
11 *Ibidem.*
12 S. Ricci, *Giordano Bruno nell'Europa del Cinquecento*, cit., p. 493. Where not otherwise indicated I follow this source, for the points the follow as well.
13 *Processo*, 177.
14 Ivi, 181.
15 A. Prosperi, *Tribunali della coscienza*, cit., p. 179, also for the stimulating notion of the "rhetoric of truth."
16 *Processo*, 189.
17 Ivi, 183.
18 Ivi, 33.
19 Ivi, 198. The reference is to an internal trial of the Dominican Order opened against Bruno in February 1576, about which he himself had spoken to the judges during the hearing of June 2.
20 Ivi, 198.
21 Ivi, 199.
22 See *supra*, pp. 19–21.
23 "Almost as if the ordinary curriculum of the documentation made the Father Commissioner forget Bruno's singular personality, his status as a philosopher and author of dozens and dozens of works, it is beyond doubt," observed Firpo, "that until that moment [February 1595] the Inquisition had virtually overlooked the open, public and incontrovertible testimony that Bruno's most intimate opinions could legitimately be drawn from his published books": *Processo*, 74.
24 Massimo Firpo, Dario Marcatto, *I processi inquisitoriali di Pietro Carnesecchi (1557-1567)*, volume II, t. 1, Città del Vaticano, Archivio segreto vaticano, 2000, p. cii.

References

Gaetano Cozzi, *Paolo Sarpi tra Venezia e l'Europa*, Turin, Einaudi, 1978.

Massimo Firpo, Dario Marcatto, *I processi inquisitoriali di Pietro Carnesecchi (1557–1567)*, volume II, tome 1, Città del Vaticano, Archivio segreto vaticano, 2000.

Vittorio Frajese, *Sarpi scettico. Stato e Chiesa a Venezia tra Cinque e Seicento*, Bologna, Il Mulino, 1994.

Giuseppe Trebbi, *Morosini, Andrea*, in *Dizionario biografico degli italiani*, cit., vol. LXXII, 2012.

7 In the Prisons of the Inquisition

Giordano Bruno remained under arrest with the Inquisition of Venice for over ten months, from the end of May 1592 to the beginning of February 1593, the date when he was extradited to enter the prisons of the Holy Office of Rome.

We know rather well what happened in the days when Bruno was brought before the Venetian tribunal of the faith, responding to the questions of the inquisitors, recounting his life and making statements: the minutes tell the story. However, we know almost nothing about what happened during the long, exhausting, empty weeks of confinement during which Bruno waited for events to unfold. Nor what lurked in the dark torpor of the cells.

Yet it was there in the prisons of the Venetian Inquisition that events took place which proved decisive for Bruno's fate.

Sequestered, he was surrounded by prisoners in the same condition as himself: desperate people, ready to use or manipulate the statements of others to earn favor with the judges, who interrogated cellmates and used actual spies.[1] Even those condemned to capital punishment often reported other prisoners or outsiders before reaching the scaffold, in an extreme attempt to delay their execution. And the Holy Office certainly did not underestimate these opportunities for investigation. In those same years the cardinal of Santa Severina censured a Neapolitan inquisitor for negligence in weighing the statements of a convict who, in order to buy time on the eve of his execution, had reported very serious heresies cultivated by a group of acquaintances.[2]

In the prisons of the Inquisition, people like Bruno who were accustomed to thinking, speaking, and provoking freely, ran commensurately high risks. A mind that was used to delving into, uncovering, and penetrating the depths of things and people could have conceived of the prisons of the Holy Office as a stage or intellectual laboratory, thus falling into a trap. Heretical priests, troubled or openly apostate nuns and friars, magicians, women and men who had been wrong to try and conceive of the world in a way different from what had been instilled in them since birth: this large and restive audience could become an attentive public for those, like Bruno, who had ambitions of changing the world with their words.

DOI: 10.4324/9781003026082-10

But hiding in this uneasy undergrowth there could also be charlatans, treacherous hustlers, and venomous spies at the service of the inquisitors, all ready to take any and every advantage of other people's errors and naiveté. Attentive ears and eyes penetrated the dark of the night; supposed friends, who with any false step could be transformed into lethal enemies.

The Secrets of the Capuchins

To understand what happened in the prisons of the Venetian Inquisition during the months of Giordano Bruno's confinement, we must once again take a few steps back in time and space to the Rome of Pope Sixtus V.

In late 1586 a short inquisitorial trial, by all appearances of little importance, took place in Rome. Until now it has not attracted the attention of historians. Furthermore, there are very few known papers to document it. In fact, only four meager decrees from the Holy Office have passed down the fact that in Rome on September 12, 1586, the Inquisition arrested a professed lay member of the Capuchin Order, Michele da Castelfranco, and his brother sub-deacon Celestino da Verona. For reasons unknown to us they were already being held in the cells at the monastery of San Bonaventura in the *rione* of Trevi, on the slopes of the Quirinal hill, when they were taken and transferred to the palazzo of the Holy Office. Shortly afterwards they were joined by another professed Capuchin layman, Pastore da Noale, who had been immediately arrested in Vicenza and from there transferred to the city of the popes.

In the months that followed friar Celestino was examined by the inquisitors and confronted with accomplices. In January 1587 all three were subjected to torture. A month later the Congregation of the Holy Office heard the case with the cardinal of Santa Severina present. After examining the trial documents and the report from Celestino's torture, Celestino and Pastore were charged with the suspicion of heresy *de vehementi*, and Michele da Castelfranco with suspicion of heresy *de levi*. The trial concluded in February of the following year with the abjuration of the unfortunate trio.[3]

We do not know the reason why two of the three men tried had been imprisoned in the Roman monastery of the Capuchins of San Bonaventura, neither do we have information about the nature of the heresy they were accused of. However, the trial must have been of some importance, as suggested by the setting in which it was held – the headquarters of the Holy Office itself – and by the fact that the offenders had first been captured by their own brothers and confined at the monastery on the Quirinal hill.

The story reveals the circulation of heterodox ideas or behaviors within the Order of Capuchins, in particular among the Venetians, in the second half of the 1500s. This is not surprising. Since its formation in the Marches in the 1520s, this branch of the Franciscan family had attracted the suspicions of the hardline members of the Roman Curia. The founders of the Capuchins immediately had problems with the justice of the faith: Matteo da Bascio was arrested and brothers Ludovico and Raffaele Tenaglia da Fossombrone were excommunicated for apostasy. It was only thanks to powerful intermediaries, among whom were the noblewomen Caterina Cybo and Vittoria Colonna, that the new Congregation of Hermit Minor Friars – called Capuchins for the new style of dress that distinguished them – obtained official recognition from Pope Clement VII in 1528.

In the fateful year of 1542, which had seen the convocation of the Council of Trent and the creation of the Congregation of the Holy Office, the Capuchin Vicar General Bernardino Ochino was summoned to Rome on suspicion of heresy. He reacted, as we know, by fleeing to Genoa: this sensational event left an indelible stain of heterodoxy on the entire Order.[4] From that point several decades would have to pass, until 1585 and the pontificate of Sixtus V, before there was a partial clearing in the relations between the Roman Curia and the Capuchins.

Pope Peretti, himself a Franciscan friar, was linked by bonds of deep friendship with Capuchin Father Felice da Cantalice: this contributed decisively to rehabilitating those Minors with the highest circles of papal Rome. Right after his friend's death in March 1587, Sixtus V would order an immediate start to the process of his canonization, which began in the month of May. This was shortly after the inquisitorial trial to which we just referred. Therefore the trial taken place in the very delicate climate of the immediate aftermath of Cantalice's death, which foreshadowed the religious rehabilitation of the Capuchins – as long as they could avoid any further compromising of their image. Perhaps this was the reason for the strict confinement endured by Celestino da Verona and Michele da Castelfranco at the monastery, as well as the severity with which the Holy Office inflicted torture: to induce them to quickly confess to the presence of accomplices who could damage the reputation of the Capuchin Order at the moment of its long-awaited redemption, when the future Saint Felice had now concluded his time on earth and the support of Sixtus V was firm and secure.

The project for the rapid canonization of Felice da Cantalice further benefitted from the support of the cardinal of Santa Severina, who apart from being the most influential member of the Holy Office also held the position as protector of the Capuchin Order. This title implied oversight of the life and turbulence inside the monasteries, in addition to the safeguarding of the image and the memory of the Capuchins. In fact, Santori opposed the burial of friar Felice's corpse, preferring the influx of the faithful and crediting the "flowing manna" that came out of the coffin with powers of personal healing. He also allowed the sister of another cardinal to make a hole in the tomb to collect the liquid that came out in a barrel and distribute it to the sick.[5] It is therefore easy to hypothesize that in those years the Holy Office collaborated institutionally in the work of rehabilitating the Capuchins, who were protected by its most senior cardinal, also carrying out the orders of the pope.

The reign of Sixtus V did not definitively dissolve the tensions between the Inquisition and the Capuchin Order, which instead re-emerged and worsened during the pontificate of Clement VIII. Even in this regard the divergence between the political-ecclesiastical positions of Aldobrandini and those of Santa Severina was profound.

The new pope viewed contemporary forms of monastic life with radical distrust, and was intensely involved in their reorganization. Very harsh judgements given during the pastoral visitation of the diocese of Rome in 1592 foreshadowed Clement's conception of the Orders, which he maintained should be marked by total poverty, strict morality of customs and the sharing of property in common according to the original spirit of the Franciscan rules.[6] Developing a broad project of reform of the Regulars, the pope also imposed legal procedures on the Capuchins that were modeled on the tribunals of faith. Thus he directly intervened in the Capuchin General Chapter of 1593 to present a first code of penal procedure for trials of brothers. This anticipated the methods of incarceration, sentencing, and the imposition of penalties officially introduced in the subsequent Chapter of 1596.[7]

Magic in the Monastery

In autumn 1592 another inquisitorial trial suddenly arose involving various monasteries whose members were accused of practicing ritual magic, which like the Roman trial of 1586–1587 saw Venetian Capuchin friars as protagonists. The proceedings were overseen by the inquisitor Gabriele da Saluzzo, Patriarch Lorenzo Priuli, and the nuncio Ludovico Taverna: the same tribunal that was judging the Giordano Bruno case in those same months.[8] While Bruno's trial took its first steps, and the still young papacy of Clement VIII began to restrict the life of behavioral freedoms granted to the members of the religious Orders, the inquisitors in Venice discovered an unsavory tangle of reticence and concealment, protections and favors granted to the Capuchins of the Serenissima by some judges of the faith, by Santa Severina himself, and by Pope Sixtus V. It was an indication that the winds were indeed changing direction.

The trial originated with the spontaneous appearance of Pietro Chiodini, a Capuchin priest and preacher, who reported episodes of invoking spirits, necromancy, and magical use of altars and blessed objects taking place in Venetian monasteries. When he gave his report, Chiodini stated that some years earlier the Order had begun an internal trial for the same crimes, led by the monastery of Verona. The Superiors in that city, however, had sent the documents containing the results of the investigation directly to Rome, bypassing the inquisitorial court of Venice, which they considered somewhat inflexible. A friar had even been punished by the Superiors with imprisonment after he threatened to present himself to the Inquisition of Venice rather than that of Padua, judged to be "friendly."[9]

Quickly summoned by the Venetian inquisitors, the Superiors of the Capuchin monastery of Verona admitted to having bypassed the inquisitorial tribunal of the Serenissima, where they preferred not to appear, instead turning directly to the Roman Holy Office. They clearly knew that there they could count on the support of Santa Severina, protector of the Order and undisputed leader of the Inquisition.[10] Regarding the accusations of magic, on September 24, 1592 father Zeno da Verona, Superior of the city's monastery, confessed to having known that

> some of our fathers along with laymen have erected an altar and that on it they have offered incense to the Demon, and that they waited for angelic visions, and baptized lodestones, and purchased afterbirth, and they bound the spirits in them.

These were serious admissions, which included the summoning of demons and thus crossed the line into black magic. Friar Zeno named brother Silvestro d'Amelia, who for his part admitted to the charges, and reported that the monastery Superiors were anything but ignorant of what happened in the friars' cells. The father guardian of Padua himself had taken part in summoning rituals. Friar Silvestro also admitted to having sent a letter to brother Andrea da Verona in which he revealed some magical formulas.[11]

The grim scenario painted by this testimony – none of which, it would seem, was extorted with torture – is aggravated by superstitions, connivance, heterodox practices, dark warnings, and reciprocal vendettas. During the favorable pontificate of Sixtus V, friars at various levels of the hierarchy in the Capuchin monasteries of the Venetian Republic sent letters, kept secrets, concealed information, and could blackmail or be blackmailed. They spoke with the inquisitors as equals and they chose which tribunals to favor, knowing they could count on protection from Rome.

This dense flow of information, threats, and fears touched the memory of Sixtus V itself. This is shown by part of the testimony that friar Cristoforo da Udine gave before the Venetian inquisitors in that September of 1592. Cristoforo responded to the question of if he knew brother Alessandro da Lugano – who was himself suspected of having taken an active role in the practice of magical arts – by explaining that in the past Alessandro had tried to report what he had seen happening in the cells by writing directly to the pope; he had asked Cristoforo to help him send the letters to Rome. Once discovered, he had been imprisoned in the monastery of Verona, landing Cristoforo himself in trouble. At that point he had no choice but to hand over the letters addressed to Sixtus V, which he had kept carefully hidden, to the Superiors.

> I will say firstly, that the said friar Alessandro was put in prison with the accusation, that certain letters that he had written to His Holiness were not found on his person; for which, as I believe, those fathers [his

> Superiors] intended to put him in prison, having foreseen that he was going to denounce them to the Holy Office. He gave me letters addressed to His Holiness, for me to hold and keep safe, and then send to Rome at the earliest convenience, and to replace these he made a sheaf of simple blank paper, but only with the heading to N[ostro] S[igno]re, placing it up a sleeve [of his religious habit], which was found here when he was put in prison. [...]
>
> The said friar Alessandro gave me one, or really two letters if I remember well, to send to His Holiness, which I have up my sleeve [...]. When the Fathers asked me for the aforementioned letters, which being addressed to the pope I did not know if it was proper to turn them over to them, and I did not want to run any risk of having to account for them and draw attention to myself however, the Provincial saying to our Fathers or them to him that I should turn them over, let go of them, I opened my arm to the aforementioned Provincial, and I said here they are you take these which I do not want to send, and so they took them.[12]

Friar Alessandro da Lugano paid for his attempt to denounce his Superiors to the Holy Office with an anguished end. Repeatedly imprisoned in the monastery of Verona, he was plunged, perhaps forever, into an obscure diagnosis of insanity. "They kept these letters for themselves, and replaced them with folded white paper – the matter led him to be eventually passed off as mad, or possessed," concluded father Cristoforo. His brother Arcangelo da Venezia instead adds, in the context of the same trial, that

> because of these writings [Alessandro] was put in prison at various times. And he was there for perhaps five years, and finally was taken from the prison [...] and was made to swear an oath in conformity with a written statement [...] to never again write to the Holy Office, nor to the Protector or to other Superiors, and with this oath he was set [...] free, and sent to the province of Milan.[13]

From that moment we lose all trace of Alessandro da Lugano.

The evidence that emerges in the Venetian trial against the Venetian Capuchins in 1592 draws a picture of an opaque universe protected by the last margins of the Orders' jurisdictional autonomy. This autonomy would be eroded by the provisions issued by Clement VIII, a pontiff who was extremely suspicious of contemporary forms of monastic life. The friars would be forced to adopt procedures for internal justice and tools of investigation similar to those of the episcopal and inquisitorial tribunals. The effort by the papacy of Sixtus V and Cardinal Santori in the second half of the 1580s to create a model of orthodoxy for the Capuchin order had by then definitively collapsed. The canonization of Felice da Cantalice was halted, to be restarted only in the 1620s. Sanctification would have to wait until the year 1712.

But what does all of this have to do with the trial of Giordano Bruno?

"Listen to the Blasphemy This Man Speaks!"

> On July 4, 1592 the Illustrious Lords of the Holy Office of Venice sent for Friar Celestino da Verona, cleric, and put him in the prisons of the Holy Inquisition at San Marco.[14]

These words, which we can read today in the *Annali* manuscripts of the provincial Archive of the Venetian Capuchins of Venezia-Mestre, report the news of Celestino da Verona's entrance in the inquisitorial jail, where he would meet Giordano Bruno. It was exactly one month after the main cycle of Bruno's interrogation had been completed on June 4, 1592.

For the inquisitors the Capuchin friar's entry into the prison was entirely providential. It was a moment when the Bruno trial was unravelling; the judges were unable to identify any witnesses or proof that could support Mocenigo's accusations, which were nearly inadmissible because they were *testis singularis*, and furthermore motivated by clear hostility. Celestino's terrible accusations against Bruno in 1593 – as we will see better later on – allowed the Holy Office to overcome this obstacle, which had undermined a trial that was already compromised by the defendant's arrest without a preliminary investigation or a citation. Celestino da Verona's entry in the inquisitorial prisons on that July 4, 1592 was the only reason that Giordano Bruno came to be sentenced to death.

But where did Celestino da Verona come from? Why was he "sent for" and put in the prison where Bruno and the case against him languished?

All we know of the Capuchin's origins is his secular name, recorded by the inquisitorial documents: Giovan Antonio Arrigoni, son of Lattanzio. We already know that in 1586, under the papacy of Sixtus V, he had been on the slopes of Quirinal hill, in the monastery of San Bonaventura: therefore outside the Venetian province where – as demonstrated by the name he chose ("da Verona") – he had professed. At the time Celestino was already in a deep dispute with the Order; an element that would distinguish his entire future story. We know, in fact, that he was first imprisoned by the brothers in 1586 and then denounced to the Holy Office for heresy. This incessant back and forth between Capuchin jails and inquisitorial prisons became a *leitmotif* of his tumultuous existence.

The case that followed his first arrest was heard by the cardinal of Santa Severina, protector of the Capuchins, who at the time was involved with the pope in a spiritual and hagiographical reassessment of the Order. It was rapidly resolved, in part due to the use of torture. The imposition of the sentence for vehement suspicion of heresy meant an abjuration, which Celestino readily signed in February 1587.

At this point we lose track of the friar, until that day on July 4, 1592 when he appears on the scene of Bruno's trial, standing out in a scenario now profoundly changed compared to that of his first inquisitorial trial in the Rome of Sixtus V. This was the moment in which the new pope, Clement VIII, had begun to make known his more severe and censorious position regarding the religious Orders. For the Holy Office, however, friar Celestino was at that point a heretic who had been reconciled at the conclusion of a prior proceeding: this meant that in the event of a second trial he would inevitably be condemned to death as a relapsed heretic.

From what can be seen in the documents, Celestino stayed clear of the trial for magical rituals and summoning demons that would shake the Venetian monasteries that autumn. However, that was the opaque context from which he came; this was the logic that presided over relations between the monasteries and the Inquisitions in the Veneto region, in addition to those between the monasteries and the Roman Holy Office and the pope. A framework of hidden and ambiguous relationships prevailed, within which it was certainly not difficult for unscrupulous individuals to win protection and powerful affiliations. Provided, that is, if one had something to offer in exchange.

The information presented by the Capuchin *Annali* reports that Celestino was "sent for." This is a phrase that cannot be considered synonymous with arrest, and which makes no reference to any accusation or proceeding. Rather it hints at an active collaboration between the friar and the "Most Illustrious lords of the Holy Office of Venice": the inquisitor Gabriele da Saluzzo, the apostolic nuncio Ludovico Taverna and the Patriarch Lorenzo Priuli. This is one of the many pieces of evidence which today lead us to believe that Celestino da Verona was an informant, probably close to the cardinal of Santa Severina, Protector of the Order, in a relationship established during the first Roman trial and cultivated under Sixtus V. Thus his entrance to the inquisitorial prisons of Venice had been artfully arranged by the inquisitors of the Serenissima, under the direction of Santa Severina, to gather new evidence and accusations against Giordano Bruno.[15]

The fierce hatred that was unleashed between Bruno and Celestino in that summer of 1592 – which emerges from the documents of the Roman phase of Bruno's trial – is not surprising. The Capuchin's mission must have called for the extortion of compromising statements from Bruno, as appears in the testimony that would be given later by the Carmelite friar Giulio da Salò, who was also a fellow prisoner with Bruno in Venice:

> While Giordano was discoursing with the prisoner friar Celestino, [I] heard [Giordano] say that Christ Our Lord had mortally sinned in this world, because he had wanted to oppose the will of the Father when, orating in the garden, he said: «*Si possibile est, transeat a me calix isse*» ["If it be possible, let this cup pass from me"]; and Francesco Marangon Napolitano was also there, and I said: "Listen to the blasphemy that man speaks!"; and it seems to me that this was September 1592 in the prison of the above.[16]

We also learn from the documents produced in the Roman phase of the trial that Bruno was forced by Celestino to descend with irritating frequency to the terrain of religious dispute, to the point that it once led the philosopher of Nola to slap him in the face.[17]

These annoying provocations did not last for long, however. On September 2, 1592 the cardinals of the Congregation, meeting in the absence of the pope but in the presence of Santa Severina, ordered that Celestino da Verona be freed from the prison in Venice, and summoned him to Rome.[18] This confirms that an unusual relationship of trust and favor existed between the inquisitorial leadership and the Capuchin friar, even though he had already been convicted on vehement suspicion of heresy. At that point it was necessary for the leaders of the Holy Office to communicate with the Veronese without intermediaries: they accordingly ordered Venice to release the friar and send him to the Roman Curia. The Congregation therefore summoned Celestino without having him officially extradited, and, from what appears in the documents, without anyone accompanying him on his journey from Venice to Rome.

Thus in early September 1592, Celestino da Verona was once again a man who was free to move about the peninsula and go to Rome in the presence of his protectors. In the meantime, Bruno remained in the Venetian prisons waiting to learn his fate.

Historian Carlo De Frede, retracing the steps that led to Rome assuming control of Bruno's trial, has hypothesized that Giordano Bruno's theatrical submission at the end of his deposition on July 30, 1592 had been staged by the philosopher after he learned of the maneuvers underway aimed at his extradition. Thus Bruno would have humiliated himself before the judges in an attempt to avoid that possibility.[19]

Perhaps this speculation can be further clarified. For Bruno, the growing awareness of the risks he was running in the Venetian inquisitorial trial could have been reinforced by the concrete view of what had been happening in the jail between June and July. He must have intuited that something strange was happening around the hated Capuchin provocateur. And he certainly drew the appropriate conclusions from the fact that Celestino da Verona, although he had been judged by the Inquisition a few years earlier and now found himself in prison again, was not only not subjected to a true inquisitorial proceeding, but was actually released from custody.

But perhaps not even the acute Bruno could imagine that Celestino's freedom had been granted in order to allow the heretic to go to Rome to meet with the leaders of Catholicism.

A Protected Enclosure

It is very likely that between Rome and Venice, a clever mastermind organized Celestino da Verona's intervention as a collaborator of the Holy Office in the trial against Giordano Bruno in the summer of 1592, which at that moment was stalled. The information arriving from Venice, via a dual channel of correspondence, had allowed Cardinal Santori to identify

Bruno as being pro-Navarre and a natural scientist: dangerous traits, which made him much like other individuals who were arrested, censured and condemned in those years by Santa Severina himself or by other members of the sacred college.

It was during these months that the serious rift developed between Pope Clement VIII and the Holy Office, between the Aldobrandini and Santori factions, between the Papal State and Spain, and between the Roman Inquisition and the King of Navarre, who by now had become Henry IV, King of France. The pontiff and the Congregation of the Holy Office clashed severely, as had already happened in the not too distant past, albeit for different reasons.[20] The pope had decided to pursue a pro-France policy, even at the cost of welcoming an overt heretic like the Bourbon back into the Roman Church. The Supreme Inquisitor intended to prevent this eventuality in any way possible, and to impede the spread of Navarre's influence on the Italian peninsula at all costs. This influence was all the more dangerous in cases such as that of the troublesome Dominican apostate confined in the Venetian prisons, where it combined with the insolent desire to know the truths of nature, regardless of those that Santori considered to be the foundations of the Christian religion and Roman authority.

Celestino da Verona, a friar who had been scrutinized, tortured and condemned at Rome in 1586–1587, who was a member of the Order of which Santa Severina was protector, and who was already settled in the Venetian Republic could at this point have represented an ideal collaborator for the Holy Office. Santori was a man who was quite convinced of the providential function of his inquisitorial work, as masterfully demonstrated by the studies of Massimo Firpo, to transform his own private work papers into an "infernal machine" capable of assembling coercive, preconceived theses, misrepresentations, circumstantial inventions, and true retroactive falsifications.[21] The Supreme Inquisitor was a judge of unshakable certainties, who believed – as had Pope Paul IV Carafa, much admired by Santori, regarding the case against Cardinal Giovanni Morone – that he did not need to have official evidence on which to base a sentence of heretical guilt. "There was no need for so many trials, writings or justifications, nor were legal terms (deadlines) required, because he knew very well what the facts were, and that this [the facts] was the true judge," Carafa stated in 1559 in reference to the Morone trial[22]; words that Santa Severina would have likely endorsed with regard to Bruno.

Having performed his function as informant and *agente provocateur* in the case against Bruno after being imprisoned, but never formally tried, by the inquisitors of the Serenissima – according to what is known from the few surviving sources[23] – Celestino went to Rome. However, he was not granted everything: there was also Clement VIII, and the Capuchin Order that the pope intended to lead back to a new morality. Thus we know that during 1593 Celestino was subjected to severe censure by the Venetian members of his Order, who were certainly given to greater circumspection after the inquisitorial trial for ritual magic the previous year, which was also brought to an close by the Venetian inquisitors without clamor or exemplary sentences.

In February of 1593 Celestino had in fact already gone back to Verona, where he returned to moving between Capuchin jails and the prisons of the Inquisition, and being tortured again with the authorization of the Roman Dicastery. The Congregation ordered that the General of the Capuchins be interrogated, with the clear purpose of investigating the conflicts between the friar and his Order, and perhaps to induce the Superior to milder counsel. Between July and October 1593 the friar continued to move between monastery tribunals and inquisitorial tribunals in both Verona and Venice, until Santori ordered him transferred to the little monastery of Colpersito in the Marches, within the secure borders of the Papal Sates. Celestino refused the injunction at first, actually provoking the direct intervention of the pontiff through the apostolic nuncio, Ludovico Taverna.

By all evidence, the embarrassments created in the Curia by the destructive confrontation between the Capuchins and the Inquisition, of which Celestino's case was a non-trivial part, required the direct intervention of Clement VIII, and was resolved by the power of the diplomatic representative of the Holy See. He had Celestino da Verona locked up in the cells of the Order in Venice, finally ordering his transfer to the Marches towards the end of 1593.[24] After such an uproar Colpersito was a protected enclosure; the turbulent Capuchin, however, was determined not to stay for very long.

Spies, Spies, and More Spies

The history of the 16th century Roman Inquisition is strewn with heretics that became informants. Such is the case, for example, of Giovan Battista Scotti.[25] Bolognese by birth, at the beginning of the 1540s he belonged to a heterodox circle of "spiritual" women and men in Napoli who were followers of Spanish theologian and reformer Juan de Valdés, who later gathered around Cardinal Reginald Pole in Viterbo. Scotti associated with Pietro Carnesecchi and Vittore Soranzo in particular – both of whom were tried by the Inquisition, the second sentenced to death in 1567 – engaging in a lively exchange of heterodox letters and books. Scotti abjured after being condemned for the first time by the Inquisition of Bologna in 1543, but continued to openly profess pro-reform doctrines. Due to new suspicions that had moved the Holy Office, he retreated to the Abruzzi and the Grand Constable of the Kingdom of Napoli, Ascanio Colonna. In 1547 he then appeared spontaneously in front of Cardinal Marcello Cervini, the future Pope Marcellus II. He confessed his errors, abjured a second time, and saw his life spared.

Giovan Battista Scotti became, we do not know when, an unscrupulous spy for the Holy Office, which paid him handsomely. Evidence remains of two payments made to him by the Inquisition in November 1551 and March 1552. There are records of his relations with the Roman Curia again in the 1560s, and around 1569–1570 the inquisitors wrote up a profile that described him with these words:

> The Holy Office has received great service from him because, in addition to his discovering the schools in Rome, Regno, Bologna, Venice, Cremona, Modena, Pisa and almost all of Italy, the Holy Office was accustomed, when it wanted to put together a case against a suspect, to sending him to get information about him. He [Scotti], in addition to the delivery of the writings he had on them [the suspects], he briefly put in writing what he knew and what the best way was to discover more: then [the Holy Office] would examine them.[26]

The life stories of Giovan Battista Scotti and that of Celestino da Verona overlapped in many ways. Both were from modest origins and were literate; the two both came from an urban center in northern Italy which had seen intense activity by the Inquisition, and were subjects of a first trial that ended with abjuration; both met the inquisitors again along the way but, despite their condition as relapsed, were not sentenced to death. Both Celestino and Scotti spent periods in isolation not far from Rome, in the Marches and in the Abruzzi; they had sinister reputations, arousing the animosity of acquaintances and fellow prisoners; and both enjoyed powerful protections and expanded geographic mobility, acting to "briefly put in writing what he knew."

Celestino da Verona, as we will see, also presented his denunciation against Giordano Bruno in writing. By giving his statement in this way the informant offered his protectors safe, unequivocal, and irrevocable evidence. It allowed the inquisitors to make corrections or additions to the texts should they become necessary at a later time. He could intervene as needed, sending papers from distant, protected, or secret places; hiding places from which he could continue to act in the shadows, without arousing the suspicions of his acquaintances or superiors, both outside and inside the monasteries.

The lives of two other characters that revolved around Giordano Bruno in the prisons of Venice and Rome were not at all dissimilar from the biographies of Giovan Battista Scotti and Celestino da Verona; both became his accusers in the Roman phase of the trial.

The first was the scholar Francesco Maria Vialardi of Vercelli, captured by Santa Severina in Genoa in 1591 on charges of clandestine Navarran activity. He was sent to Rome, where he entered the prisons of the Inquisition on May 6, 1592. There he became acquainted with Bruno, discussing questions of religion with him and – according to what the Italian philosopher himself would later testify – provoking him with heretical statements.[27] Bruno also associated him with his other controversial accuser, friar Francesco Graziano, asserting that Vialardi had

> many times said horrible words against God, Religion, and the Church, and to this I respond [or really to the heretical declarations that the judges were at that moment impugning to Bruno] they bring to mind the proposals of the said [Vialardi and Francesco Graziano], who used to bother me with this and other doubts.[28]

Graziano and Vialardi also contribute to defining the profile of the informant that we have drawn from the comparison between Scotti and Celestino da Verona. They were both educated men: the first, who was from Udine, wrote letters for a fee and copied books[29]; the second boasted a broad acquaintance with the humanities and natural philosophy, and was also a prolific writer on a broad variety of subjects, including: zoology, Italian geography, and literature. Celestino was a professed cleric and sub-deacon; therefore he knew Latin well and was trained in theology. Graziano, imprisoned in Venice with Bruno, was summoned to the Roman Holy Office because his name had been mentioned by one of the witnesses cited by Celestino. He gave a wide ranging and bitter deposition against Bruno, including the subject of blasphemy: he spoke of "very horrible blasphemies" and of outrageous gestures Giordano directed at heaven and repeated "more than twenty-five times."[30]

Bruno claimed that both Graziano and Vialardi were rabid atheists, albeit disguised. This extremely serious accusation, lodged by Bruno and accompanied by detailed circumstances,[31] does not, however, appear to have impacted the legal status of either, who in all probability were under the protection of the inquisitors. Both, in fact, were granted unusual clemency by the tribunals that judged their cases of faith. Graziano first stood trial in Venice in 1584–1585, concluding with abjuration *de formali* for various heresies – including the alleged illegitimacy of the so-called Donation of Constantine, which argued for the temporal power of the pontiff and his spiritual supremacy over clerics – and a sentence of life in prison.[32] However, the sentence was revised, because he was tried by the Inquisition a second time. Notwithstanding these very serious precedents, on March 27, 1593 he was not condemned to death, but rather once again to life in prison.[33] In this case the sentence was also commuted as early as 1598, with the obligation that he resided in Venice: therefore sooner than the ordinary eight-year period after which a sentence of life in prison was normally re-evaluated if the prisoner showed signs of repentance.[34]

Vialardi, in addition to being released unconditionally from prison by the Holy Office in 1595, boasted in a letter to the Grand Duke of Tuscany in 1597 about the comfortable treatment he had enjoyed in the Roman prisons of the inquisition where he had been with Bruno. "I was very well treated for rooms, [with] convenience for study and anything, they did not deny me the holy sacraments, nor company, nor visitors, nor writing, and I was well liked by the cardinals." After his release, even the 300 *scudi* of debt accumulated from paying for his upkeep during 61 months of luxurious confinement was forgiven.[35]

After being released from prison, Francesco Maria Vialardi became an informant for the Grand Dukes of Tuscany. He received confidences, and gave information and counsel to the cardinal of Santa Severina on the subject of business with the Curia and the pontiff's diplomatic decisions[36] as well as the processes of the Holy Office. For example, on November 2, 1599 he wrote to Grand Duke Ferdinand I de' Medici:

> I was with S[anta] Severina a little today, who told me that he did not know that Campanella is a prisoner, but thinks that he saved himself among the Turks, and that the author of giving up spaces to the Turks in Calavria [*sic*] is the Viceroy, who was in Cosenza, is Spanish, and who, along with his wife and children cannot be found.[37]

And again, on December 15 of that year:

> Santa Severina created a Congregation of 20 cardinals *de propagatione fidei*, where it was resolved to send [...] certain preachers [...] to Germany according to the recollections I gave S[anta] Severina from my friend Gaspar Nertusio, who was made a Catholic and died a short time ago.[38]

While Giordano Bruno was heading for the stake, a former Navarran heretic presented the Supreme Inquisitor Santa Severina with an informer recently "made a Catholic" who would help him propagate the true faith, and proudly wrote about it to the devoted Grand Duke of Tuscany, Cardinal Ferdinand.

This is how the world worked at the heart of the Counter-Reformation.

Geography of a Venetian Trial

When the Venetian Inquisitors secured Giordano Bruno in their prisons, they were faced with two big problems: the inadequacy of the evidence against the accused, and the questionable viability of Giovanni Mocenigo's testimony. The cardinal of Santa Severina himself, in legal opinions written in previous years, had observed the authoritative guidance expressed by the *Directorium inquisitorum*: *testes singulares*, even when combined with a defendant's bad reputation, were not a sufficient basis for sentencing: at most they could be the premise for canonical purgation – a sort of absolution in the absence of proof.[39]

It is wholly evident, however, that the Venetian judges were nevertheless aware – partly due to their experience and inquisitorial intuition, and partly thanks to channels of information that could not be officially used in the trial – that Bruno was a heretic. They quickly succeeded in persuading Rome of this, as well as the Supreme Inquisitor Santa Severina, who in all probability coordinated a plan to gather new denunciations and testimony via the networks of informers he had built over the preceding years, starting with the Capuchin order of which he was the Protector.

The results of this strategy – applied countless times in the history of the Inquisition – were clear before long. However, to bring them to completion it was worth waiting for the dangerous Navarran to be extradited to Rome. It was necessary to put pressure on the Venetian authorities by all means to get Bruno secured in the Roman prisons – at that point the trap could be sprung. This is precisely what happened.

Before taking leave of Venice and moving our gaze to the imposing Roman palazzo of the Holy Office and its prisons, where Bruno was transferred at the end of February 1593, we must examine one last important aspect of the trial phase that took place in Venice.

The information cited from the Capuchin *Annali* confirms that on July 4, 1592 friar Celestino da Verona was "sent for" and placed "in the prisons of the Holy Inquisition at San Marco." The last part of the notation is a clue that can shed light on an important aspect of Bruno the trial: the Venetian prisons in which the philosopher was confined were not – as historiography has traditionally maintained – the cells of the Dominican monastery of San Domenico in the *sestiere* of Castello, located near the point of Sant'Elena.[40] Bruno was actually held in the new prisons of the Holy Office built near the Palazzo Ducale.

In the second half of the 16th century in Venice, the so-called New Prisons over the Ponte della Paglia were already under construction, and were completed between 1600 and 1605. Only after their completion were they connected directly to the Palazzo Ducale by the little bridge that would become famous with the name "Bridge of Sighs." At the rear of the New Prisons, at a corner with the Calle degli Albanesi, the so-called Premises of the Holy Office (Luoghi del Sant'Officio) were soon built: offices and a few cells available to the ecclesiastical tribunal, whose existence is still shown on 18th century maps, before they were demolished.[41] That structure was adjacent to the first section of the New Prisons, completed beyond Rio di Palazzo by the second half of the 1570s. The first prisoners were transferred there in the following decade.[42]

The Luoghi del Sant'Officio were already completed in 1592 and so could accommodate Celestino da Verona and Giordano Bruno. This idea is also recalled by a persistent 19th century oral tradition – still accepted to this day by tourist guides – which numbers Bruno among the famous guests of the notorious "Piombi" of the Palazzo Ducale.

This is not a minor detail, since, if definitively proven, it moves not only the place of detention, but also the location where the inquisitorial tribunal met to interrogate Bruno. In all probability the trial did not take place in the monastery of San Domenico – a poor place, which would have been uncomfortable for the members of the tribunal and the illustrious witnesses – but rather in the same building as the New Prisons. Here there were rooms alongside the prison set aside for use by the Holy Office, as shown on the 18th century map. Furthermore the Bruno trial documentation does not contain a passage that specifies where the first meetings of the inquisitorial tribunal and the first three depositions of the prisoner took place. Only in the fourth deposition, the second to be conducted on June 2, 1592, do we find that the minutes begin with the phrase "*in domo et locum carcerum Sanci Offici*,"[43] which can be supposed to be the Luoghi del Sant'Officio in the New Prisons.

In the Italy of the late 16th century it was actually rather common for Inquisition trials to take place in the episcopal palazzo or nearby, especially where – as in the case of Milan, which follows the topography of Venice in this regard – the Dominican monastery to which the inquisitor belonged was far from the city center. The same thing happened, for example, in Ravenna, Vercelli, Como, and at Piacenza in the early 1600s. During this period, in a letter circulated to all the bishops of cities with an inquisitorial office, the cardinals of the Roman Congregation resolved that

> to quell or settle the differences that are wont to arise between the bishops and the inquisitors over the place to assemble congregations for cases of the Office [...], notwithstanding any custom, albeit immemorial, or contrary in style, the inquisitors must move to the palazzo of the bishops and there assemble congregations for the cases under the control of the Holy Office, when those same bishops want to attend them personally.[44]

Perhaps the entire Venetian geography of the Bruno trial must be reconsidered, repositioning the spaces and the balances of power intrinsic to the individual locations. The nucleus of the Ducal prisons "beyond the Rio" was not far from the residence of the apostolic nuncio: palazzo Gritti in San Francesco Della Vigna, which the Republic of Venice presented to Pope Sixtus V in 1586.

Even the more secluded palazzo of the Patriarch, then located in Campo San Pietro, again in the *sestiere* of Castello, could have lent itself to hosting some meetings of the tribunal and Bruno's first depositions themselves, at which the Venetian Ordinary was sometimes present personally. Lorenzo Priuli's coat of arms remains on the portal of the building to this day. A Venetian diplomat, Priuli was elected Patriarch by the Senate in August 1590, and only later consecrated as a priest, and then bishop. In 1583 he had been ambassador to Paris at the court of Henry III, precisely when Bruno was living there.[45]

Perhaps Priuli had already heard talk of Bruno during his years in France; it's possible that since that time he had been aware of his political orientation. Certainly he must have been disturbed to learn the Bruno was back in

Venice. Andrea Morosini, owner of the "*ridotto*" attended by Bruno, once he took the office of "public historiographer" of the Republic of Venice, would celebrate Priuli as a prudent diplomat who was sincerely convinced of the necessity of close collaboration between Venice and the Holy Office. More recent studies also identify Priuli as the first Patriarch truly committed to introducing the canons and decrees of the Council of Trent into the Venetian Church, raising the moral standards of the clergy and reducing the autonomy of ecclesiastic life in the Serenissima as compared to Rome.[46] His intervention in the Bruno trial could perhaps constitute a piece of this political and diplomatic identity, which at that moment was still being defined, and would fully unfold in the years to come.

Notes

1 An interesting case of the use of testimony from fellow prisoners by the Spanish Inquisition in a trial is presented by Giovanna Fiume, *L'impossibile riscatto di Aly del Marnegro, «Turco vero»*, in «Quaderni storici», 2012, n. 140, pp. 385–424, especially on pp. 399 ff.

2 Giovanni Romeo, *Aspettando il boia. Condannati a morte, confortatori e inquisitori nella Napoli della Controriforma*, Florence, Sansoni, 1993, pp. 23 ff. and 51–52.

3 Germano Maifreda, *Giordano Bruno e Celestino da Verona. Un incontro fatale*, Pisa, Edizioni della Normale, 2016, pp. 77–78.

4 Miguel Gotor, *Santi stravaganti. Agiografia, Ordini religiosi e censura ecclesiastica nella prima età moderna*, Rome, Aracne, 2012, pp. 233 ff.; Id., *Tradizione inquisitoriale e memoria eterodossa: un cartello di sfida di Bernardino Ochino al cardinale Carafa (1543-1628)*, in «Archivio italiano per la storia della pietà», 1999, n. 12, pp. 89–142. For an overall historical interpretation of the Counter-Reformation canonization procedures one may start with Simon Ditchfield, *Liturgy, Sanctity and History in Tridentine Italy: Pietro Maria Campi and the Preservation of the Particular*, Cambridge, Cambridge University Press, 1995.

5 On the devotion of Sixtus V, see the entry on *Felice da Cantalice* written by Sergio Rivabene in *Dizionario biografico degli italiani*, cit., volume XLVI, 1996; M. Gotor, *Santi stravaganti*, cit., p. 249.

6 See Miguel Gotor, *I beati del papa. Santità, Inquisizione e obbedienza in età moderna*, Florence, Olschki, 2002, pp. 116–119.

7 See the *Introduzione* a *Registrum Scripturarum della Procura generale dell'Ordine cappuccino 1599–1613*, edited by Giuseppe Avarucci, Rome, Istituto storico dei Cappuccini, 2011, pp. 22 and 35.

8 They were not, as often happened, all present at every deposition: for a session of the complete court, on October 3, 1592, see Archivio di Stato di Venezia (from here on ASVe), *Savi all'eresia (Sant'Ufficio)*, box 69, folder «Cappuccini di Venezia», fol. 12*v*.

9 ASVe, *ibidem*, minutes of the spontaneous appearance on September 4, 1592, fol. 1*r*.

10 ASVe, *ibidem*, hearing of Zeno da Verona, September 22, 1592, fol. 2*r*–*v*.

11 Ivi, fol. 39*v*.

12 Ivi, fols. 10*r*–11*v*.

13 Ivi, fol. 16*r*.

14 APCVM, *Annali*, A-BB, fol. 12*r*. Thanks to Father Remigio Battel for his assistance in consulting these sources.

15 I have elaborated on these aspects in G. Maifreda, *Giordano Bruno e Celestino da Verona*, cit., to which I refer in the interest of brevity.
16 *Processo*, 263.
17 The Veronese, during the repetitions, would state "There were words between us, and once he even slapped me in the fact, but I forgave him" (ivi, 299).
18 Città del Vaticano, Archivio della Congregazione per la dottrina della fede (from here on ACDF), So, *Decreta* 029, fol. 281/2*v* [*sic*], 2 settembre 1592. The following day, September 3, in *feria quinta* with Clement VIII present, Celestino's case was not addressed.
19 C. De Frede, *L'estradizione di Giordano Bruno da Venezia*, cit., p. 410.
20 See *supra*, p. 70.
21 See the work done on the *Compendium* of the Morone trial in M. Firpo, *Inquisizione romana e Controriforma*, cit., pp. 435–448.
22 Ivi, p. 396.
23 G. Maifreda, *Giordano Bruno e Celestino da Verona*, cit., pp. 111–112.
24 Ivi, p. 105.
25 See la *Nota biografica* in Massimo Firpo, Dario Marcatto, *Il processo inquisitoriale del cardinal Giovanni Morone. Nuova edizione critica*, volume 1: *Il processo d'accusa*, with the collaboration of Luca Addante, Guido Mongini, Rome, Libreria Editrice Vaticana, 2011, *passim* and M. Firpo, *Inquisizione romana e Controriforma*, cit., *passim*.
26 M. Firpo, *Inquisizione romana e Controriforma*, cit., pp. 266–267.
27 The reference study on Vialardi remains L. Firpo, *In margine al processo di Giordano Bruno*, cit.
28 *Processo*, 272.
29 As emerges from the testimony in his first trial for heresy: ASVe, *Savi all'eresia (Sant'Ufficio)*, box 53, folder «Graziano Francesco», fol. 1*r*, testimony of Rinaldo de Vanti given April 22, 1584.
30 *Processo*, 273.
31 «Et prosequitur recensere haereses, quas Gratianus et Vialardus tenebant » (*Processo*, 272).
32 See ASVe, *Savi all'Eresia (Sant'Ufficio)*, box 53, folder «Graziano Francesco », fols. 29*r*–33*r*, abjuration of April 4, 1585.
33 *Processo*, 53 and 66–67.
34 On the reconsideration of the sentence of perpetual imprisonment as irremissible after eight years, see J. Tedeschi, *The Prosecution of Heresy*, cit., pp. 147–155.
35 See *Processo*, doc. 51, pp. 271–272. The letter of 1597 to Ferdinando I is cited by L. Firpo, *In margine al processo di Giordano Bruno*, cit., pp. 345–346.
36 See, for example, Archivio di Stato di Firenze (from here on ASFi), *Mediceo del Principato*, *filza* 3623, letter by Vialardi of May 29, 1599 in un-numbered pages:

> *Quanto a cardinali [...], [Francesco di] Gioiosa ha mandato a posta in Francia per aver licenza dal re d'andarvi a ordinar il fatto suo disordinato per lo fratello fattosi Capuccino, S. Sev[erin]a m'ha detto, che questo è un colore, ma che il papa il manda in Francia per negocij, non si sa quali, e che il Duca Capuccino viene qua.*
>
> As far as cardinals [...], [Francesco di] Gioiosa has sent to France for the king's license to go there to sort out the messy affair of the brother who become a Capuchin, S. Sev[erin]a told me that this is a pretense, and that the pope sent him to France for business, no one knows what, and that the Capuchin Duke is coming here.
>
> (p. 1*r* of the letter)

37 ASFi, *Mediceo del Principato*, *filza* 3623, pages un-numbered, fol. 1*r* of the letter dated November 2, 1599.

38 Ivi, fol. 1*r* of the letter from December 15, 1599.
39 S. Ricci, *Il sommo inquisitore*, cit., p. 216.
40 See, for the exact location of the prisons, the 18th century view of Venice that reproduces the one by Vincenzo Coronelli of 1697, published in *Giordano Bruno 1548-1600. Mostra storico documentaria. Roma, Biblioteca Casanatense 7 giugno-30 settembre 2000*, Florence, Olschki, 2000, p. 189.
41 Giovanni Scarabello, *Carcerati e carceri a Venezia nell'età moderna*, Rome, Istituto della Enciclopedia italiana, 1979, p. 91.
42 Umberto Franzoi, *Le prigioni di Palazzo Ducale a Venezia*, Milan, Electa, 1997, *passim* and, for the phase of the construction of the New Prisons, Giovanni Scarabello, *La pena del carcere. Aspetti della condizione carceraria a Venezia nei secoli XVI-XVIII: l'assistenza e l'associazionismo*, in *Stato, società e giustizia nella Repubblica di Venezia (sec. XV-XVIII)*, edited by Gaetano Cozzi, Rome, Jouvence, 1980, tome I, pp. 317–376, p. 325, note 3. For further arguments in favor of this hypothesis I refer to G. Maifreda, *Giordano Bruno e Celestino da Verona*, cit.
43 *Processo*, 171. The fifth Bruno hearing (June 3) was held "*in loco supradicto*" (ivi, 184), while the remainder do not specify the place where the session was held. None of the other records from the questioning of witnesses offers information in this regard.
44 E. Bonora, *L'Archivio dell'Inquisizione e gli studi storici*, cit., pp. 982–983.
45 Regarding Bruno in Paris, see pp. 22–23.
46 Giuseppe Trebbi, *Priuli, Lorenzo*, in *Dizionario biografico degli italiani*, cit., volume LXXXV, 2016.

References

Simon Ditchfield, *Liturgy, Sanctity and History in Tridentine Italy: Pietro Maria Campi and the Preservation of the Particular*, Cambridge, Cambridge University Press, 1995.

Massimo Firpo, Dario Marcatto, *Il processo inquisitoriale del cardinal Giovanni Morone. Nuova edizione critica, volume 1: Il processo d'accusa*, with the collaboration of Luca Addante, Guido Mongini, Rome, Libreria Editrice Vaticana, 2011.

Giovanna Fiume, *L'impossibile riscatto di Aly del Marnegro, «Turco vero»*, in «Quaderni storici», 2012, n. 140, pp. 385–424.

Umberto Franzoi, *Le prigioni di Palazzo Ducale a Venezia*, Milan, Electa, 1997.

Giordano Bruno 1548–1600. Mostra storico documentaria. Roma, Biblioteca Casanatense 7 giugno-30 settembre 2000, Florence, Olschki, 2000.

Miguel Gotor, *Tradizione inquisitoriale e memoria eterodossa: un cartello di sfida di Bernardino Ochino al cardinale Carafa (1543–1628)*, in «Archivio italiano per la storia della pietà», 1999, n. 12, pp. 89–142.

Miguel Gotor, *I beati del papa. Santità, Inquisizione e obbedienza in età moderna*, Florence, Olschki, 2002.

Miguel Gotor, *Santi stravaganti. Agiografia, Ordini religiosi e censura ecclesiastica nella prima età moderna*, Rome, Aracne, 2012.

Germano Maifreda, *Giordano Bruno e Celestino da Verona. Un incontro fatale*, Pisa, Edizioni della Normale, 2016.

Registrum Scripturarum della Procura generale dell'Ordine cappuccino 1599–1613, edited by Giuseppe Avarucci, Rome, Istituto storico dei Cappuccini, 2011.

Sergio Rivabene, *Felice da Cantalice*, in *Dizionario biografico degli italiani*, cit., volume XLVI, 1996.

Giovanni Romeo, *Aspettando il boia. Condannati a morte, confortatori e inquisitori nella Napoli della Controriforma*, Florence, Sansoni, 1993.

Giovanni Scarabello, *Carcerati e carceri a Venezia nell'età moderna*, Rome, Istituto della Enciclopedia italiana, 1979.

Giovanni Scarabello, *La pena del carcere. Aspetti della condizione carceraria a Venezia nei secoli XVI-XVIII: l'assistenza e l'associazionismo*, in *Stato, società e giustizia nella Repubblica di Venezia (sec. XV-XVIII)*, edited by Gaetano Cozzi, Rome, Jouvence, 1980, tome I, pp. 317–376.

Giuseppe Trebbi, *Priuli, Lorenzo*, in *Dizionario biografico degli italiani*, cit., volume LXXXV, 2016.

8 Before the Throne of Peter

Faustus. Most sacred Patron of the Church of *Rome*
By full consent of all the reverend Synod
Of Priests and Prelates, it is thus decreed:
That *Bruno*, and the Germane Emperour
Be held as Lollords, and bold Schismatiques,
And proud disturbers of the Churches peace.
And if that *Bruno* by his owne assent,
Without inforcement of the German Peeres,
Did seeke to weare the triple Dyadem,
And by your death to clime Saint *Peters* Chaire,
The Statutes Decretall have thus decreed,
He shall be straight condemn'd of heresie,
And on a pile of Fagots burnt to death.[1]

In scene eight of Christopher Marlowe's *Doctor Faustus* there is a dialog between Raymond, the King of Hungary, Pope Adrian VI, and a character named *Saxon Bruno*, who is presented before the pontiff in chains, awaiting his judgement. Even though the profile of Marlowe's "Saxon Bruno" is far from that of Giordano Bruno, it may be possible that this passage was inspired by the tragic story of the Italian philosopher. The mention of the stake, the connection with the Germanic world symbolized by the Emperor and the character's name itself may not be accidental.[2]

The difficulty finding echoes of Giordano Bruno's trial in the testimony of his contemporaries – both before and after his burning at the stake – is indicative. On one hand it is certainly due to the secrecy with which the Inquisition operated: in general no news should have leaked from the palazzi of the Holy Office until the moment of sentencing. Moreover, at that time there was nothing comparable to today's "public opinion" which could be scandalized, or circulate written comments regarding the workings of ecclesiastical or secular justice. Europe's silence about Bruno's fate is also a sign of the limited circulation of his works[3] and, at an even deeper level, of the isolation in which he lived. Bruno's work had been harsh, difficult, and against the current. His own restless wandering, his lack of roots within the ranks of power, and his

DOI: 10.4324/9781003026082-11

intellectual non-conformity prevented his reputation from establishing itself and thus from benefitting from influential protectors.

So, apart from a few students and some Venetian interlocutors, few would have been aware of the fact that in that second half of 1592 the government of the Serenissima was deciding to extradite the accused to Rome for heresy. Allowing Bruno to be dealt with directly by the supreme inquisitors, gathered before the throne of Peter.

A Question of Opportunity

The request for Bruno's extradition was made by the Holy Office in mid-September 1592, after the Venetian Inquisition had to acknowledge that it was necessary to move the trial to be heard by the tribunal of Rome. This was not by decision of the Congregation, since as shown by a deletion in the original text of the Venetian decree, «in executionem literarum illustrissimi Cardinalis Sanctae Severinae» [in execution of the letter of the illustrious Cardinal of Santa Severina] this was the direct, personal initiative of the cardinal prefect of the Holy Office.[4]

We cannot dwell too long on the extradition negotiations between Venice and the Holy See, which occupied their respective diplomats in the second half of 1592 and ended with Rome's victory in January 1593. The rare surviving documents allow us to reconstruct of only a few hints about the precise nature of the hard negotiations that took place between the government of the Republic and the papal curia.

However, the minutes from the session of the *Collegio dei Savi* of Venice on September 28, 1592, the body which was responsible for the decision regarding the extradition, are of particular interest. That day, the vicar of the patriarch of Venice, the inquisitor Gabriele da Saluzzo, and one of the Inquisition's lay magistrates presented themselves before the *Collegio*, which consisted of the *Savi* and other authorities of the Serenissima. What was said on that occasion, therefore, allows us to get an idea of what the Venetian Holy Office thought of Bruno after having heard the witnesses and the defendant's depositions.

Reading the document confirms our suspicions. The Venetian inquisitorial tribunal appears convinced – regardless of the facts that emerged in the trial – that the accused was guilty of very serious crimes. Although we cannot rule out the possibility that the inquisitors may have exaggerated the trial evidence for the occasion in order to secure Bruno's extradition (but then we would have to ask why the Holy Office in Rome so doggedly wanted to try a philosopher whose heresy had been, until then, only tenuously proven), it is striking to see that Bruno was presented to the judges that day in these terms:

> Bruno da Nola, accused not only of heresy, but also of [being a] heresiarch, having written various books, in which he greatly praises the

> Queen of England and other heretic princes, wrote some things concerning a particular of the religion which are not suitable, even if he was speaking philosophically; and that he was apostate, having first been a Dominican friar, who lived for many years in Geneva and England, and who in Napoli and other places has been investigated for the same charge.[5]

We learn from the minutes of this session that Bruno was presented to the Venetian authorities by the inquisitors as a heretic and a heresiarch primarily because of his books – which in reality were almost completely unknown to the judges – and not for his alleged verbal statements, or rather those reported by Mocenigo. We further discover that the cornerstone of Bruno's defense (that he had spoken "philosophically" about matters of religion) was, even at the beginning of the trial, considered unsatisfactory. Thus he had constructed it in vain; and – based on the canons of Lateran V[6] – so it would remain in the years that followed.

Equally expressive is the deposition that the papal nuncio Ludovico Taverna gave before the *Collegio della Repubblica* itself, a few days before Christmas 1592. He also unhesitatingly repeated what were considered to be Bruno's certain crimes, referring primarily to the books. The bishop of Lodi added – in contradiction of what had emerged in the trial[7] – that Bruno's status as "public heresiarch," was well known, "and not just concerning simple articles, but around the incarnation of Our Savior and the most Holy Trinity."[8]

Between the end of the year and the beginning of 1593 the Venetian government, faced with the pressure being applied by Rome, finally decided to allow the extradition. This was done taking note of the very serious accusations of which the prisoner was – according to the inquisitors – guilty, as well as in the context of a policy of diplomatic compliance that was being established between Venice and the Holy See in that period. In fact, beyond the myth of the Serenissima as a protector of those accused in cases of faith, in the second half of the 16th century Venice did not really have a consistent attitude regarding requests from the inquisitors. In some cases they offered no resistance to the will of the Holy Office; others, instead, they firmly and successfully opposed – in particular where the requests for extradition concerned members of the Venetian elite. In the 16th century Venice held to the principle of not allowing Rome to try suspects, only to abandon it in order to present the release as an act of gratuitous generosity. This approach allowed the Venetian rulers to choose whether or not to resist Roman requests depending on the particular, contingent circumstances.[9]

Those opportunities, in the end, also decided Bruno's case. The letter sent by Doge Pasquale Cicogna on January 9, 1593 to his Roman ambassador, the famous Paolo Paruta, communicating the decision to him and asking him to present it to the pope, is eloquent in this regard. "We have moved quickly to satisfy His Beatitude in this request," he emphasized, enjoining the diplomat to go to Clement VIII and "that this be represented to the Pontiff as the result of our reverent and filial deference towards His Beatitude." Paruta promptly executed, responding: "I informed His Holiness what Your Serenity committed to me on the subject of friar Giordano Bruno [...] with those circumstances that seemed to me to better demonstrate of Your Serenity's desire to do what pleases him" and again "a greater expression of the Republic's observance toward him."[10]

Giordano Bruno set sail from Venice on February 19, 1593, bound for Ancona. He reached Rome eight days later. He was confined to the cells of the Holy Office, situated within the severe and imposing palazzo that is still today home to the Congregation for the Doctrine of the Faith, immediately to the south of Saint Peter's.

The deep discontinuity introduced into the trial by Giordano Bruno's relocation to Rome risks being minimized in our eyes. From one prison to another, from one Inquisition to the other, from one tribunal to the other; not much seems to have changed. The Roman Holy Office, preparing to adjudicate Bruno's heresies, found itself faced with the same problems that had vexed their Venetian colleagues. Outwardly – as we will see shortly – not much seemed to happen on the scene at the beginning of 1593.

But in Bruno's mind everything must have changed. In Venice, the philosopher – who aspired to contributing to the political-religious reform of Europe – faced a Dominican friar, the Patriarch, and a diplomatic representative of the pope; the last two being often absent from the sessions and replaced by delegates. In Rome, on the other hand, Bruno was in the presence of the highest authorities of the Catholic Church: the leading lights of the religion that – as he had written and often repeated – "he liked more than the others."[11] The Holy Office was the most important Discastery of that Church, as well as its supreme tribunal, even more so after the reforms introduced by Sixtus V. The pope was its leader. The cardinal inquisitors met each week in his presence. For Bruno, a philosopher of the religious and political renewal of Europe and a theorist who considered the Catholic Church itself to be in need "of great regulation, and which was not doing well," and who had predicted "that soon the world would see a general reform of itself," having just returned from his lengthy wanderings on the continent and now finding himself in Rome to be judged by the Holy Office could have been seen by the philosopher as the long awaited opportunity to begin putting his plans in action.

He needed, however, to find the right times and ways to speak with the pope and the most illustrious members of his court, among whom numbered the most subtle and aggressive theologians, philosophers, and jurists of Christianity. This was a very tough challenge, which Bruno's insatiable curiosity and volatile personality could only have found seductive. It was a challenge that required a careful strategy, which Bruno had plenty of time in the long years of imprisonment to meditate upon and calmly prepare.

The image of an inmate of the inquisitorial prisons who finds a way to reflect and formulate a plan for the trial or even a political plan – in short, to carry on a material and mental life similar that of a free person – can be perplexing. However, we must first recall that the habits and material conditions for work and meditation to which our forebears were accustomed were quite different than ours today: for example, during his months of confinement in the prisons of the Padua Inquisition (1594–1595), where he was also tortured, Tommaso Campanella wrote four works in Latin.[12]

We must also take into account the fact that the function of prisons in the early modern era was rather different from what it is today. When Bruno was imprisoned, the primary purpose of his confinement was not punishment, but rather temporary custody of the accused while awaiting trial. Prisons assumed their current function only in subsequent centuries, becoming institutions meant for the detention of criminals who had already been through a criminal trial. However, the prisons of the 1500s – both secular and ecclesiastic – were not only tools of custody for the tribunal when it opened a proceeding, but were also a source of profit for the businesses that managed them, typically on contract. Each tribunal was responsible for one or more prisons; the tribunal that arrested a criminal had full ownership of his trial and corresponding incarceration. The contractors earned money from the bureaucratic organization of the trial as well as from the daily maintenance of the prisoners. The *birri*, for their part, profited from the incarcerations, being paid based on the so-called *incerti*, that is to say, depending on the number of prisoners that they were able to bring in. Arguments and disputes could break out between the tribunals and police, who were incentivized to bring in the highest number of inmates, especially wealthy ones. Prison expenses and trial costs were for the most part paid by the prisoners or their spouses; therefore, during the course of the trial well-off detainees could maintain a decent standard of living.[13]

The prisons of the Holy Office also functioned based on these organizing principles. The defendant's detention by the inquisitors was not for the purpose of punishment (imprisonment *ad poenam*), but rather to prevent flight (imprisonment *ad custodiam*). Rivers of ink have been spilled, often with apologetic aims, boasting of the "good treatment" of offenders – and of Bruno himself – in the inquisitorial prisons; the ample size and lighting of the spaces or the generosity of the concessions, like the weekly shave, the changing of linen or the daily ration of wine for detainees of the Inquisition. Such accounts fail to recall that these services were delivered by for-profit contractors, and that, except for cases of extreme poverty, the expenses were paid by the detainees themselves at the end of the trial. A rather different treatment was reserved for someone who was judged guilty, and therefore severely deprived of freedom as a punishment: in these cases the confinement was often spent on the papal galleys, living in conditions so degraded that most did not survive beyond a few years.

The prisons of the Roman Inquisition were certainly not a normal accommodation, even if they were less gloomy and uninhabitable than the image passed down by the *leyenda negra*.[14] But for our purposes what is more important to highlight is the fact that daily life in the prisons, which included common outdoor time, allowed for a dense circulation of information, and the formation of a genuine prison culture. In 1567, a few months before being sent to the scaffold, Pietro Carnesecchi confessed to Santa Severina that he had "covertly and furtively" written various letters while he was in the Roman inquisitorial prisons, sending them to the outside in secret "by way of one who is not of my house nor is my servant [...] without having them seen and signed by the father commissioner."[15] One of Bruno's accusers, Francesco Graziano, in a passage from an interrogation related to a Venetian trial he was subject to in 1584, told the inquisitors of reading texts with heretical themes while in the cell, and discussing them with his fellow inmates:

> [...] I speak of the sermons of Hieronimo Pistoria, which in one sermon tells the opinions of various heretics, which I saw, and read in prison, which is in prison, and I read in prison [*sic*], and while he read [those sermons] he would speak to the prisoners, repeating the opinions of the heretics, and still did so when he would read of the evils of our faith, and I have seen this book if not in prison and I had never seen it before.[16]

Pressed by the judges about these readings and interpretations, Graziano repeated that he had practiced them "in prison, which those prisoners say that they had been granted by the Father inquisitor"; proof of a daily interaction between prison culture and the direct influence of the inquisitors, an element which deserves more in-depth study. We know that Bruno himself, in the years of his incarceration, gave impassioned lectures on the infinity of the universe and the plurality of worlds to Antonio Stigliola and Tommaso Campanella, as well as engaged in religious disputation, at least with Vialardi.[17]

The testimony of other inmates, which was used by the judges in the trials, demonstrates how and to what extent the intertwining of discussions and emotions bound the unfortunate together during the long days and nights in prison. They compared each other's cases and the attitudes of the judges: "I fear severity much more than I hope for the fairness of these my lords," wrote Carnesecchi, for example, in one of the letters he had tried to get out of the prisons of the Roman Holy Office, "making the conjecture from seeing how they act with others that are in the same situation as I am, so that they do not show themselves more ill-disposed towards me than otherwise." "What makes me extraordinarily afraid of the severity of my lords," confided the imprisoned protonotary again, "is that they deprived these two priests of their benefits, which even if they bear some guilt, they still do not even have Christ crucified."[18]

Another of the missives written by Carnesecchi in the Roman prisons gives us a glimpse of the emotional state of an inmate who, like Bruno, saw his trial passing slowly and struggled between doubts and discouragement, requests for help, and the desire to react and fight for his own salvation:

> I had proposed from the beginning that I would enter in here to stay for as long as it pleases God to get me out, that is not to win my liberation with any sort of human means of favor, it seeming to me that the other time [on the occasion of the preceding inquisitorial trial] that I had in the same situations sinned in trusting too much in men and too little in God, although with good success.
>
> Now, won from such a long tedium in prison and in part frightened by the strictness used by this tribunal against defendants who are in the same position that I am in, I changed not yet in everything but in a relevant part: I mean to say that as I believe trusting too much in human help to be a drawback, so I believe that at the meeting it is a temptation from God to disparage them in everything, and above all not to make use of those means and instruments that God's providence apparently assigns to everyone so that he can make use of them according to his needs.[19]

Two decades before Bruno, lying in the same cells, the Florentine nobleman could thus also describe the strategy that – while he pleaded for the support of the Duke of Florence, Cosimo I – he was setting up for his defense. "The clue that they have had against me again, and which was the cause for my sudden capture, was having written to the late Lady Giulia [Gonzaga] [...] that I was tempted to go to Geneva," Carnesecchi clarified to himself and to his correspondents a few months before being sentenced to death.

> But I deny the consequence, showing in the same letters that my intention was not to remain there, but to stay in that place temporarily during the life of Paul [IV] in case I wasn't able to stay safely in Venice, nor as a result in other places in Italy.[20]

Even in the extraordinary graffiti and drawings that survive in the prisons of the Palermo Inquisition there are frequent references to the outcomes of the author's and others' trials among the prayers, invocations, and talismans.[21] Prisoners scoured the graffiti they found left behind for information, asking, for example – as Carnesecchi always did – about the "practices followed here by this Holy Office, which never seizes things if not from the fugitives and those who have relapsed, whose lives are also taken."[22] Messages, books, and money could enter the cells[23] and be used to corrupt guards and servants, or to buy paper for writing, which itself could at times be stolen during depositions, as also happened with pens and sealing wax; the ink itself was often made from charcoal and vinegar.[24] Meanwhile, in the outside world, exactly as happens today, news about imprisonments, depositions and trials became the object of curiosity, gossip, or real accusations which – in the most sensational cases – circulated in the most important courts of Europe. Just as, for example, Francesco Maria Vialardi wrote to the Grand Duke of Tuscany on July 3, 1599, referring to the most talked about case at the time, that involving the family of Beatrice Cenci:

> The woman De Cenci, who washed the bloody shirt, sheets and mattresses has confessed, and they confronted her and the girl [making them confess together] in Torre di Nona, and the girl was brave. But it was added that a friar of San Domenico confessed at the last minute, that he had lodged in his cell a certain Cap[tain] who is her relative, who told him, that for love de' Cenci had murdered their father.[25]

Celestino's Denunciation

When the cardinal inquisitors of the Supreme Inquisition managed to secure Giordano Bruno in the Roman prisons, they found themselves faced with the same problems confronted by their colleagues in the Venetian Holy Office: insufficient evidence against the defendant and doubts about the usability of Giovanni Mocenigo's charges, him being a sole, hostile witness whose allegations had not been corroborated by any of the summoned witnesses.

Thus the trial continued to languish, along with the accused, in the Roman palazzo of the Holy Office. We know that on April 12, 1593 the prison officials ordered Bruno to send his manuscripts and books to Cardinal Girolamo Bernerio, a former inquisitor of Genoa known as l'Ascolano.[26] This action, however, was not a prelude to a search for and systematic purgation of the volumes Bruno had printed abroad. Such a purge was prevented by nearly insurmountable obstacles: the impossibility of identifying witnesses against him; the extreme difficulty in tracking down the most compromising of Bruno's works, which, furthermore, were theoretically complex, had been printed abroad, and had only circulated within elite intellectual contexts. Moreover, a systematic investigation of Bruno's book production would have involved jurisdictions in northern Europe, in the face of which even the most powerful papal tribunal was forced to stop.

At that moment the cardinal inquisitors were also occupied by other important issues. In France, on July 25, 1593, Henry of Navarre had abjured in the hands of the Archbishop of Bourges, receiving his pardon. At that point his opponents in Rome, who were well represented in the Holy Office by Santori and Cardinals Deza and Bernerio, could see that it would be increasingly difficult to argue the intransigent line for denying the validity of Henry IV's abjuration. The pro-French cardinals even persuaded Clement VIII to receive a delegate of the French king in Rome for the first time, in order to discuss his position on the matter.[27] All of this suggested that, sooner or later, the Bourbon would reach reconciliation with Rome. The authority of the Holy Office and that of Santori personally would emerge – they may have feared – seriously compromised.

In 1593 the inquisitorial trial against il Nolano again came to a halt. This did not, however, lead to a resolution of the case. In an ordinary inquisitorial trial, the abjuration of what had emerged in Venice and a relatively mild sentence would, at that point, have been a plausible outcome. The Roman Holy Office's wait and see policy certainly derived from the belief that there was still much to discover in that case, and perhaps also from the hope – or certainty? – that some new event would come along to break the logjam.

That event came. A document was sent to Rome, probably in the second half of 1593,[28] that would deal a very serious blow to Bruno's situation in the trial, erasing any possibility of his being freed, and incalculably aggravating the accusations against him. It was a sweeping written denunciation ("*in scriptis*," the trial documentation states with certainty), lost to us today, by a fellow inmate of Bruno's in Venice: the Capuchin friar Celestino da Verona.

The new complaint advanced 13 venomous charges: 10 more than those contained in Mocenigo's denunciations.

1. That Christ mortally sinned when he prayed in the garden refusing the will of the Father, when he said *Pater, si possibile est, transeat a me calix iste.*
2. That Christ was not placed on the cross, but was hanged on two pieces of wood in the style of a hanger, which was used back then and was called a gallow.
3. That Christ is a dog, a horned fucking dog: he said that the one who governed this world was a traitor, because they did not know how to govern it well, and raising his hand made the fig sign at heaven.
4. There is no Inferno, and nobody is damned to eternal punishment, but that with time everyone is saved, adding the words of the Prophet: *Nunquid in aeternum Deus irascetur?*
5. That there are more worlds, that all the stars are worlds, and the belief that this world is alone is very great ignorance.
6. That, when bodies die, the souls are transmigrated from one world to another of the many worlds, and from one body to another.
7. That Moses was a very cunning magician and, because he was very expert in the art of magic, easily beat Pharaoh's magicians; and that he faked having spoken with God on Mt. Sinai, and that the law given by him to the Jewish people was imagined and forged by him.
8. That all of the Prophets had been cunning men, false and liars, and that for this they had come to bad ends, that is, they had been justly condemned to a reviled death, as they deserved.
9. That appealing to the Saints is ridiculous and not to do it.
10. That Cain was a good man, and that he deservedly killed his brother Abel, because he was a cruel villain and killer of animals.

11 That, if he was forced to return to being a friar of S. Domenico, he wants to blow up the monastery where he will be, and, that done, he wants to immediately return to Germany or England among the heretics to more comfortably live in his way and there plant his new and infinite heresies. About which heresies I intend to product as witnesses Francesco Ieronimiani, Silvio canonic of Chiozza and friar Serafino of Acqua Sparta.

12 That the one who made the breviary, or rather ordered it, is an ugly dog, a fucking goat, brazen, and that the breviary is like an out of tune lute, and that in it are contained many profane and inappropriate things, and that it is not worthy of being read by good men, but rather should be burned.

13 That what the Church believes, none of it can be proven.

> *Allegat in contestes fratrem Iulium de Salò, Franciscum Vaia et Matthaeum de Orio, concarceratos* [cited as witnesses friars Giulio da Salò, Francesco Vaia and Matteo da Orio, fellow inmates].[29]

The three inmates cited by Celestino were quickly heard by the Venetian inquisitor, since – unlike the Capuchin, who by now had been moved to the Marches – they were still imprisoned in Venice. They did not confirm all of the friar's accusations; they downplayed or omitted some, but they added others, among which was the disrespecting of relics. The Neapolitan carpenter Francesco Vaia added that there was a further witness to Bruno's boasting in the Venetian prisons, Francesco Graziano, who we have cited many times; he too was heard, and further worsened Bruno's position.

As we saw before in reference to Mocenigo's accusations, major scholars of Bruno's work are disposed to acknowledging the substantial veracity of the denunciation sent to Rome by Celestino, diminished though it may be by the limited culture of the interlocutor and by his evident malice.[30] Of the thirteen total accusations made by Celestino, only three – the erroneous opinions about Christ, the multiplicity of worlds, and the transmigration of souls – had already been advanced by the Venetian patrician. Ten were new, and included erroneous opinions about Scripture, the saints, the prophets, the existence of the inferno and the use of the breviary. There was also the accusation that Bruno, in case he was treated with clemency and sent to a Dominican monastery, would have chosen heresy and flight: this confirmed the suspicion that the philosopher was a heresiarch, and that he had elaborated a plan of religious reform that was intolerable for the leadership of the Catholic Church.

Arriving at a moment when the case against Bruno was temporarily suspended, allowing hope for a mild resolution, Celestino's flood of accusations set the judicial machinery back in motion. The Capuchin friar's act can therefore be considered the decisive element in the trial of Giordano Bruno. In addition to dumping a heap of new charges on the accused's head, it also irreparably damaged the two strongest pillars of his defense: the existence of only one witness and the ostentatious sincerity of his repentance.[31] These pillars had seemed unbreakable to the Venetian inquisitors, but it was a voice belatedly raised from Venice itself that managed to decisively knock them down.

The flood of accusations brought against Bruno by Celestino da Verona re-energized the trial and secured its legal legitimacy. Now there were two accusers: both of them hostile, but on this point the judges could turn a blind eye. One of them was a heretic who had already been investigated and abjured in Rome in 1587: but this too could be overlooked.

This natural philosopher and Navarran heresiarch had to be made into an example with his sentencing, as soon as possible. The rapprochement between France and Clement VIII was making giant steps, and risked thwarting everything in which Santa Severina had believed, along with his great teachers before him, the papal inquisitors Paul IV and Pius V. The readmission of the Bourbon into the Catholic Church would end the devastating succession of religious wars of the second half of the 16th century in the worst possible way, placing a relapsed heretic on the throne of France. A Calvinist would take the title of "Most Christian King" and the prestige of the Inquisition would be shattered. It was absolutely intolerable.

At the end of 1593 witnesses who had been imprisoned with Bruno in Venice were questioned, and gave testimony that was anything but benevolent. Bruno was also deposed again; before the turn of the year he was subjected to 15 interrogations, during which – we know from indirect sources – he returned to clarifying his positions on the Trinity, and most of all defended himself from the Capuchin's corrosive accusations, strongly denying them or proposing clarifications and articulations – not always convincingly – concerning the disputed issues. On the major point of the multiplicity of worlds and creation *ex nihilo*, Bruno reiterated that his philosophy did not conflict with the faith and the theology of Creation.[32] Mocenigo's accusations were then revisited in light of the new elements in the trial. The prosecution's scheme became clear, assuming precise articulations and more insistent rhythms. At the beginning of 1594 the so-called repetition of the witnesses took place: the reiteration of the questioning with the purpose of exposing contradictions and unmasking false accusers. Celestino himself was called for a repeat examination, which was carried out, in what form we do not know, by the inquisitor of Venice. He repeated his accusations point by point.

Celestino da Verona's denunciation of Giordano Bruno, this decisive chapter for all of Italian history, was incredibly – or perhaps emblematically – written by an opaque figure; a prior offender who for years had oscillated between prisons and torture, rejection, and exile. The evolution of this ferocious, definitive attack inevitably involved a game of favors, exchanges, and extortion. The accuser, we learn from the Capuchin *Annali*,[33] remained in the inquisitorial prisons of Venice until September 18, 1593. If he denounced Giordano Bruno during this period he did not do so *in scriptis*, but rather in the context of an oral deposition, which at the time he was in the ideal conditions to provide. The document that arrived in Rome at the end of 1593 could therefore have been *written* by Celestino either when he was in the Venetian Capuchin jail by order of the apostolic nuncio, or more likely after he had been moved to the secure monastery in the Marches, under the close supervision of the cardinal of Santa Severina's trusted superiors.

The decisive attack against Bruno was certainly launched after February 1593, the month in which he was extradited to Rome, and at which time the Capuchin was struggling with the inquisitorial and monastery prisons between Verona and Venice. The now discovered collaboration between friar Celestino da Verona and the Holy Office was probably the cause of his turbulent relations with the Capuchin Order and his constant alternation between the monastery prisons and inquisitorial prisons during those months. The denunciation against Bruno could have been the price that he paid to win back his freedom and save his life at the end of that two-year period, protected within a guarded enclosure, from which – as we will see further on – he attempted to escape in the summer of 1599, immediately returning to the scene of Giordano Bruno's trial.

There may have been other reasons why Celestino's denunciation was presented only at that moment. The Capuchin had to be summoned to Rome to meet in person with one or more representatives of the Holy Office; it is plausible that this took place towards the end of 1592. For the supreme inquisitors, however, it was at that point preferable to await developments in the now imminent transfer of Bruno's trial to Rome. Entrusting Bruno to the direct jurisdiction of the Roman Inquisition presented various advantages: it removed the government of the Serenissima and its representatives, who occupied seats in Venice's inquisitorial tribunal with full powers, from the calculus of the trial; it guaranteed almost unlimited power to the cardinal inquisitors of the central Dicastery, whose will could only be overruled by the pronouncements of Clement VIII. It was also preferable to wait for the waters to calm in the controversy between the Inquisition of Venice and the Capuchins who were accused of magical practices before introducing Celestino into the Bruno trial. That mess involved the late Pope Sixtus V and Santa Severina himself, who in the past had neglected to inform the inquisitors of Venice about local internal processes of the Order.

In 1593, Celestino continued to be empowered by the protection guaranteed by figures who, as Santa Severina did, extended the regime of *ad personam* protections and mediations established under Pope Sixtus V. The benevolence of the Cardinal Protector probably aroused the suspicions of Aldobrandini, a pontiff who had never tried to conceal his mistrust of the monasteries. For this reason too Santori would loathe him until the end of his days. "A cruel man has died," wrote Francesco Maria Vialardi, the associate of Santa Severina who had been investigated, to the Grand Duke of Tuscany on the day of Clement VIII's death. "Totally interested for his own, mortal enemy of the friars, one who had something bad to say about everyone, and in a position of holiness was a great hypocrite."[34]

One Eye on Rome, One on Venice

Those inquisitors who at that point would have preferred to quickly reach an exemplary sentence and abjuration of Bruno found a serious obstacle in their path.

In the first place, in 1594 the infuriated Giovanni Mocenigo produced another denunciation, which revolved around the accusation that in *Cantus Circaeus* Bruno had intended to represent the Roman pope as a type of "pig."[35] This had to be noted. Later on – perhaps in connection with this new complaint – the Holy Office was forced, by order of Clement VIII, to begin the retrieval and censorship of Giordano Bruno's books. The fact that this phase of the proceeding, crucial in the context of a trial against a philosopher who had written and published a great deal, was only launched in Rome, only in 1594, and only by the direct will of the pope, is another indication of the inquisitors' lack of desire to investigate Bruno's authentic religious condition given the urgency of reaching a sentence as soon as possible. His guilt was too certain: the political situation in the Curia and in France too delicate.

Thus between March 1595 and December 1597 groups of theologians and councilors were commissioned to perform a detailed evaluation of the themes expressed by Bruno in the printed works of his that could be found. The positions expressed in his books were the subject of new interrogations. It is possible, albeit unlikely, that in this phase the defendant was subjected to torture.[36] Meanwhile, the cardinals of the Supreme Inquisition copied and re-examined all of the trial documentation. The Tribunal procurator drafted a list of charges based on these documents. This was the so-called *Sommario*, one of the most important documents we have today that testifies to the evolution of the Roman phase of the trial. That list, appropriately edited, may have served the defendant in crafting questions to ask his accusers during the *interrogatoria,* meant to challenge informers and better clarify circumstances and events. Unfortunately, none of these papers has survived. The *interrogatori* regarding the censures and the examination of the defendant's responses probably occupied all of the year 1597.

The examination of the books written by Bruno was hardly exhaustive. The surviving documentation, containing the accusations that the Inquisition formulated after having gathered and read some of Bruno's texts, has allowed Luigi Firpo to charge the judges with "inadequate diligence employed in the research of the books, with such paltry results that they do not in any way justify the extreme slowness of the review."[37] The inquisitors found themselves with very little in hand: the *Cantus Circaeus*, the *De minimo*, the *De monade*, the *De la causa*, and the manuscript *De' predicamenti di Dio*. Obviously the judges sensed that Bruno had written many more titles, but they were either unable to procure them or were not very interested in doing so. This negligence seems, once again, to echo the previously cited words that Paul IV uttered from his death bed in 1559 to speed up the deliberation of the trial against Cardinal Giovanni Morone as much as possible: "There was no need for so many trials, writings or justifications, nor were legal terms (deadlines) required, because he knew very well what the facts were, and that this [the facts] was the true judge."[38]

In 1598 there was a long interruption of the trial in connection with the preparations for the solemn voyage of Clement VIII and various cardinals of the Holy Office to the new embassy of Ferrara, which had been annexed to the Papal States after the extinction of the main branch of the House of d'Este. Only after mid-December of that year did the pope return to Rome, welcomed by the torrential rains that culminated in the disastrous Christmas flood of the Tiber. The deliberation of the case against Bruno could therefore have only been started in January of that fateful year of 1599.

> It was not rare for investigations, rather than starting from the beginning with a sufficiently defined hypothesis of crime, to spend a long time searching for possible crimes. Moreover, the timeframe could be further extended because the public ministries did not always possess the knowledge or skill to resolve [cases] in a reasonable time frame.[39]

This analysis, formulated by an authoritative jurist, who is specifically an expert in Mafia trials – and so discussing problems in the modern Italian criminal justice system – shows how some of the important issues that underlie the prosecution of the inquisitorial trial of Giordano Bruno reappear intact in the present.

Let us leave the judges of the Roman Holy Office to attend to their complex procedures, and turn our gaze away from Rome. In order to understand what happened in the decisive moments of the Bruno trial, we must not rely on a perspective that is completely centered on the Roman palazzi where his endless months of waiting were spent. Outside those walls, life continued its tireless swirl: stirring up small and large events that historians who are interested in this trial have overlooked for too long.

We have already seen that Bruno's terrible accuser, Giovan Antonio Arrigoni *alias* Celestino da Verona, spent the period 1594–1599 in the little Capuchin monastery of Colpersito at San Severino Marche. He remained there – in all likelihood without interruption – until May 1599.

Now we will take a look at what happened in Venice after Bruno's extradition. As was customary, the inquisitor who had launched the trial, Gabriele da Saluzzo, left the tribunal after several years of activity. His successor was the Dominican friar Giovanni Vincenzo Maria Arrigoni, who, after occupying the position of vicar of the Holy Office in Brescia, settled in Venice on February 4, 1595. He remained in that office until Clement VIII named him bishop of Sibenic, in Dalmatia, in August 1599.[40]

Here we will open a very brief parenthesis that does not directly regard Bruno, but helps us understand the climate in which his trial took place. The new inquisitor of Venice, who had just taken office, brought to light an interesting case of prison informants. Just days after his arrival on February 21, 1595 he was able to question two ecclesiastics who were confined in the prisons of the bishop of Padua along with Ottavio Longo da Barletta. Longo is a well-known figure in the history of the Inquisition because he was Tommaso Campanella's most bitter accuser; exactly what Celestino da Verona was for Giordano Bruno. The inquisitor Arrigoni discovered that Longo was "an atheist" and unreliable, and that he, in the usual conversations between prisoners, had confessed to one of his fellow inmates "that what he had testified against [...] Campanella was a lie, and that he wanted to ask his forgiveness if he knew how to save his life." Longo had given this false deposition intending to reach the number of 28 Lutherans that he had promised to report to the Inquisitor of Vicenza in exchange for obtaining his release from prison.[41]

The parallel between the dual role played by the accusers of Campanella and Bruno during their respective trials in Venice confirms that the procedural technique very probably inflicted on Bruno – the use of informers who could be influenced and blackmailed – was far from infrequent.

Thanks to his professional expertise the new Inquisitor of Venice quickly earned an excellent reputation. When the apostolic nuncio Ludivico Taverna, the second member of the tibunal that had tried Bruno, was preparing to leave la Serenissima in 1596, he wrote an *Instruttione finale* meant for his successor. In this document he describes Arrigoni as "vigilant, assiduous, of great integrity, very intelligent and practical," as well as "very well informed." "Your Most Reverend Signoria can trust him," concluded Taverna, addressing the incoming nuncio, "as I have always found him to be a good man."[42]

The esteem which the inquisitor also enjoyed from the government of the Republic is demonstrated by the fact that he was soon considered by the Venetian Senate to be worthy of being assigned the bishopric of Sibenic, in Dalmatia. This happened a little less than two years after his arrival in Venice. At the time, the ordinary who occupied this office at Sibenic, Vincenzo Bassi, appeared to be dying. Bassi was disliked by the Serenissma authorities for having excommunicated the Venetian Rector of Sibenic in 1590, in the context of a controversy we cannot follow here.[43] However, Bassi defied all expectations and regained his health. Arrigoni was consecrated as bishop of Sibenic only when the ordinary who was so unpopular with the Republic was finally transferred to the diocese of Andria on May 25, 1599.[44]

To avoid overly complicating this mosaic of events, at the moment we will not explain why developments in Arrigoni's ecclesiastic career could have affected Bruno's fate. We shall return to reflect on these elements further on. For now we will simply observe that Celestino da Verona and the new inquisitor of Venice bore the same name and surname: Giovanni Arrigoni. At the current state of research we cannot demonstrate a close kinship between the two men; neither can we hypothesize the Capuchin's membership in the wider Arrigoni *familia* or faction, which originally hailed from the Bergamo area. However, we must not forget that in that period it was not necessary to be a close relative to belong to the same domestic or parental unit; one could also be a part of it by ancient customs and acquaintances, recommendations, affiliations of various types, or simple cohabitation. The leading cardinals of the 1500s gathered true courts in their palazzi households that included not only blood relatives, but dozens or even hundreds of people, often paid and employed in a wide variety of tasks and missions.

The Arrigoni *familia* included, among others, branches in Brescia and Mantua – home of the new Inquisitor of Venice – and a powerful Roman branch, which counted another cardinal inquisitor among its most illustrious members: Cardinal Pompeo Arrigoni, who, after having pursued his ecclesiastical career in the service of Cardinal Odoardo Farnese and earning a degree in law at Padua, was made a cardinal by Clement VIII in 1596. He immediately became part of the Congregation of the Holy Office. He participated in the commission set up in Rome to annul the marriage between Henry of Navarra and Margherita di Valois, defended the interests of Philip II, and was considered one of the leading exponents of the pro-Spanish faction in the Curia; a faction that was led, as we well know, by the cardinal of Santa Severina.[45]

Families, Kinship, and Careers: What Revolved Around Bruno?

Let us continue unraveling some of the events that took place on the peninsula while Giordano Bruno and his trial languished in Rome. The small movements, secondary in appearance, must not escape us, because they allow us to capture the true texture – made up of relatives, relations, factions, and alliances – of that complicated system of power which today we call the Old Regime.

We have seen that at the end of October 1593 Celestino da Verona was yet again incarcerated in the Capuchin monastery at Venice for refusing to move to the Marches. In doing so he violated – without too much concern for the consequences – an injunction from the most powerful inquisitor of the second half of the 16th century, the cardinal of Santa Severina. It was the apostolic nuncio, Ludivico Taverna, Clement VIII's diplomatic representative, who wanted him in custody. Celestino was once again imprisoned in precisely the weeks when his written denunciation reached Rome, revitalizing the Bruno trial. Taverna could therefore, in that crucial step, act as an intermediary between Rome and Venice: getting the Bruno trial underway once more and, at the same time, ensuring that the will of a pope who was extremely suspicious of the religious Orders was done. After this episode, Celestino was temporarily silenced in the confines of the tiny Capuchin monastery of Colpersito, but only after having signed the denunciation against Bruno, which was promptly sent to Rome.

Ludovico Taverna was an aristocrat from Lombardy who had served as nuncio in Spain between 1581 and 1586, shortly after having become bishop of Lodi. He had embarked on diplomatic service in Venice on April 23, 1592, exactly one month before Giordano Bruno's arrest, holding the office for four years until April 1596. His nephew, called Federico or Ferrante, was named a counselor of the Holy Office at the end of 1593, right as his uncle was occupied with the Celestino da Verona affair. Ferrante's career progressed thanks to the close patronage relationship that Taverna had with the Aldobrandini, and in particular with the nephew, Cardinal Pietro. Thanks to his nomination to the Holy Office, Ferrante Taverna could attend the entire trial of Giordano Bruno and assume decision making power,[46] undoubtedly debating the case periodically with his uncle, who had led the trial of the same defendant in its Venetian phase and who was just as close to the papal family.

What's more, Ferrante Taverna became Governor of Rome in 1599, an office that his uncle Ludovico had previously occupied in the 1570s.[47] This is another element of continuity between the careers of uncle and nephew; and this too, concerned the Bruno trial, albeit indirectly. The Governor, representing the so-called "Secular Arm," was, in fact, the one who formally took charge of the prisoner at the moment he was sent by the inquisitors to be executed at the stake or beheaded. It had been the practice in Rome since the Middle Ages, following a canon of the Lateran III (1179) that prevented ecclesiastic tribunals from carrying out cruel punishments, that those condemned by a tribunal of the faith would be handed over to a secular prison. In this way it was possible to pretend that the bloody execution was carried out by a secular authority, preserving – from a purely superficial point of view – the letter of the conciliar canon. So, the unfortunates in Rome who were sent to their death were normally transferred to one of the secular prisons in the city for several hours; almost always to the prisons of Tor di Nona or Corte Savella. They were then taken to be decapitated by the Governor's troops, sometimes in front of Castel Sant'Angelo, or led to the stake in Campo de' Fiori.

Ludovico Taverna and his nephew Ferrante both held important offices that put them in the position of deciding and agreeing upon the development of some important steps in the trials of Bruno and others under investigation at the time, from their start to their tragic conclusion. Although the documents available to date do not allow us to fully illuminate these contiguities, they do contribute to tracing the general climate of close collusion on which the processes of the Holy Office hinged in that era.

The fact that there were significant similarities between the ascent of the Arrigoni and Taverna families contributes to further clarifying the picture. Both the aforementioned Cardinal Pompeo Arrigoni and Ludovico Taverna undertook their ecclesiastical careers as secretaries for Cardinal Odoardo Farnese (1573–1626), a direct descendant (great-grandson) of Pope Paul III and son of Alessandro, the Duke of Piacenza and Parma. Other Arrigoni family members in Milan who were related to Cardinal Pompeo collaborated closely with the Tavernas: Pietro Paolo Arrigoni, nominated president of the Senate of Milan by Charles V in 1557, shared the responsibilities of administering the Ambrosian Republic with Grand Chancellor Franceso Taverna in a crucial period in the life of the State.[48]

What happened in those years to the third member of the inquisitorial tribunal that opened the Bruno trial and guided its Venetian phase? He also left the city on the lagoon, shortly after the departure of the nuncio Taverna. Patriarch Lorenzo Priuli, in fact, was made a cardinal in June 1596.

The nephew of two Doges, and a former ambassador to Rome, Spain, France and Tuscany, Priuli was a consummate secular politician. In May of 1579 he was chosen by the Venetian Senate as the ordinary ambassador to Henry III, at whose court he would reside until April 1582; there he had the opportunity to meet Giordano Bruno and to gain in-depth knowledge of the religious problems tormenting France. In his final report, read in the Senate in June 1582, he illustrated the profound political crises of the crown and of the whole society, insightfully predicting the future strengthening of Catholicism to the detriment of the Huguenots.[49]

The successive *cursus* of offices held by Priuli in Venice is impressive: in 1586 he became a Ducal counselor and a Governor of the University of Padua; in 1587 he was appointed to be a sage of the Council and superintendent of the *Zecca* (the Mint); in 1588 he was one of the commissioners elected by the Senate to oversee the construction of the Rialto Bridge. In 1589–1590 he was *podestà* (mayor) of Brescia. It is surprising that he was able to support the costly mayor's office on the mainland and the even more onerous ambassadorships for all these years, coming from a patrician but not a wealthy house: in 1582 he and his brothers reported an annual income of 772 ducats. It is therefore probable that in order to obtain all these offices and honors he was deeply indebted, jointly – as happened in these cases – with his own family.

At the beginning of the 1590s Priuli was an able, unmarried diplomat, much appreciated both by the Venetian Signoria as well as the Holy Office. This allowed him to open doors for his ecclesiastical career, sanctioned on August 4, 1590 with his appointment by the Senate as Patriarch of Venice. Only then did he put himself *in sacris*, and thanks to an apostolic indulgence to shorten the prescribed period, took possession of the office on January 27, 1591. Just over five years later he would be made a cardinal.

Once he became a cardinal, Lorenzo Priuli continued to occupy himself with Venetian business in the Curia. In that same summer of 1596 he had to confront – collaborating with inquisitor friar Giovan Vincenzo Maria Arrigoni – the dispute between Rome and la Serenissima over the application of the Index of prohibited books, which that year had been newly compiled in an updated edition. The *Dechiaratione delle regole dell'Indice delli libri prohibiti*, which incorporated many demands made by the government of the Republic, was approved by the Venetian Senate in September of that year, and is considered his political masterpiece: the mature fruit of the wise balance established by its talented mediator on the very delicate terrain of relations between the Roman Curia and the Republic of Venice.

The climate of rapprochement between Venice and Rome, which to some degree had been inaugurated by Bruno's extradition, had reached an important milestone. Priuli was a brilliant diplomat, who in a few decades had passed from the embassies of Venice to the most secret chambers of the Roman Church, where he was intent on applying the Tridentine canons notwithstanding the bottlenecks imposed by the Venetian government. As such he was hardly inclined in those years to follow the fate of the presumptuous Navarran friar whom he may have glimpsed in Paris, had certainly encountered in the inquisitorial tribunal of the Serenissima, and who was now languishing in the palazzo of the Holy Office. The great story had to run its course.

Notes

1 *The Complete Works of Christopher Marlowe.* Second edition, edited by Fredson Bowers, volume II, Cambridge, Cambridge University Press, 1981, p. 192.
2 It is not certain that the piece was written by Marlowe's own hand before his death, which took place in 1593. We do know, however, that it was inserted in the text no later than 1602: see S. Ricci, *Giordano Bruno nell'Europa del Cinquecento*, cit., p. 511.
3 Again in the 17th and 18th centuries the Congregation of the Index, which also banned all of Bruno's works, did not include it among the books for which it periodically issued public reminders of the prohibition on reading them; nor, in the same period, were exemptions granted from the Index on the prohibition of reading Bruno's works. These are clear indications of his very small readership: L. Spruit, *Due documenti noti e due documenti sconosciuti*, cit.
4 See the decree of the Inquisition of Venice of September 17, 1592, and the related corrections, reported in *Processo*, doc. 21, p. 201 and note 1.
5 *Processo*, 202.
6 See *supra*, pp. 33–34, p. 68.
7 See *supra*, pp. 91, 106.
8 *Processo*, 208.
9 C. De Frede, *L'estradizione di Giordano Bruno da Venezia*, cit.
10 *Processo*, 212–214.
11 See *supra*, p. 26.
12 L. Firpo, *I processi di Tommaso Campanella*, cit.
13 See Michele Di Sivo, *Sulle carceri dei tribunali penali a Roma: Campidoglio e Tor di Nona*, in *Carceri, carcerieri, carcerati. Dall'Antico regime all'Ottocento*, edited by Livio Antonielli, Soveria Mannelli, Rubbettino, 2006, pp. 9–22 and Id., *Il braccio del tribunale: birri e carcerieri a Roma tra Cinque e Seicento*, in *La giustizia dello Stato pontificio in età moderna*, edited by Maria Rosa Di Simone, Rome, Viella, 2011, pp. 259–266, both with broader bibliographical indications, also by the same author.
14 A floorplan of the palazzo of the Holy Office acquired by Pius V in 1566 and immediately restructured and reported in Daniel Ponziani, *Interessi architettonici: i palazzi dell'Inquisizione*, in *Rari e preziosi. Documenti dell'età moderna e contemporanea dall'archivio del Sant'Uffizio*, edited by Alejandro Cifres, Marco Pizzo, Rome, Gangemi, 2009, pp. 86–105, p. 99.
15 See the hearing of March 8 in M. Firpo, D. Marcatto, *I processi inquisitoriali di Pietro Carnesecchi*, cit., volume II, tome III, p. 1263; some of the letters that were sent clandestinely but never received because they were intercepted by the

inquisitors are published in ivi, p. 1237 ff. The prisoner was able to at least receive a response in prison: in the letter written from prison to Antonio Del Migliore in Rome, "from you know where," February 19, 1567, Carnesecchi however invites the interlocutor to "continue to write, addressing the letters in the usual way, so that I will in any case get it very soon" (ivi, p. 1248).

16 ASVe, *Savi all'eresia (Sant'Ufficio)*, box 53, folder «Graziano Francesco», fol. 23*v*. Girolamo da Pistoia (1508–1570), a preacher of the Observant friars who was attracted to the ideal of the reform of Fransicanism proposed by the Capuchins, he was a theologian to Pius V; he comforted and led Pietro Carnesecchi to the scaffold. His corpse was moved in 1583 to the church of San Franscesco di Caserta at Cardinal Santori's expense. His sermons were printed for the first time at Bologna in 1567. See the entry *Girolamo da Narni* by Dario Busolini in *Dizionario biografico degli italiani*, cit., volume LVI, 2001.

17 S. Ricci, *Giordano Bruno nell'Europa del Cinquecento*, cit., p. 520.

18 See The previously cited letter to Antonio Del Migliore of February 19, 1567, in M. Firpo, D. Marcatto, *I processi inquisitoriali di Pietro Carnesecchi*, cit., volume II, tome III, p. 1247.

19 Letter to Vincenzo Parpaglia, Rome, "from you know where," February 28, 1567, reported ivi, p. 1250.

20 Ivi, p. 1252.

21 Until now this reality has mainly been explored in reference to the Spanish inquisitorial prisons of Sicily: see Maria Sofia Messana, *Inquisitori, negromanti e streghe nella Sicilia moderna (1500-1782)*, Palermo, Sellerio, 2007, pp. 240 ff.

22 This is again cited from the letter to Antonio Del Migliore of February 19, 1567, in M. Firpo, D. Marcatto, *I processi inquisitoriali di Pietro Carnesecchi*, cit., volume II, tome III, p. 1248.

23 As appears in letter from Carnesechhi to his servant Antonio Testa, again from the prisons of the Holy Office on March 6, 1567:

> Antonio, dirai al calzettaro che quando verrà a calzarmi faccia motto a quell'amico il quale io li commessi che salutasse in nome mio accioché, havendomi da fare intendere qualche cosa, lo possa fare per lui. Et tu darai li duo scudi che harai havuti da messer Paulo [Poltri] al guardiano che me li porti. [...] Se messer Paulo ti darà un libro per mandarlo a Ferrara, tu me lo manderai qui dentro, rivolto nei panni quando saranno bianchi. Et non dubitare di niente, perché non è cosa che importi quando fusse trovata: ma non ci è pericolo di questo dando li panni al guardiano.
>
> Antonio, would you say to the linen man when he comes to get my linen to have a word with my friend to whom I commend him and greet him my name so that, having something to make me understand, I can do that for him. And you will give the two scudi that you got from Paulo [Poltri] to the guard that brings them to me. [...] If mister Paulo gives you a book to be sent to Ferrara, you can send it to me here within, wrapped in the sheets when they are clean. And there is no need to doubt anything, because it is not important if it was found: but there is no danger of this giving the sheets to the guard.
>
> (ivi, p. 1261)

We do not have confirmation that these transactions actually took place, but the missive denotes that they were considered possible by the prisoner, who also received while in prison – as confessed by Poltri – "«il Concilio tridentino in sextodecimo et il Cathecismo ad parocos in folio» (see la *Nota critica* dei curatori, ivi, volume II, tome I, p. lxxxvii).

24 The thefts and the manufacture of ink were always carried out by Carnesecchi: see the same *Nota critica*, cit., p. lxxx.

25 ASFi, *Mediceo del Principato, filza* 3623, un-numbered pages, fol. 1*v* from the letter dated July 3, 1599.
26 L. Spruit, *Due documenti noti e due documenti sconosciuti*, cit., p. 471.
27 S. Ricci, *Giordano Bruno nell'Europa del Cinquecento*, cit., p. 513.
28 Regarding the arguments that led Firpo to propose this date, see *Processo*, 46.
29 We do not actually have access to the document with Celestino da Verona's charges. This is the reconstruction made by Firpo in *Processo*, 47–48.
30 Michele Cilberto, asking "why Bruno behaved this way, breaking all the safeties and preparing a good part of the wood that would burn him in Campo de' Fiori with his own hands" recalls

> the ire, the true anger, the resentment that Giovanni Mocenigo had spurred with his denunciation [...] in the situation in which he found himself once imprisoned [...]. It is in this environment that the anger [...] spills over into a furious attack against all around him
>
> (Interpretazione del Processo di Giordano Bruno, cit., p. 341)

31 *Processo*, 48–49.
32 S. Ricci, *Giordano Bruno nell'Europa del Cinquecento*, cit., pp. 516–517.
33 G. Maifreda, *Giordano Bruno e Celestino da Verona*, cit., p. 105.
34 ASFi, *Mediceo del Principato, filza* 3624, un-numbered pages, fol. 1*r* of the letter dated March 3, 1605.
35 S. Ricci, *Giordano Bruno nell'Europa del Cinquecento*, cit., p. 519.
36 See the arguments presented by Firpo in *Processo*, 78–79; see also F. Beretta, *Giordano Bruno e l'Inquisizione romana*, cit., p. 42.
37 *Processo*, 85–86.
38 See *supra*, p. 144.
39 See the interview given by Giuseppe Fiandaca on the occasion of the publication of *Prima lezione di diritto penale*, Rome-Bari, Laterza, 2017, in «La Lettura», June 25, 2017, p. 11.
40 ASVe, *Savi all'eresia (Sant'Ufficio)*, box 153, list of «Inquisitori domenicani», fol. 1*r*; the date is confirmed in other places in the disorganized documentation contained in the same envelope.
41 See the new documentation published in Giovanni Angeli, *Lettere del Sant'Ufficio di Roma all'Inquisizione di Padova (1567-1660), con nuovi documenti sulla carcerazione padovana di Tommaso Campanella in appendice (1594)*, edited by Antonino Poppi, Padua, Centro studi antoniani, 2013, pp. 141–147.
42 See the text of the *Instruttione finale* for the new nuncio Antonio Maria Graziani, Venezia, March 22, 1596, in *Nunziature di Venezia*, volume XIX: *La nunziatura di Ludovico Taverna (25 febbraio 1592-4 aprile 1596)*, edited by Sergio Pagano, Rome, Istituto italiano per l'età moderna e contemporanea, 2008, pp. 822–823. This edition of the correspondence maintained by Taverna during his years as nuncio in Venice has not brought to light any previously unknown documents concerning Bruno, nor any references to events regarding Celestino da Verona.
43 Gian Battista Michiel, a Venetian captain engaged in the war against the Uskoks, in his position of rector of Sibenik refused to deliver a priest who had been tried by the local Inquisition to Bishop Bassi, instead imprisoning the inquisitor himself; he was thus excommunicated. See the letter about this from nuncio Taverna to the cardinal Secretary of State Cinzio Aldobrandini (November 28, 1592) published ivi, pp. 135–136.
44 On the events surrounding the bishopric of Sibenik relating to Arrigoni, see Brian S. Pullan, *The Jews of Europe and the Inquisition of Venice, 1550-1670*, Oxford, Blackwell, 1983, p. 58 of the Italian edn. For the dates, see Conrad Eubel, *Hierarchia catholica Medii et recentioris Aevi*, volume III, *Saeculum XVI ab anno 1503 complectens*, ed. altera, edited by Ludovicus Schmitz-Kallenberg, Regensburg, sumptibus et typis Librariae regensbergianae, 1923, p. 299. The

date of May 25, 1599 is derived from the same work, p. 103, where the date of Bassi's nomination to the diocese of Andria is reported with what is clearly the wrong year as May 25, 1598, which is incompatible with what is stated on p. 299, and confirmed by the ACDF documentation on Arrigoni. The date of Arrigoni's papal election to the bishopric of Sibenik is instead set on August 19 by Giovanni Michele Cavalieri, *Galleria de' sommi pontefici, patriarchi, arcivescovi, e vescovi dell'Ordine de' predicatori*, tome I, Benevento, nella stamperia arcivescovale, 1696, p. 551.

45 See the entry on *Arrigoni, Pompeo* by Gaspare De Caro in volume IV of *Dizionario biografico degli italiani*, cit., 1962 and the remaining bibliography cited by T.F. Mayer, *The Roman Inquisition*, cit., pp. 41 ff. The direct descent of the Roman branch from the Milan branch has been questioned by some genealogists (see ivi the entry by Giuseppe Martini about *Arrigoni, Simone*); it should, however, be noted that at the time it was still common to call Cardinal Arrigoni "*Milanese*": see, for example, the very accurate report of the Venetian ambassador Giovanni Gritti, in *Le relazioni degli ambasciatori veneti al Senato durante il secolo decimosesto*, cit., p. 352.

46 As attested to by the *Decreta* of the Holy Office, which records its presence in the Congregation for the whole period that runs from the visit to Bruno in prison in December 1593 up to his release to the Secular Arm on February 8, 1600 (see *Processo, passim*).

47 Having become a cardinal with the title of Sant'Eusebio, Ferrante would also be a judge in the first trial of Galileo Galilei in 1616. See l'*Introduzione* a *Nunziature di Venezia*, cit., pp. v–xxx; T.F. Mayer, *The Roman Inquisition*, cit., *ad vocem* e *Processo, passim*. The Holy Office decree of February 8, 1600 lists him among those present as «*reverendus pater dominus Ferdinandus Taberna Mediolanensis gubernator Urbis*» and in fact states: «*Contra fratrem Iordanum Brunum [...] fuit lata sententia, idemque fuit relaxatus Curiae saeculari reverendi patris domini Gubernatoris praesentis in eadem Congregatione*» (*Processo*, 345–346).

48 See the entry by Nicola Raponi, *Arrigoni, Pietro Paolo*, in *Dizionario biografico degli italiani*, cit., volume IV, 1962.

49 See the entry by G. Trebbi per il *Dizionario biografico degli italiani*, cit., 2016, from which I take the information that follows.

References

Giovanni Angeli, *Lettere del Sant'Ufficio di Roma all'Inquisizione di Padova (1567-1660), con nuovi documenti sulla carcerazione padovana di Tommaso Campanella in appendice (1594)*, edited by Antonino Poppi, Padua, Centro studi antoniani, 2013.

Dario Busolini, *Girolamo da Narni*, in *Dizionario biografico degli italiani*, cit., volume LVI, 2001.

Giovanni Michele Cavalieri, *Galleria de' sommi pontefici, patriarchi, arcivescovi, e vescovi dell'Ordine de' predicatori*, tome I, Benevento, nella stamperia arcivescovale, 1696.

The Complete Works of Christopher Marlowe. Second ed., edited by Fredson Bowers, volume II, Cambridge, Cambridge University Press, 1981.

Gaspare De Caro, *Arrigoni, Pompeo*, in *Dizionario biografico degli italiani*, cit., volume IV, 1962.

Michele Di Sivo, *Sulle carceri dei tribunali penali a Roma: Campidoglio e Tor di Nona*, in *Carceri, carcerieri, carcerati. Dall'Antico regime all'Ottocento*, edited by Livio Antonielli, Soveria Mannelli, Rubbettino, 2006, pp. 9–22.

Michele Di Sivo, *Il braccio del tribunale: birri e carcerieri a Roma tra Cinque e Seicento*, in *La giustizia dello Stato pontificio in età moderna*, edited by Maria Rosa Di Simone, Rome, Viella, 2011, pp. 259–266.

Conrad Eubel, *Hierarchia catholica Medii et recentioris Aevi*, volume III, *Saeculum XVI ab anno 1503 complectens*, altera ed., edited by Ludovicus Schmitz-Kallenberg, Regensburg, sumptibus et typis Librariae regensbergianae, 1923.

Giuseppe Fiandaca, *Prima lezione di diritto penale*, Rome and Bari, Laterza, 2017.

Giuseppe Fiandaca, article in «La Lettura», June 25, 2017, p. 11.

Maria Sofia Messana, *Inquisitori, negromanti e streghe nella Sicilia moderna (1500-1782)*, Palermo, Sellerio, 2007.

Nunziature di Venezia, volume XIX: *La nunziatura di Ludovico Taverna (25 febbraio 1592-4 aprile 1596)*, edited by Sergio Pagano, Rome, Istituto italiano per l'età moderna e contemporanea, 2008.

Daniel Ponziani, *Interessi architettonici: i palazzi dell'Inquisizione*, in *Rari e preziosi. Documenti dell'età moderna e contemporanea dall'archivio del Sant'Uffizio*, edited by Alejandro Cifres, Marco Pizzo, Rome, Gangemi, 2009, pp. 86–105.

Brian S. Pullan, *The Jews of Europe and the Inquisition of Venice, 1550-1670*, Oxford, Blackwell, 1983.

Part 3

"A Willing Martyr"

9 The Choice

Why did Giordano Bruno allow himself to be burned at the stake by the Inquisition on February 17, 1600? What exactly happened during the last year of that very long trial? More than four centuries after the death of the greatest Italian philosopher of the Renaissance, the circumstances of the final year of his life still appear mysterious to us. Many, too many, questions remain unanswered.

Michele Ciliberto, one of the leading scholars of Bruno's life and work, forcefully sums up the progress of the trial:

> during eighty months of imprisonment – first in Venice, then at Rome – [Bruno] waged, day after day – and with all the tools available to him – a bitter fight not to succumb, not to abjure, not to die. [...] Bruno decided to turn the tables, and chose to go to the stake when he felt definitively trapped, without any real possibility of saving himself or his philosophy.[1]

When, we must now ask ourselves, was this trap sprung? What exactly happened at that moment, how was it reached, and why? For what reason did Bruno – unlike another contemporary philosopher and scientist, Galileo Galilei – after having fought for so long to affirm his truth, decide in the end to withdraw into obstinacy and accept the final consequences of the sentence inflicted by the inquisitors, up to the torture of being burned alive? Why, especially after having repeatedly declared his willingness to abjure – as in fact he had already done in Calvinist Geneva – did he not offer a superficial repudiation of part of his work in order to save his life?

These are the questions we will now explore – with the awareness that they will probably never be conclusively answered – and try to construct some hypotheses which further research can confirm or disprove. It can perhaps be assumed that for a long time these same questions have not had a home in the historiographical debate out of respect for the sort of lay martyrology that arose around the figure of Bruno in the first decades of unified Italy.[2] Emphasizing the inequities of the religious justice imposed on the populations of the peninsula by the Roman Church between the Middle and Modern Ages, this martyrology has embraced an almost neutral interpretation

DOI: 10.4324/9781003026082-13

of Bruno's death as being the mere result of heroic intellectual consistency. Yet the tragic implications of self-sacrifice were very clear to the Italian "martyrs of free thought"[3] who paid dearly for defending their ideas during the religious crisis of the 16th century. Bernardino Ochino, the vicar general of the Capuchins who fled the Inquisition, wrote about this with clarity in the famous letter he sent to the poetess Vittoria Colonna in the fateful year of 1542, explaining to her the reasons for his flight:

> because I would have to either deny Christ or be crucified. The first I would not wish to do, the second yes, with his grace, but when he wills it. I will gladly go to my death, but I do not have that spirit now.[4]

It has perhaps been these same reflexes of Italian political and cultural history and identity that have obscured the facts of how Bruno tried to save the fundamental core of his philosophy during the eight years of his trial, going so far as trying to engage in debate with the inquisitors; and repeatedly declaring his full willingness to repent, both in the Venetian phase and especially in the Roman phase of the prosecution. But in the end he decided to turn the tables and allow himself to die – as we read from one of the reports published just a few days after his burning at the stake – "a willing martyr":

> Thursday morning in Campo di Fiore the wicked Dominican friar da Nola was burned alive, about whom it has been written in the past: a very obstinate heretic, and having at his whim formed various dogmas against our faith, and in particular against the Holy Virgin and Saints, stubbornly wanted to die in his wickedness; and said that he died a willing martyr, and that his soul would ascend with the smoke to paradise. But now he will see if he told the truth.[5]

Bellarmino the Jesuit

In this chapter we will quickly review the events of the trial in the year 1599 and the information that attests to the death of Giordano Bruno at the stake in Campo de' Fiori in February 1600. These are crucial aspects for understanding the outcome of the trial, unquestionably influenced by the events of the last year of the convict's life. In the following chapter we will present some aspects of these events which in our opinion remain obscure. At the end of the book we will try to throw some glimmers of light on them.

Only in January 1599, in the harsh atmosphere of popular hostility towards the Aldobrandini family, now exacerbated by disastrous flooding, did the hearing of the case begin to take shape in the Holy Office. The judges did not agree on the procedure to employ for reaching a sentence, neither, probably, on the extent of the defendant's guilt. The tribunal therefore entrusted the task of re-examining all of the trial documentation to the Jesuit Roberto Bellarmino, a notable theologian and consultant to the Congregation of the

Index and the Holy Office, and author, since the early years of the 1570s, of an *Index haereticorum*, which attests to his deep understanding of religious heterodoxy. Bellarmino grew closer to the omnipresent Giulio Antonio Santori, granting him various consultations on the subjects of Hebrew books and reform of the Roman Ritual.[6] An expert censor, the Jesuit had risked being censored himself: only the very brief pontificate of Urban VII (the shortest in history, lasting less than 13 days in September 1590) managed to block the order placing the first volume of his *Controversiae* in the Index.[7] He was then made part of the commission charged with amending the *Talmud*, and worked on the revision of the "Vulgate" Bible in 1591.

In the years 1591–1596 Bellarmino took part in the censorship proceeding brought by the Congregation of the Index against the book *Nova de universis philosophia* by Francesco Patrizi of Cherso: the previously cited philosopher was protected by Clement VIII, and taught at the University of Rome at the request of the pontiff. The case of Patrizi – whose summons to the Capitoline *studium* had raised so many hopes for Bruno – was the first occasion that the future Jesuit cardinal confronted cosmological theses that had not up to that time been condemned by the Roman Church. The two censors charged with examining the text were a Dominican and a Jesuit: the first applied harsh and scholastic criticism; the second – Bellarmino – proved to be more open and tolerant towards Patrizi's cognitive method and language. In spite of this, Cardinal Francisco de Toledo (who was also Jesuit) proposed closing the case with a total ban on the work, which was later commuted by the Congregation of the Index into a milder interdiction.[8]

Recalling the Patrizi affair helps us to understand the turn that the Bruno trial will take. First of all, it represents the immediate precedent for Bellarmino's censorship of the philosopher from Nola: both natural philosophers dealt with cosmological questions, even though Bruno despised Partizi and his work. For Bellarmino, the work of prohibiting the *Nova de universis philosophia* led to the maturation of the theory *consensun omnium*, which established the cognitive supremacy of Church tradition over the natural sciences. In the trial against Bruno this position was taken by Clement VIII himself, who personally intervened at the Holy Office on February 4, 1599, deciding that some of the propositions traceable to Bruno's work could be considered heretical based on the authority of the Church Fathers and canon law, even if they had not been explicitly condemned by Roman ecclesiastical tribunals.[9] This would, moreover, be the theoretical basis of the first Roman trial against Galileo, opened in 1615 because of his heliocentric views, even though neither the Holy Office nor the Index had ever officially pronounced against this category. Bellarmino, writing at the time to the Calabrian provincial of the Carmelites, Paolo Antonio Foscarini – according to whom Biblical cosmology was not considered part of the Catholic faith, and the Bible therefore had to be reinterpreted in accordance with the new astronomical discoveries – stated that geocentrism was an article of faith, even if it was only indirectly expressed in Scripture. Heliocentrism was therefore to be considered heresy, and the following year Galileo was admonished by the Inquisition to abandon his cosmology, or be penalized with the opening of a case against him.[10]

Therefore, it is important to note that the decisive phase of the Bruno trial began in the context of a now established theoretical and doctrinal hardening in the Catholic Church which lay at the center of a Counter Reformation which had not only seen the Holy Office position itself in the heart of the system of papal government and justice, but had also seen the centralization in the Roman Curia of the power to adjudicate which theological positions and, more broadly, which cultural positions could be considered legitimate and orthodox. It was a vision of a top-down and fundamentally authoritarian Church, arising from the reaction caused by the European religious crisis of the 1500s; a vision still barely permeated by the spirit of moral renewal and pastoral care affirmed by the Tridentine canons, but founded instead on the primacy of obedience. It was an ecclesiastical conception that could not be reconciled with that of the humanist and renaissance philosophy of open debate, of which Bruno considered himself to be the last, and for certain aspects, the supreme heir.

Other harbingers of the Bruno trial can be found in the procedure of censoring Patrizi's work that involved Bellarmino. As has been mentioned, there was a direct confrontation between a Jesuit theologian and a Dominican: this aspect will be repeated at the beginning of 1599 in the context of the Bruno trial. This is a point that studies about Bruno have never emphasized, but which seems to be significant. In Rome, beginning on February 22, 1599, the investigation into the alleged heterodoxy of the work *Concordia liberi arbitrii cum gratiae donis* by the Jesuit Luis de Molina was resumed by request of the leaders of the Dominican Order, who wanted it banned. The first session of the ad hoc open congregation to establish if the book was to be considered orthodox was inaugurated that February 22 by the Jesuit and Dominican Generals of the Orders, respectively, Claudio Acquaviva and Ippolito Maria Beccaria.

The long and subtle controversy – which involved issues that were extremely delicate due to their heretical assonances, including grace and free will – had begun in 1593. It had been initiated by the Dominican Friars, who charged Molina's text and by extension, the entire Society of Jesus with heterodoxy. The Jesuits had aroused suspicion and been subject to inquisitorial proceedings since their formation in the 1530s, and the Spanish Dominicans condemned the *Esercizi spirituali* by Ignatius Loyola, who was tried eight times by Spanish, French, and Italian religious courts.[11] The controversy over the *Concordia*, which opened the same year that Bruno was extradited to Rome, overtook the storm triggered by the ascent of Henry of Navvare to the throne, and would conclude only in 1607, under Paul V.

As mentioned, the clash soon extended from the subject of Molina's volume to theses about grace and predestination presented by the lawyers for both parties; and, from here, to a more general indictment of Jesuit orthodoxy. To understand this important aspect, we must forget the apologetic and hagiographic image which the followers of Loyola in later centuries have offered of their Order's origins. Shadows and light are instead projected on the bond that certainly came about in the context of the religious crisis of the 1500s between the first followers of Ignatius and the heresy of the *alumbrados* in Erasmian Spain, and in the France of Francis I, where the evangelism of Lefèvre d'Etaples fermented and Calvin was trained.

The particulars of the new Ignatian Institution generated bitter internal conflicts in the Roman Curia while Paul III was judging its admissibility in 1539. Some cardinals deemed the absence of common dress and communal choral recitations of the breviary to be suspect expressions of anti-monastic undertones dangerously close to the ideas of Luther and Erasmus. Other elements considered questionable were the insistence on the itinerant and free apostolate carried out in poverty; the peculiar contemplative *forma vitae*, which lacked, among other things, obligatory corporal penance; the use of the controversial *Esercizi spirituali* itself; the more general religious and ideological distinctiveness founded on the myth of the primitive Church; and the emphasis on an allusive "way of proceeding" which in many respects is still not clear today. Emblematic of these suspicions is the venomous *informatio* written by the Commissioner General of the Holy Office, Teofilo Scullica da Tropea in the 1540s, pointing at Loyola as a "Lutheran" who "could be burned alive," and accusing the group of Jesuits, which he defined as "Illuminated [...] priests," of sodomy and violating confessional secrecy. As a result, once the cardinal inquisitor Gian Pietro Carafa (Pope Paul IV, 1555–1559) reached the pontifical throne he launched a war against the "Jesuit difference" that would continue to be prosecuted by popes coming out of the inquisitorial ranks into the 17th century.[12]

But let us return to the controversy over the *Concordia* by the Jesuit Luis de Molina and its possible influence on the Bruno trial. After an initial phase that was favorable to the Dominicans, in 1598 the Jesuits were able to reopen the case thanks to a wide ranging diplomatic maneuver, avoiding what looked to be a certain conviction. Between December 1598 and January 1599 the Company's most important theologians arrived in Rome; Molina himself addressed an appeal to the pope to justify his work in terms of opposition to Luther and Calvin. Clement VIII received letters in support of the Jesuits from Phillip III, from the Empress, and from Archduke Albert of Austria, governor of the Low Countries: the controversy over grace had by now taken on political depth. Not only was the honor of the two Orders at stake, but also their theological, political, and educational roles within the post-Tridentine European Catholic Church. An oppressive atmosphere prevailed in the Roman Curia in those days. Bellarmino's position on the *Concordia* can be identified by what he wrote in a memorandum directed to the pope in 1597, previewing the line of defense adopted in 1599: turn the indictment of the entire Order that the preachers had launched at the Jesuits with subtle arguments for conversion back on the Dominicans.[13]

The two fundamental procedural passages in the events of Bruno's inquisitorial trial – his arrest in Venice and the hearing of the case – therefore took place during the two major political-religious crises to strike the papacy in the 1590s: the clash between the pope and the Holy Office regarding the king of France Henry IV of Bourbon, and the resumption of the investigation of the *Concordia*. The first split saw Santa Severina and the group of prelates loyal to him at its center; the second found Bellarmino as the protagonist, involved in the dispute in two ways: both as consultor for the commission, and as a member of the Company of Jesus, always disliked by the inquisitors and now newly accused by the Dominicans. The pontiff and the cardinals of the Holy Office, delegating the identification of the clauses which Bruno would have to abjure to Bellarmino in precisely the moment at which the controversy between the Jesuits and the Dominicans was boiling up once again, thus risked transforming – we do not know how consciously – the Bruno trial into a sort of extension of the controversy itself, and consequently into one of the test beds of Jesuit orthodoxy.

In the clashes and meetings between the leadership of the two Orders, the Bruno case – himself a Dominican friar – may have been used as tool for indictment, or even of blackmail. The hypothesis that to some degree the tensions between the Jesuits and the preachers had repercussions on the Bruno trial could be confirmed by the fact that the Dominican General, Ippolito Maria Beccaria – as we will soon see – took a leading role both in the Congregation that had to evaluate the orthodoxy of the *Concordia* as well as in the tribunal that deliberated the trial of Giordano Bruno. However, this was a very peculiar position to assume.

There is little doubt about the fact that the transfer of advisory powers in the Bruno trial into Bellarmino's hands had been decided by the pontiff. Clement VIII placed the utmost trust in the Jesuit concerning questions of science and theology. Called to Rome by Aldobrandini at the beginning of 1597 as a papal theologian and consultor to the Holy Office, Bellarmino appears for the first time in the Bruno trial documentation conducting a visit to the prison on March 24, 1597: a visit during which the philosopher was admonished to cease his "ravings" about the multiplicity of worlds.[14]

In all probability the Jesuit and Clement VIII discussed the progress of the case against Bruno in the middle and final months of 1598, when Bellarmino accompanied the pontiff on his visit to the embassy of Ferrara. In the Curia it was clear to all what a strong influence the future cardinal exercised on a pope who had not been kind to the Jesuits, criticizing the activities of the Company in years past with the accusation of being "fallen from its primitive fervor" and submitting its general, Claudio Acquaviva, to an commission of inquiry which ultimately exonerated him of all charges.[15] During the months spent in the Este city, however, Bellarmino found a place among the dignitaries of the most intimate circle around Aldobrandini: those who could speak directly with him without the mediation of his omnipotent nephew Pietro.[16] Furthermore, in 1600 the theologian would send Pope Clement a brief of just a few pages, known by the title *De officio primario summi pontificis* and destined for broad diffusion in Rome. This was a very harsh

> indictment of the management of the system of power in the Church, a document of great religious and emotional importance and, at the same time, a test of the intellectual independence and the confidence which he enjoys[ed] with Clement VIII.[17]

The Jesuit must have worked very hard to win this confidence.

The list of clauses for Bruno to abjure drawn up by Bellarmino was delivered to the prisoner on January 18, 1599. Clement VIII had returned to Rome, accompanied by his circle, exactly one month prior; his arrival was immediately followed by the dramatic flooding of the Tiber. Realistically, therefore, Bellarmino had already begun working on the extensive Bruno trial documentation while in Ferrara,[18] when he was in direct contact with the pope whom Giordano Bruno had called "a gentleman because he favors philosophers."[19] This was an educated pontiff, who had long understood that the Bruno trial had as its protagonist an intellectual with depth, whose works he himself – as we have seen – had wanted to obtain by searching book stores across half of Europe. After all, Clement VIII was a ruler who, as the Venetian ambassador Dolfin wrote in 1598, "wants to know everything, read everything and order everything."[20] Thus he could have thought that it was the moment to place the trial in the hands of a trusted advisor, thanks to whom a decision would finally be reached.

In reality Bellarmino did not go much beyond the points elaborated by the theologians who had intervened in the preceding years in his reappraisal of the Bruno trial papers, and so based his conclusions on the mostly sloppy work done by the censors in the period 1595–1597. At the end of the examination, he proposed that the tribunal submit to the accused a list of eight clauses which had been judged to be heretical, to be abjured on pain of a death sentence for impenitence. Unfortunately this list has not come down to us. We only know that it was delivered to the prisoner on January 18, 1599, with notice that he had six days to decide to abjure them. As we have already noted,[21] the assertions identified by Bellarmino included crucial nodes of Bruno's work, and undermined the foundations of the latter's philosophical system. At that point it seemed that the philosopher was faced with the tragic alternative between abjuration and death, along with a complete censorship of his works that – at least in Catholic countries – could be permanent.

But perhaps a third way was possible.

The Way to Salvation

On January 25, 1599, after having read the eight clauses, Bruno declared himself willing to revoke them, but then presented a written brief in his defense. In early February, perhaps after that brief had been read, the Congregation once again ordered the accused to abjure the eight clauses within 40 days. On February 15 Bruno stated that he did "acknowledge the said eight clauses as heretical and to be ready to abhor them and abjure them at a time and place that pleases the Holy Office."[22]

On April 5 – during the visit to the prison – the prisoner presented another written statement to the inquisitors. It became clear that the Holy Office's hope for closing the trial was a vain illusion, and that the skilled philosopher, after having already spent seven years in dismal imprisonment, could have played that game forever.

At that point, ensnared by Bruno's desperate desire to save himself and his thought using the few tools available to him, namely debate and persuasion, the Congregation of the Holy Office reacted by imposing yet another abrupt halt to the trial's progress. Although the notary added the phrase "the case has to be presented"[23] alongside Bruno's name on the certificate for the court visit to the prisons of the Holy Office on April 5, 1599 – thus confirming, in the language of the inquisitorial bureaucracy, that the final sentencing hearing had been scheduled – the actual proceeding was again halted for almost six months. Bellarmino, who in the meantime had been made a cardinal by Clement VIII, did not report the contents of the brief Bruno sent to the Congregation in April until a meeting on August 24, held in the residence of Santa Severina, the palazzo di Montecitorio.[24]

Why, unlike what had happened in January, was the trial halted for almost five months when faced with Bruno's second brief from April? What delayed the official examination of the document until the end of August? It is difficult to imagine that this long period was spent without anything happening, because the resumption of the trial in September also brought a definitive acceleration. The documents available to us are, however, silent on the matter.

The three weeks between August 24 and mid-September 1599 thus proved to be decisive for Giordano Bruno's fate. On the 24th, when the brief the philosopher had written in the spring was read in Congregation, Bellarmino noted new heresies.[25] Having heard the report, the Congregation made the definitive decision to present the case for final discussion at the first assembly where the pontiff was in attendance.

At the same time, on that August 24 the Holy Office voted to grant Bruno's request to be given glasses, pen, paper and ink in his cell, while not allowing him, evidently for reasons of security, to have a knife or a sharpener and a compass[26]: this is a clear indication of the fact that the prisoner was considering producing another brief. This fact is extremely important, because it demonstrates that Bruno meant to continue his pursuit of the tactic he had deployed in January of writing letters of argumentation in his own defense to the inquisitors. Thus on August 24, Bruno had not yet decided to doom himself by refusing abjuration, the prelude to a death sentence.

In the meantime September 6 arrived, when the Holy Office – without the presence of the pontiff – decided to assign the final discussion of the trial to the following meeting. The outcome would therefore be decided at the session on Thursday, September 9, 1599.

That day the inquisitorial Congregation was faced with making a final decision: what to do about the case against Giordano Bruno? What value should be attributed to the accusations and the evidence gathered?

At the time almost all the members of the tribunal expressed support for the idea of subjecting Bruno to torture. This proposal, far from representing a form of cruelty or punishment against the accused, was in fact aimed at helping him. By stating the need to acquire more information, certified by the trust placed in torture as a tool for producing truthful confessions, the majority of the judges had tacitly admitted that the evidence gathered over the long years of the trial was not sufficient for reaching an informed decision.

At this point, however, there was a dramatic turn of events. Although all the consultors of the Holy Office declared themselves in favor of, or at least not opposed to, the idea of torturing Bruno, Clement VIII instead decided to grant the offender a final "*terminus ad resipiscendum*" (period to repent).[27] So, in that very delicate moment, there was a break between the trial strategy proposed by the panel of judges and that chosen by the pontiff, the leader of the Holy Office, which of course prevailed. Bruno would not have another possibility to speak out, albeit under torture, on the charges against him. The tribunal was now, by will of the pope, obliged to rule based on what had emerged up to that point.

How do we interpret what took place that September 9, 1599?

Let us take a look at the actions of the aforementioned General of the Domenicans, Ippolito Maria Beccaria, who had regularly attended the sessions of the Congregation up to January 12 and in February, just when the *Concordia* controversy was resuming. At the behest of Clement VIII he had worked alongside Bellarmino and the Commissioner of the Holy Office in compiling the eight clauses that Bruno would have to abjure.[28] At the session of September 9 Beccaria also expressed his support for torture, administered severely and repeatedly ("*torquendus nedum semel vel bis*"), at the completion of which Bruno would have to be judged based on the deposition he gave ("*ex his quae deponet iudicetur*") between the torments.

Even Beccaria, particularly because he was the General of the Order to which the accused belonged, advanced this proposal with the purpose of helping Bruno. Claiming no confidence in the results of the entire procedure, based as it was on testimony given by opaque characters like Celestino da Verona and Francesco Graziano, he wanted to give Bruno a final chance to absolve himself from the most damning accusations. The General knew that Bruno's accusers were *criminosi*, and – as dictated by the established procedural doctrine and judicial practice of common law – their testimony could not be considered fully credible. As we read in the draft of the

September 9 decree, the Commissioner General of the Holy Office himself, Alberto Tragagliolo confidently stated "*quod non possit habere alios testes nisi carceratos criminosos*" ("that [in the trial] no other witnesses were found except prisoners who had committed crimes"). The Procurator Fiscal and the Assessor also stated their opinion that the subject of investigation was not guilty of the principal charges. For this reason everything called for the use of torture.

The pope's rejection of this idea, far from the desire to favor the offender, therefore meant that Bruno was deprived of the last chance to demonstrate his orthodoxy and, as a result, the full recognition of the legal value of the accusatory structure, launching a re-examination of the confessions given, among others, by his main accuser, Celestino da Verona.[29] As we will see later, this paradoxically happened while Celestino was confined in the same prisons of the Roman Holy Office, already sentenced to death and awaiting his execution at the stake.

The session of September 9, 1599 therefore concluded with the decision to again order Bruno to abjure the eight clauses, on penalty of death. That was done the following day, September 10, when the prisoner was once more brought before the judges. At this encounter Bruno officially declared that he had written a new brief addressed *directly to the pope* ("*memoriale missum sanctissimo Domino Nostro*"), but that at the same time he acknowledged his errors and was ready to do whatever the tribunal ordered ("*quod intendit recognoscere eius errores et facere totum et quicquid ei iniunctum fuerit a sancta Ecclesia catholica Romana*").[30]

So it would appear that, at least until September 10, Giordano Bruno demonstrated a strong will to emerge from the trial, which by now had tormented him for seven years, alive. He produced a new written statement and declared himself ready to abjure. The third brief he delivered that day, this time addressed directly to the pope – an important detail – would be read by the judges at the September 16 session. September 10, 1599 is therefore, according to the current state of the documentation, the *terminus post quem* of Bruno's decision to refuse abjuration. On that day he simultaneously showed himself to be broadly deferential to the inquisitors, as well as eager to clarify his positions with a new brief. Not at all ready, therefore, to be sent to the stake as a "willing martyr."[31]

Only after that September 10 would the philosopher enclose himself in stubborn and definitive silence. At that point the situation in the trial worsened. Between the end of September and the first days of October the peremptory injunction was repeated, as an extreme mediation against his now clear obstinacy.[32] The philosopher therefore made his conclusive and irrevocable decision to close off any communication with the tribunal, refuse abjuration and go willingly to the stake between September 10th and 30th of 1599. From September 16 on, the date his new brief was read in Congregation and he was once again asked for a retraction, Bruno no longer sought any further debate with the judges.

At that point, on November 17, the Holy Office ordered that the hearing of the case should proceed, as the accused's impenitence had been established. Despite General Beccaria's attempts at persuasion, the philosopher never revisited his decisions. On December 21, during the customary pre-Christmas visit to the prisons, he was questioned about his material needs and again invited to submit to abjuration. He replied that he had no desire to do so, nor did he believe that he had anything to retract.[33]

On January 20, Clement VIII ordered that the case be closed with a capital sentence. The apostate friar Giordano Bruno was at that point formally judged to be an unrepentant and pertinacious heretic. He would be delivered to the Governor of Rome's men (the so-called "Secular Arm") to be led by them to the scaffold.

Before this happened, one last attempt at reconciliation with the Catholic Church remained. This was normally instigated by confraternities of clerics and laymen whose mission consisted of giving comfort to condemned prisoners and accompanying them to the scaffold. The comforters collected the condemned from the secular prison that had received him in his passage to the Secular Arm. At that point they were obliged to make every effort to convert the prisoner: uninterruptedly, up to the last moment of the offender's life, even while he was burning on the stake. The medieval inquisitorial manual *Directorium inquisitorum* specifies that an execution can be suspended and the already lit fire extinguished if the condemned shows repentance, and there is no lack of historical cases to prove the effectiveness of this practice.[34] In Rome it was the archconfraternity of San Giovanni Decollato that saw to this painful office. Members of this group took Bruno from the prison of Tor di Nona during the night between the 16th and 17th of February 1600, tasked with attempting a final reconciliation before accompanying him to the stake.

Even if the condemned impenitent could not receive Communion, the three masses and the Eucharistic sacrifice called for by the rules of the archconfraternity were fully part of this mission. A lack of repentance was, by the same rules, set as a barrier for the celebration of the masses: "In a case where someone does not want to convert," we read in the *Regolamenti che si praticano in Roma dalla Arciconfraternita di San Giovanni Decollato nell'esecuzione di giustizia*, "the obstinate is moved to another place, leaving only those who are willing, warning that if none of them wanted to convert, they may not celebrate Mass until they show signs of repentance."[35] But, in Bruno's case all was in vain. What took place that night is certified by the registries of the confraternity:

> At hour of 2 in the night it was conveyed to the Company that in the morning justice had to be done to an impenitent, but at 6 in the night the comforters and the Chaplain of Sant'Orsola gathered and went to the jail of Torre di Nona, entered our Chapel and performed the usual orations, and the one who was condemned to death was delivered to us, that is:

> Giordano son of the late Giovanni Bruni, an apostate friar from Nola di Regno, and unrepentant heretic. Who has been urged by our brothers with all charity, and for who they summoned two Fathers of San Domenico, two of the Jesuits, two of the new Church and one from San Giordano, who with all affections and much doctrine showed him his error, has in the end remained in his accursed obstinacy, his brain and intellect traversed by a thousand errors and vanities; and so much did he persevere in his obstinacy that from the Ministry of Justice he was led to Campo di Fiori, and there he was stripped nude, lashed to a stake and was burned alive, always accompanied by our Company, chanting the litanies, and the comforters up to the final moment encouraging him to leave his obstinacy with which he finally ended his miserable and unhappy life.[36]

This document, whose authenticity is incontestable, proves that the fire at Bruno's stake was actually lit. Interpretations which persisted to the end of the 19th century suggesting the possibility of the philosopher's last minute liberation therefore have no historical basis.[37]

In recent years, moreover, the entry in the records of the Tribunale del Governatore – the head of the Secular Arm – that certifies Bruno's execution has been discovered and published, accompanied by a drawing of the condemned surrounded by flames at the lit stake, this too prepared by the notary of the secular court (Figure 12.1, p. 220).[38] This sketch, as acutely noted by Nuccio Ordine, would seem to represent the condemned dressed in a tunic: in appearance this would contradict the records of San Giovanni Decollato, according to which he "was led to Campo di Fiori, and there he was stripped nude, lashed to a stake and burned alive."[39] It is possible, however, to think that the horizontal line in the drawing which crosses the body of the condemned at the neck level does not depict the top of a robe, but rather the so-called "*borello*" or "*borelo*": a collar used to fasten the condemned to the execution stake and keep his face firmly turned toward the public and the comforters. The *borello* appears in various representations of contemporaneous live burnings. Some of these pictures also show how, as an alternative to the *bordello*, two holes were made in the stake of punishment, through which were passed a rope to fasten the victim's neck, producing the same visual result.[40]

Both of these tools could have been represented by the notary with that horizontal line on Bruno's neck, with the sketching of the tongues of fire that could have perhaps produced the illusion of a tunic.

The Procedural Scheme

The events of that last year in the trial of Giordano Bruno were decisive in determining its outcome. This is demonstrated by, among other things, the text of the death sentence imposed by the Holy Office, although it only survives in a sort of partial copy, in the form of the draft composed by notary Flaminio Adriani, which served as the basis for preparing the copy of the sentence authorizing the execution that would be delivered to the Secular Arm,.

One of the functions of the sentencing document was to explain the reasons for the condemnation: it is therefore significant that in its preparations the inquisitorial tribunal focused almost exclusively on elements that emerged in the last year of the trial. Let us read attentively.

> You being, friar Giordano, son of the late Giovanni Bruno da Nola in the kingdom of Napoli, professed priest of the order of san Domenico, at your age of about 52 years, the accusations made against you in the Holy Office of Venice eight years ago are:
>
> That you have said that it was a great blasphemy to say that the bread transubstantiated into flesh, etc. *ut infra.*
>
> The clauses were presented to you, on the 18th of January 1599 in the congregation of the lord Prelates assembled in the Holy Office and you were assigned the term of six days to deliberate and then respond if you wished to abjure the aforementioned clauses or not; and then on the 25th of the same month, being again in the same assembled congregation and place, you responded that, if the Holy See and the Holiness of our Lord have declared the eight clauses as definitively heretical, or His Holiness granted them as such, or by the Holy Spirit defines them as such, you were disposed to revoking them; and then immediately you presented a writing addressed to His Holiness and to us, which (as you said) concerned your defense; and subsequently, on the eighth of the month of February 1599, it was ordered again that you be given the said eight clauses, as in effect was proposed to you on the 15th of that month, and that, acknowledging them as heretical and wanting to abjure them, you were to be received in penitence, furthermore, that you were given the term of forty days to repent yourself; and you said at the time that you acknowledged the said eight clauses as heretical and to be ready to detest them and abjure them in a place and time that pleased the Holy Office, and not only the said eight clauses, but also that you were prepared to make every obedience around the others that have been placed before you; but then, you having put other writings into the records of the Holy Office and addressed to the Holiness of Our Lord and to Ourselves, from which it manifestly appears that you stubbornly persevere in your above mentioned errors.
>
> And having [also] been notified that you were denounced in the Holy Office of Vercelli, that while you were in England you were taken for an atheist and that you have composed a book of *Trionfante bestia*, you were on the 10th of the month of September 1599 given the term of forty

> days to repent yourself, after which we would proceed against you as ordered and commanded by the sacred Canon; and you still remaining obstinate and unrepentant in your aforementioned errors and heresies, the most reverend friar Ipolito Maria Becaria, a general, and the father friar Paolo Isaresio of Mirandola, procurator of the order of your said religion, were sent to you so that they would admonish and persuade you to recognize these your grave errors and heresies; nonetheless you have always persevered pertinaciously and obstinately in your said erroneous and heretical opinions.
>
> For which, having been seen and considered in the trial formed against you and the confessions of your errors and heresies with pertinacity and obstinacy, since you deny being such, and all the other things to be seen and considered: first proposed your case in our general congregation done before the Holiness of Our Lord under that of the 20th of January just passed, and voted and resolved, we have reached the sentence below, [...].[41]

Almost all of the surviving text of the sentence against Giordano Bruno, from which only the list of the convict's doctrinal errors was excised, probably due to the rigorous protection of inquisitorial secrecy,[42] consists of a meticulous recapitulation of the events of 1599. Luigi Firpo, the historian who published the reference edition of the trial documentation immediately after the end of the Second World War, has already observed that

> Bruno's attitude over the course of 1599 is illuminated [...] by a full coherence: not a monolithic kind of constant denial, but the human and lively coherence of the long alternating dispute with the judges and even more with himself. It is not foolish stubbornness, nor the petulance of an obsessive writer that are revealed by his behavior, but a firm will to not be suffocated, an anxiety to be understood, and a painful arc from hope, to astonishment, to desperation.[43]

Luigi Firpo attributes the famous phrase that the philosopher turned on the inquisitors after having heard the pronouncement of the sentence to Bruno's final "painful disillusionment": "Perhaps you pronounce the sentence against me with greater fear then I feel in receiving it." This striking prophecy was referred to (in Latin) in a letter written from Rome by an eye witness to the burning, the German Humanist Kaspar Schoppe – who had recently converted to Catholicism – to his friend Konrad Ritterhausen. A note sent to Duke Virgilio Orsini immediately after the execution of Bruno also reported that "he finally said to Cardinal Santa Severina [...] that with great joy he understood his sentence was to be burned, while by comparison it was with bitterness and displeasure that they had read it to him." It may therefore be considered highly probable that Bruno spoke a similar phrase in the days before his trip to the scaffold.[44]

Retracing the entire arc of events over the eight years of the trial of Giordano Bruno, we see that it can be broken down into five phases.

The first stage of the trial consists of the period between Bruno's arrest in Venice (May 23, 1592) and the completion of the first round of questioning of witnesses and the prisoner (June 23, 1592). The Venetian judges, among whom were the apostolic nuncio and the patriarch of Venice, perhaps because they had been forewarned that the philosopher was a dangerous heretic, perhaps because they were aware, albeit indirectly, of his history and his writings, had accepted Mocinego's denunciation despite its being legally tainted as the product of a sole and hostile accuser, and had immediately arrested Bruno. They were unable to find witnesses to confirm the charges, and their suspicions, but were soon strengthened in their convictions by support from Cardinal Santa Severina in Rome, who at the time was a severe persecutor of Navarrans and natural philosophers. In this phase, while awaiting the still uncertain outcome of Rome's extradition request, the Venetian tribunal launched a proceeding based on the scarce available evidence. However, at the completion of this first phase of the investigation the inquisitors found themselves at a dead end, without evidence or testimony to support their expectations.

The second step of the trial can be identified in the period between Bruno's return to court in Venice, which ended with his declaration of penitence and full willingness to abjure (July 30, 1592), and his successful extradition to Rome. Thus this stage ended with the accused's entry into the prisons of the Roman Inquisition (February 27, 1593). After this eventful phase, there was a new obstacle: the Roman inquisitors were confronted with the same problems left unresolved in the Venetian phase of the trial. Like their counterparts in the inquisitorial tribunal of the Serenissima, even the Holy Office of Rome did not concern itself with tracing and censoring Bruno's works until the pope himself ordered them to proceed in this direction.

The third phase involved the investigation carried out – albeit very slowly – based on the charges in Celestino da Verona's denunciation (dated by Firpo in autumn 1593), which finally allowed the judges to proceed to the real development of the trial, up to the start of the hearing of the case. The offender immediately reacted by declaring himself willing to abjure, but he also produced two briefs in his defense. At the end of this phase there was third halt in the process, between the spring and summer of 1599. In fact, once it became clear to the inquisitors that Bruno intended to employ a tactic of reconsideration and negotiation which would delay sentencing, the second brief delivered by the prisoner was not read in Congregation immediately, as had happened with the first. Instead they waited – for reasons unknown to us – until the end of August 1599, thus halting the procedure for hearing the case.

A fourth phase of the trial can be identified in the period between the resumption of internal discussions at the Holy Office (on August 24, at Santa Severina's palazzo) and Bruno's final appearance before the inquisitors

(September 10, 1599). After that September 10, when "Giordano had to be even more compliant than usual,"[45] declaring in writing that he wanted to acknowledge his errors and was ready to do anything that the Catholic Church ordered ("*totum et quicquid ei iniunctum fuerit a sancta Ecclesia catholica Romana*"[46]), he produced a third brief in his defense. His reprise of this combination of a written statement of defense and spoken willingness to abjure led to a new, albeit short, suspension of the trial.

The case was set back in motion towards its definitive outcome by the prisoner's final decision – we do not know when or why – to refuse abjuration, at the cost of his life. Girodano Bruno, despite repeated injunctions to retract heretical clauses, withdrew the willingness for reconciliation that he had declared before the tribunals since July 1592, and repeated several times in 1599. He was thus condemned to death, with the sentence executed on February 17, 1600.

What we will now show is that these five phases, divided by four periods of stalemate, were invariably punctuated – and, perhaps, always resolved – by the appearance on the scene of the trial of a figure already known to us: the obscure Capuchin friar, Celestino da Verona.

Notes

1 M. Ciliberto, *Italia laica*, cit., p. 145.
2 In the *Introduction* I have already quoted Anna Foa's study *Giordano Bruno*, cit.; see also Ead., *La memoria di Giordano Bruno e l'Italia: spunti per una riflessione*, in *Giordano Bruno nella cultura mediterranea e siciliana dal '600 al nostro tempo. Atti della Giornata nazionale di studi, Villa Zito, Palermo, 1 marzo 2008*, edited Alberto Samonà, Palermo, Officina di studi medievali, 2009, pp. 11–20.
3 The reference is to the volume published with this title by the erudite Piedmontese Antonio Betolotti (1891) and the collection of the same name inaugurated in 1910 with the work by Arturo Labriola, *Giordano Bruno. Con prefazione storica di Lucio Vero*, Rome, Podrecca e Galantara, 1910.
4 Cited by Susanna Peyronel Rambaldi, *Una gentildonna irrequieta. Giulia Gonzaga fra reti familiari e relazioni eterodosse*, Rome, Viella, 2012, p. 237.
5 *Processo*, doc. 73, p. 356.
6 S. Ricci, *Il sommo inquisitore*, cit., p. 398. The date of the cardinal is in T.F. Mayer, *The Roman Inquisition*, cit., *ad vocem*. See also the entry dedicated to *Roberto Bellarmino* by Franco Motta in *Dizionario storico dell'Inquisizione*, cit., volume III.
7 Guido Mongini, *I gesuiti e i papi nel Cinquecento tra crisi religiosa e Controriforma*, in *I gesuiti e i papi*, edited by Michela Catto, Claudio Ferlan, Bologna, Il Mulino, 2016, pp. 19–51, p. 47.
8 See Saverio Ricci, *Le procès de Giordano Bruno par l'Inquisition*, in «Lexicon Philosophicum», 2014, n. 2, pp. 97–125.
9 *Ibidem* and the entry by L. Fedi on *Processo*, cit.
10 On the vast debate regarding the trial of Galileo one can today begin with Vittorio Frajese, *Il processo a Galileo Galilei. Il falso e la sua prova*, Brescia, Morcelliana, 2014 and the edition edited by Sergio Pagano of *I documenti vaticani del processo a Galileo Galilei (1611-1741)*, Città del Vaticano, Archivio segreto vaticano, 2009.

11 See the recent Guido Mongini, *Maschere dell'identità. Alle origini della Compagnia di Gesù*, Rome, Edizioni di storia e letteratura, 2017.

12 See the works of Guido Mongini, now collected in *«Ad Christi Similitudinem ». Ignazio di Loyola e i primi gesuiti tra eresia e ortodossia*, Alessandria, Edizioni dell'Orso, 2011 e Id., *I gesuiti e i papi nel Cinquecento*, cit., pp. 19–51, citations from p. 42. On the weighty symbolic inheritance of Loyola and the efforts to escape it, see Michela Catto, *La Compagnia divisa. Il dissenso nell'ordine gesuitico tra '500 e '600*, Brescia, Morcelliana, 2009; Silvia Mostaccio, *Spiritual Exercises: Obedience, Conscience, Conquest*, in *The Oxford Handbook of the Jesuits*, edited by Ines G. Županov, New York, Oxford University Press, 2019, pp. 75–104.

13 F. Motta, *Bellarmino*, cit., pp. 484 ff. and 569.

14 See the entry by L. Fedi on Bellarmino in *Giordano Bruno. Parole, concetti, immagini*, cit.

15 G. Mongini, *I gesuiti e i papi nel Cinquecento*, cit., p. 48.

16 F. Motta, *Bellarmino*, cit., p. 567.

17 Ivi, pp. 568 and 576–577. See also Stefano Tabacchi, *Nomine vescovili e ruolo del papa in un dibattito curiale di inizio Seicento*, in *Religione, cultura e politica nell'Europa dell'età moderna. Studi offerti a Mario Rosa dagli amici*, edited by Carlo Ossola, Marcello Verga, Maria Antonietta Visceglia, Florence, Olschki, 2003, pp. 263–275. This closeness would come to a halt when, for reasons that are still not clear, Bellarmino was sent by the pope to oversee the diocese of Capua (1602–1605), from which he would return only after the elevation of Paul V.

18 Perhaps thanks to one of the copies of the so-called *Sommario* that – as demonstrated by Luigi Firpo – were made available after 1597 for internal use by the Holy Office: *Processo*, 3 ff.

19 Ivi, 248.

20 I quote from the entry by A. Borromeo, *Clemente VIII, papa*, cit.

21 See *supra*, p. 4.

22 *Processo*, 94.

23 Ivi, doc. 58, p. 320.

24 Ivi, doc. 59, pp. 323–325.

25 Ivi, doc. 59, p. 325.

26 Ivi, doc. 59, p. 324. The phrase «quod ei dentur pennae, carta, atramentum et perspicilia, non tamen culter aut circinus» is reproduced in the beautiful summary copy referred to in point (b) of p. 325.

27 Ivi, doc. 61, pp. 327–329, p. 329.

28 His name appears for the first time in the documents published in ivi, 309; on the papal nomination, see ivi, doc. 56, p. 315: «Sanctissimus decrevit quod dicto fratri Iordano intimentur a Patribus theologis, videlicet a reverend patre Generali dicti ordinis fratrum Predicatorum, a patre Belarmino et a patre Commissario, propositiones istae tanquam haereticae et contra fidem catholicam [...]».

29 This is the interpretation proposed by D. Quaglioni, *«Ex his quae deponet iudicetur»*, cit., pp. 306 ff.; see also *Processo*, 328.

30 We learn this from the record relative to the following session of the Holy Office on September 16, where the declaration that he gave in that circumstance was read. See *Processo*, doc. 62, pp. 329–331, pp. 330–331:

> [In causa] fratris Iordani Bruni de Nola ordinis Predicatorum, lecto ultimo examine ac declaratione facta, quod intendit recognoscere eius errores et facere totum et quicquid ei iniunctum fuerit a sancta Ecclesia catholica Romana, nec non memoriale missum sanctissimo Domino Nostro.

The date of September 10, with reference to the last examination of Bruno, can be deduced from the copy of the sentence to which we will refer shortly.

31 This evidence unfortunately weakens the suggestive hypothesis formulated by Lucia Boschetti (*Lo Spaccio nel processo a Bruno*, in *Favole, metafore, storie. Seminario su Giordano Bruno*, edited by Olivia Catanorchi, Diego Pirillo, Introduction by Michele Ciliberto, Pisa, Edizioni della Normale, 2007, pp. 281–351, p. 292) according to which it was learning that the inquisitors had obtained a copy of Bruno's volume *Spaccio de la bestia trionfante* – which almost certainly happened in the summer of 1599 – that led the philosopher to close himself definitively in silence and the refusal to abjure that September 10.

32 *Processo*, 101.

33 As the Congregation's decree of January 20, 1600 reports: «consentire nolebat, asserens se nunquam propositiones haereticas in suis scripsisse aut protulisse» (ivi, doc. 65, pp. 336–339, p. 338).

34 See Vincenzo Lavenia, *Eretici sentenziati e 'reincorporati'. Sacramenti, grazia e conforto in alcune norme delle Inquisizioni*, in *Misericordie. Conversioni sotto il patibolo tra Medioevo ed età moderna*, edited by Adriano Prosperi, Pisa, Edizioni della Normale, 2007, pp. 153–187, p. 163. On the multiple techniques of conversion even *in extremis*, also see Vincenzo Paglia, *La morte confortata. Riti della paura e mentalità religiosa a Roma nell'età moderna*, Rome, Edizioni di storia e letteratura, 1982, pp. 89 ff. and 116 ff.

35 Ivi, p. 185.

36 Archivio di Stato di Roma (from here on ASR), *San Giovanni Decollato*, volume 16, fol. 87*r*.

37 The reference is to the booklet by Théophile Desdouits, *La légende tragique de Jordano Bruno*, Paris, Ernest Thorin editeur, 1885. Regarding the difficulty in opening the archives of the Roman confraternity, which had long been closed to the requests of scholars, and were opened by order of the government of Francesco Crispi, see Achille Pognisi, *Giordano Bruno e l'Archivio di San Giovanni Decollato*, Turin, Paravia, 1891. For the notices attesting to Bruno's death, see *Processo*, 355–356 in addition to other documents we will examine ahead.

38 Michele Di Sivo, Orietta Verdi, *Bruno e Celestino da Verona. Le immagini del rogo nelle carte criminali dell'Archivio di Stato di Roma*, in «Bruniana & Campanelliana», 2012, n. XVIII, n. 2, pp. 519–527.

39 Nuccio Ordine, *E il notaio «fotografò» Giordano Bruno sul rogo*, in «Corriere della Sera», April 17, 2011, p. 39.

40 For example in the engravings that over the course of the 1500s illustrated different editions of the *Book of Martyrs* by John Foxe, available in various editions, including a modern edition that can be consulted on the site www.johnfoxe.org, edited by the John Foxe Project at the University of Sheffield.

41 *Processo*, doc. 66, pp. 339–344. Firpo considers "completely unjustified" the accusations of manipulation of the text previously advanced by Spampanato (ivi, 138, note 46).

42 Ivi, 99.

43 Ivi, 110.

44 Ivi, doc. 71, pp. 348–355, p. 351; Federica Favino, *«Et sta per brugiarsi un relasso ostinato»: una testimonianza inedita intorno alla condanna di Giordano Bruno*, in «Galilæana. Journal of Galilean Studies», 2010, n. VII, pp. 85–95, p. 85 and p. 90, note 20, which reports the testimony of a "conte di Ventimiglia," a student of Bruno's, published by Domenico Berti in the second edition of *Giordano Bruno da Nola. Sua vita e sua dottrina*, Turin, Paravia, 1889, p. 326 and note 1, which confirms how Bruno yelled at the judges "you are more afraid sentencing me than I, hearing myself condemned."

45 As Luigi Firpo writes in *Processo*, 98.

46 Ivi, doc. 62, pp. 329–331, p. 331.

References

Domenico Berti, *Giordano Bruno da Nola. Sua vita e sua dottrina*, Turin, Paravia, 1889.

Lucia Boschetti, *Lo Spaccio nel processo a Bruno*, in *Favole, metafore, storie. Seminario su Giordano Bruno*, edited by Olivia Catanorchi, Diego Pirillo, Introduciton by Michele Ciliberto, Pisa, Edizioni della Normale, 2007, pp. 281–351.

Michela Catto, *La Compagnia divisa. Il dissenso nell'ordine gesuitico tra '500 e '600*, Brescia, Morcelliana, 2009.

Théophile Desdouits, *La légende tragique de Jordano Bruno*, Paris, Ernest Thorin editeur, 1885.

Michele Di Sivo, Orietta Verdi, *Bruno e Celestino da Verona. Le immagini del rogo nelle carte criminali dell'Archivio di Stato di Roma*, in «Bruniana & Campanelliana», 2012, n. XVIII, pp. 519–527.

Federica Favino, *«Et sta per brugiarsi un relasso ostinato»: una testimonianza inedita intorno alla condanna di Giordano Bruno*, in «Galilæana. Journal of Galilean Studies», 2010, n. VII, pp. 85–95.

Anna Foa, *La memoria di Giordano Bruno e l'Italia: spunti per una riflessione*, in *Giordano Bruno nella cultura mediterranea e siciliana dal '600 al nostro tempo. Atti della Giornata nazionale di studi, Villa Zito, Palermo, 1 marzo 2008*, edited Alberto Samonà, Palermo, Officina di studi medievali, 2009, pp. 11–20.

John Foxe, *Book of Martyrs*, The John Foxe Project at the University of Sheffield, www.johnfoxe.org.

Vittorio Frajese, *Il processo a Galileo Galilei. Il falso e la sua prova*, Brescia, Morcelliana, 2014.

I documenti vaticani del processo a Galileo Galilei (1611-1741), edited by Sergio Pagano, Vatican City, Archivio segreto vaticano, 2009.

Arturo Labriola, *Giordano Bruno. Con prefazione storica di Lucio Vero*, Rome, Podrecca e Galantara, 1910.

Vincenzo Lavenia, *Eretici sentenziati e 'reincorporati'. Sacramenti, grazia e conforto in alcune norme delle Inquisizioni*, in *Misericordie. Conversioni sotto il patibolo tra Medioevo ed età moderna*, edited by Adriano Prosperi, Pisa, Edizioni della Normale, 2007, pp. 153–187.

Guido Mongini, *«Ad Christi Similitudinem». Ignazio di Loyola e i primi gesuiti tra eresia e ortodossia*, Alessandria, Edizioni dell'Orso, 2011.

Guido Mongini, *I gesuiti e i papi nel Cinquecento tra crisi religiosa e Controriforma*, in *I gesuiti e i papi*, edited by Michela Catto, Claudio Ferlan, Bologna, Il Mulino, 2016, pp. 19–51.

Guido Mongini, *Maschere dell'identità. Alle origini della Compagnia di Gesù*, Rome, Edizioni di storia e letteratura, 2017.

Silvia Mostaccio, *Spiritual Exercises: Obedience, Conscience, Conquest*, in *The Oxford Handbook of the Jesuits*, edited by Ines G. Županov, New York, Oxford University Press, 2019, pp. 75–104.

Franco Motta, *Roberto Bellarmino*, in *Dizionario storico dell'Inquisizione*, cit., volume III.

Nuccio Ordine, *E il notaio «fotografò» Giordano Bruno sul rogo*, in «Corriere della Sera», April 17, 2011, p. 39.

Vincenzo Paglia, *La morte confortata. Riti della paura e mentalità religiosa a Roma nell'età moderna*, Rome, Edizioni di storia e letteratura, 1982.

Susanna Peyronel Rambaldi, *Una gentildonna irrequieta. Giulia Gonzaga fra reti familiari e relazioni eterodosse*, Rome, Viella, 2012.
Achille Pognisi, *Giordano Bruno e l'Archivio di San Giovanni Decollato*, Turin, Paravia, 1891.
Saverio Ricci, *Le procès de Giordano Bruno par l'Inquisition*, in «Lexicon Philosophicum», 2014, n. 2, pp. 97–125.
Stefano Tabacchi, *Nomine vescovili e ruolo del papa in un dibattito curiale di inizio Seicento*, in *Religione, cultura e politica nell'Europa dell'età moderna. Studi offerti a Mario Rosa dagli amici*, edited by Carlo Ossola, Marcello Verga, Maria Antonietta Visceglia, Firenze, Olschki, 2003, pp. 263–275.

10 The Mysteries of the Capuchin

The events of 1599 were fatal not only for Giordano Bruno, but for his bitter and ambiguous accuser, friar Celestino da Verona as well, who was also sent to be burned at the stake by the Inquisition that year, on a warm mid-September Roman night.

However, while the last year of the philosopher's life is at least intelligible in its time frame and internal sequence of events, up to their tragic conclusion, the Capuchin's fate is wrapped in a web of unsettling mysteries. There are very few documents available today that track the path leading to the death of the Capuchin. These documents were all produced by the Holy Office, and as such are affected by interpretive problems which we now must carefully address.

Scholars of the Bruno trial have never directly related what happened to the philosopher in that dramatic year of 1599 with the contemporaneous events that cost the Veronese friar his life. The scarce documentation known until now concerning Celestino's last inquisitorial interactions was not published by Luigi Firpo among the Bruno trial documents, but was rather confined to brief notes in his introductory essay. Firpo thus established an interpretive gap which persists to this day. While information regarding Celestino da Verona in reference to the years 1592–1594 is considered directly relevant to the Bruno trial – this was the period of their common imprisonment, Celestino's deposition *in scriptis* against Bruno and its oral repetition – the final years of the Capuchin's life are not normally seen as related.[1]

But perhaps things were more complicated than that.

Outside the Protected Enclosure

We shifted our attention away from the life of Capuchin friar Celestino da Verona at the end of his long period of oscillation between monastery and inquisitorial tribunals in Verona and Venice during the year 1593. At this point the Protector of his order,[2] the cardinal of Santa Severina Giulio Antonio Santori, decided to have him transferred to a small monastery located within the borders of the Papal States. Celestino refused the order at first, provoking the direct intervention of the pontiff or his people through the

DOI: 10.4324/9781003026082-14

apostolic nuncio Taverna. The latter – evidently acting not as an inquisitor, but as the diplomatic representative of the pope – had Celestino locked up in the cells of the Capuchin order in Venice until he was moved to the Marches.

Celestino da Verona's denunciation against Giordano Bruno reached Rome at the end of 1593. It was therefore written either while the accuser was in the Capuchin jail in Venice by order of the nuncio or, more likely, once he had arrived at the secure monastery in the Marches, under the attentive surveillance of the Cardinal Protector's trusted superiors. Celestino da Verona's now discovered collaboration with the Holy Office was very likely the cause of his turbulent relations with his Order between 1592 and 1593. The denunciation against Bruno may have been the price that he paid, at the end of those two years in a guarded enclosure, to regain his freedom and save his life. He tried to escape in the late spring of 1599, precisely while Bruno's trial was stalled. It is possible that this was not a simple coincidence.

Now we will retrace what happened to Celestino da Verona in that fateful year of 1599, with the caveat that these events are known only from partial and fragmentary Inquisition sources; as such (as I tried to demonstrate in the Introduction) they are characterized by precise limits and potential distortions.

On May 6, 1599 the friar sent a request from San Severino Marche, where he had probably remained since the end of his trials in Venice, to be called to testify before the Holy Office. This was an apparently inexplicable and suicidal act. Celestino had already been involved in at least one prior formal inquisitorial proceeding in Rome, back in 1586–1587. During this trial he had been tortured, and it closed with a severe sentence of abjuration *de vehementi*. While in the Republic of Venice, between 1592 and 1593, he had also entered the prisons of the Inquisition more than once, and was tortured again on least one further occasion.[3] These are very serious developments, which suggested the friar's possible relapse into heretical positions. Taken together with his previous abjuration *de vehementi*, there is no way, on the legal and procedural level, that these events could have resulted in another full acquittal.[4] Torture was normally used by the tribunals of the Holy Office in two cases: either when the evidence seemed to unequivocally indicate guilt that the accused stubbornly denied but was unable to disprove, or when the offender had admitted his guilt but the tribunal had reason to believe that the confession had not been complete. In both cases, as historian John Tedeschi has observed, "it is difficult to imagine that a trial which made use of torture could conclude if not in only one way," that is, condemnation.

For these reasons – and not only for these, given the turbulent personal relations between the Veronese Capuchin and the leadership of his Order, as well as the embarrassments he had caused in the past for the cardinal of Santa Severina, attracting the pontiff's attention – it was unquestionably better for Celestino to remain silent and safe at the little monastery of Colpersito. There he could hope for an eventual softening of the tribunal's positions, which sometimes revisited sentences after five years[5] to evaluate their possible reduction, based on the prisoner's conduct in the interim.

According to canon law of the time, a second trial that did not demonstrate the full innocence of the accused normally implied the imposition of the death penalty on the relapsed heretic, as had often happened over the course of the century that was now coming to an end. According to some inquisitorial procedure manuals, delivery of the accused to the Secular Arm required that the he had abjured *de formali* in the first trial, or rather with complete certainty of his condition as a heretic. Others, however, considered all heresy transferable to the second sentence, regardless of the type of the first abjuration. Following this often applied procedural orientation, Celestino, who had abjured *de vehementi* in Rome and had been subjected to torture and other imprisonments in 1592–1593, would have been at considerable risk of a death sentence.[6]

Therefore, it appears inexplicable that in May 1599 the Capuchin would have asked to be heard again, not just by the Holy Office, but in the dreaded Roman forum itself, in the presence of the supreme inquisitors and the pope. Evidently he must have believed that what he had to say should not be heard by the local inquisitors, but directly by the cardinals of the Roman congregation, and even by the pope. The cardinals, moreover, immediately agreed to receive him: a further indication of the fact that to the Holy Office he was not only an obscure Capuchin relegated to a remote monastery at the margins of the pontifical domains. In fact, the Congregation called Celestino directly to Rome after a meeting on June 3, to allow him to testify "*quae sibi occurrunt*."[7]

At that point another of the many events which are difficult to decipher in the last months of the life of Giordano Bruno's main accuser took place. On June 20, the inquisitor in Venice received an anonymous letter which he brought to the attention of the pope. This letter has not survived and thus its contents are unknown to us. On July 8, 1599 Clement VIII personally ordered a handwriting analysis of the original letter during a session of the Congregation, summoning the superiors of the Capuchin Order and reviewing written statements among trial documents deposited in the archives of the Holy Office, all aimed at demonstrating that the anonymous letter had actually been written by Celestino da Verona.[8]

The friar was certainly already in Rome that July 8: in fact, he was questioned by the inquisitors on July 9 and 11. On July 15 his depositions were read *per extensum* in Congregation. Their contents must have been particularly serious or shocking, because at the end of the reading the pope "renewed" the obligation (*renovavit praeceptum*) – which had therefore been invoked previously – for those present to maintain the strictest silence around the entire case (*servandi secretum, ne quisquam audeat loqui de causa praedicti fratris Celestini*[9]). Just 20 days later, on August 5, in what has been called by Luigi Firpo an "unusual summary procedure,"[10] Clement VIII decreed that a death sentence be prepared against Celestino da Verona as a relapsed, unrepentant, and persistent heretic.

All the subsequent formal acts against Celestino were completed by the Holy Office with unusual rapidity.

On August 19 the prisoner presented his self-defense, albeit in vain, given that the death sentence had already been ordered by the pope. This hearing had only been scheduled, therefore, to respect procedure. On August 24 – at the same meeting of the Congregation that saw the reading of the brief Bruno had delivered in April – the inquisitors signed the death sentence. At that same session on August 24 permission was given to the comforters, several Capuchin friars and preachers, along with some Jesuit priests, to visit the friar's cell "*pro eius conversione*," that is, to induce him to repent of his sins before the execution of the sentence, and so at least obtain the benefit of decapitation in prison before being burned. Once again, the decree of August 24 imposed the strictest silence on the clerics ("*imponatur silentium de non revelando*"[11]).

The fact that the Capuchin was granted a "defense" – or, as provided for in the procedural rules, a forum for the accused to submit briefs and legal opinions signed by lawyers, their own pleadings, exonerating documents or lists of favorable witnesses to the tribunal[12] – demonstrates that in July 1599 a genuine proceeding was organized against the friar by the Holy Office. On the other hand, it is hard to believe that this was any more than a mock trial, given that the "defense" granted to Celestino was useless, considering the pope had already sentenced him to death, and that everything happened far too quickly for the tribunal to be able to develop a formally admissible proceeding. The way events unfolded, with the order to draw up the friar's death sentence pronounced by Clement VIII on August 5, and the signing of the sentence itself by the cardinals of the Congregation on the 24th, leaves no doubt that the prime mover of this unusual summary death sentence was the pope himself. By all indications – and for reasons incomprehensible to us – the pontiff wanted to end the earthly affairs of the unfortunate friar as soon as possible.

The absolute public silence imposed by the Holy Office around the figure of Celestino even broke the traditional rules for delivering the condemned to the Secular Arm, which had been done for centuries following a Lateran III canon that prohibited ecclesiastical tribunals from inflicting severe penalties, and thus calling for a condemned prisoner to be moved to a secular prison prior to execution. This issue also merited special attention from the pope, and was debated at the session of August 24. Contrary to any practice normally applied in Rome in the early modern age, and once again by the direct intervention of Clement VIII, it was decided that the prisoner would not be moved to one of the secular Roman prisons (usually Tor di Nona or Corte Savella) before being led to the stake, but would be taken to Campo de' Fiori directly from the prisons of the Holy Office.[13]

The short time that separated the imposition of the death sentence (August 24) and its execution (September 16) is also completely incongruent.

The *Directorium inquisitorium* called for the condemned to be converted at any cost, both for the benefit of his soul and to avoid the heretic becoming a martyr of faith in the eyes of the population by accepting the horrible sentence of being burned alive at the stake that was mandatory for unrepentant relapsed heretics. Eymerich prescribed that unconfessed and unreconciled heretics should be left in prison for six months, "*et frequentius admonendi, quod in corpore et anima cremabuntur, ac perpetuo damnabuntur et similia.*" He also introduced the practice of the inquisitor and the bishop visiting the cell of the condemned, in addition to relatives and the comforters.[14] In Giordano Bruno's case, as we have seen, the attempts to persuade him to abjure went on for some months, with reiteration of the terms of resipiscence throughout all of autumn 1599 until January 1600.

Even the performance of Celestino da Verona's execution was shrouded by every possible caution. A quick resolution on September 2 formally established modifications to the ordinary procedure, specifying that the comforters were to go directly to the palazzo of the Holy Office, and that from there the friar would be led to Campo de' Fiori.[15] By explicit order of the pope the official sentence of August 24 was not read before a crowd of people in Campidoglio or some other public place, as was typically done for sentences of people who were not of high rank. It was instead read in great secrecy inside the offices of the tribunal of faith ("*Sanctissimus D. N. ordinavit quod sententia contra eum legatur in S. Officio*"[16]).

Celestino da Verona was led to the stake at the end of the night between the 15th and 16th of September 1599, thus minimizing the possibility for the Holy Office to make a show of his execution. These circumstances are corroborated by the certification produced by the archconfraternity of San Giovanni Decollato, which we will look at a little later, and additionally by three reports written by *menanti* (a type of precursor to today's journalist or reporter) who worked for the Duke of Urbino and the Grand Duke of Tuscany; or rather by professional informants whose accounts are considered to be fully reliable by historians of 16th–17th century Rome.[17]

The first two reports sent to the Duke of Urbino on Saturday September 18 read as follows:

> Thursday morning in Campo di Fiori at dawn at the hour of 9 a certain Veronese was burned, with the habit of a Capuchin friar, who although he was not a cleric, had taken the aforementioned habit for himself. His sin was formal obstinate heresy, and so he was burned at night because the French Ambassador did not want these kinds of executions to happen in front of his palazzo, not because he did not want to see heretics burned, as he says with malice, but to not hear or see that horror.
>
> Thursday morning in Campo di fiori before day a wretched member of the Veronese Nation, pretending to be cleric, who was a perfidious heretic, imprisoned for 8 years by the Inquisition, was burned alive, without ever wanting to renounce [his religious convictions].[18]

Both of these statements note the strange pre-dawn execution of a death sentence by the Roman Inquisition. The first reporter even sensed the need to justify the anomaly, referring to an implausible *diktat* of the French Ambassador Brulard de Sillery, whose residence at the time was palazzo Orsini, at the entrance to via de' Giubbonari[19]: Henry IV's diplomatic representative, just a few years after the king's reconciliation with the Holy See, had no interest in getting mixed up in the Inquisition's execution of a Capuchin friar. It does not appear that – not even in the case of Giordano Bruno – the French Ambassador ever wanted to or could have imposed such conditions on the conduct of what was a crucial event for ecclesiastical and secular justice in the Old Regime.[20]

It was, in fact, the cardinal of Santa Severina himself who formulated, in the anti-heretical treatise *Pro confutatione*, the thesis of the essential importance of the public punishment of heretics as an instrument of popular education and dissuasion:

> In fact I believe – he wrote in that office – that the wise of the world have justly said that the pain of just one should be the fear of many, such that the others, edified by the example of the pain, abandon heresy or deny and abjure it, or at least do not teach it. And so the punishment of heretics is worthwhile and useful: in fact, just as the good strive to do good for the love of virtue, so do the bad, to say it with Horatio, cease their delinquency due to the fear of pain.[21]

Very careful evaluations normally took place between Santori and the pope regarding the public forms of carrying out the death sentences of the Holy Office. For example, a note written by Santa Severina to Clement VIII in preparation for a consistorial hearing of June 1597 points out the inadvisability of having a repentant prisoner decapitated in jail: "if [the condemned] repents then he is not burned alive, but dead; but cutting his head off in the jail and not in public is the wrong way, for the bad example that follows it."[22] Not even the possibility that the impenitent heretic could engage in religious propaganda in front of the crowd could induce the tribunals to hide the execution. The offender's tongue could be held in a *giova* (a muzzle), which, if we are to believe the *avviso di Roma* of February 19, 1600, is what happened to Giordano Bruno. His execution, just a few months following that of Celestino, took place in the customary fashion; in daylight and before a large crowd of people.[23]

The third report that confirms the nocturnal execution of Celestino da Verona was penned by Francesco Maria Vialardi, who after his release from prison by the Holy Office became an informant for the Grand Duke of Tuscany. In a brief passage of a long letter written to Ferdinando I on September 24, 1599, he noted:

> at Campo Vaccino a woman who had murdered her son was put to death, and at Campo di Fiore a friar Antonio, formerly a Capuchin

> from Verona, was burned in the night, a most villainous man who dared to say that CHRIST O[ur] L[ord] had not redeemed the human race.[24]

This is the only source that gives an indication, obviously presumptive, of the heresies perpetrated by the Capuchin. It is, moreover, noteworthy that the informant knew and cited Celestino's baptismal name, Antonio: to our knowledge this had been reported only in the most secret decrees and probably in the Congregation's sentence, which, of course, due to the pope's specific instructions regarding absolute secrecy in the case, was not read in public.

Another element common to the three reports about Celestino da Verona's death is the fact that all of them, while emphasizing the condition of impenitence in which he died, erroneously state that he was a layman. Vialardi speaks of "a friar Antonio formerly a Capuchin from Verona"; the first reporter from the *avvisi* (now to be found in the *carte urbinate* in the Vatican Library) wrote that "a Veronese was burned, with the habit of a Capuchin friar, who although he was not a cleric, had taken the aforementioned habit for himself"; the second instead reported that "a wretched member of the Veronese Nation, pretending to be a cleric," or really pretending to belong to an Order, "was a perfidious heretic."[25] Why did they all repeat this error?

The idea that the person burned at the stake in Campo de' Fiori on the night between September 15 and 16, 1599 was a layman is apparently disproved by the certification of the laicization of Celestino da Verona that is found in the registries of the *Depositeria camerale pontificia* for the two year period 1599–1600, preserved today in the State Archive of Rome. This document proves that Celestino, as a subdeacon, was subjected to laicization, the canonical penalty imposed by the Catholic Church annulling ordination. However, the laicization that took place is not on its own certain proof of the execution of the death sentence, given that this penalty could be inflicted on clerics who had committed serious crimes without sending them to the scaffold.[26] The laicization for which we have certification was performed by Maltese Jesuit and bishop of Sidone *in partibus* Leonardo Abel or Abele (1541–1605), who for decades was a pupil of the cardinal of Santa Severina, who had ordained him in 1582.[27]

It is important to note that the documents present in the *Depositeria camerale* are not actually ecclesiastical certifications of canonical laicization. Instead they are records accounting for the Camera Apostolica's reimbursement of the expenses incurred by Bishop Abel in the imposition of the sentence. Let us read the two certifications relative to the laicization of Bruno (which he was subject to as a Dominican friar) and that of Celestino da Verona:

> O[n] the 14th similar to above to the aforementioned [month of March 1600], said he had laicized fra' Giordano Bruni heretic 2 *scudi*.[28]
>
> [...]

> On the [5th] the aforementioned [month of October] 2 [*scudi*] and 40 [*baiocchi*] to be sent as above [or from the vicegerent] to the below mentioned [monsignor de Sidonei] for having laicized fra' Xoffaro [read Cristoffaro] da Verona who was burned *scudi* 2:40.[29]

We learn that the payment of the money owed to the bishop of Sidone for the laicization of Celestino was made on October 5, 1599, a little less than 20 days after the burning, along with a payment of 25 *scudi* for provisions owed to the same ecclesiastic for the preceding three months. This quarterly payment was disbursed regularly for all of 1599,[30] attesting to the fact that a continuing financial relationship existed in that period between the bishop of Sidone and the Camera Apostolica.

Yet another – and not the last – inconsistency in the documentation concerning the end of Celestino da Verona's life is that here he is called Cristoforo: had the laicized friar's place of origin not been noted, we would not be able to attribute the record to the Capuchin. It is hard to believe that this was just an ordinary writing or transcription error, considering the rarity and canonical relevance of the laicization procedure, as well as the fact that the registrations were intended to be a permanent record of its imposition. Bruno and Celestino certainly underwent the so-called real laicization, reserved for the most serious crimes; verbal laicization was prescribed for less serious sins or sentencing in absentia.[31]

The Veronese may have benefited from the procedure called for in the case of *clericus in minorisbus*, which was a laicization in the sole presence of the bishop or, after the Council of Trent, of an ecclesiastic designated as his representative. This could be done in a public church, but also in a private chapel, and was completed by the shaving of all the parts of the body that had received chrism, not only for symbolic reasons but also to avoid leaving any remnant of tonsure.[32]

It should be noted that in Bruno's case the payment of money to the bishop of Sidone was made by mandate of the Governor of Rome: this because the laicization of a cleric sent to the Secular Arm had to take place with a ceremony in a church *praesente iudice saeculari* (in the presence of a secular judge). Indeed, on the canonical level laicization was the true definitive moment of the offender's passage from the hands of the ecclesiastical tribunal to the Secular Arm, which would execute the death sentence.[33] In the case of "Cristoffaro" da Verona the rite was not reimbursed by mandate of the Governor but rather the vicegerent of the Camera Apostolica: or by the pontiff. This is because Clement VIII had expressly ordered that Celestino was not to be transported to the secular prisons, but rather led to the stake from the palazzo of the Holy Office to Campo de' Fiori.

Even here, however, an enigma presents itself: the documents of the Archconfraternity of San Giovanni Decollato show that the person led to the stake on September 16, 1599 was met by the comforters in the prisons of Corte Savella.

Celestino as Bruno?

The registries of the archconfraternity of San Giovanni Decollato also confirm the nocturnal unfolding of the burning at the stake of Celestino da Verona. For the date of Wednesday, September 15 we read:

> [In the margin: "Justice for an unrepentant heretic burned alive"]
> At the hour of one in the night notice was given that the following morning justice must be done to a heretic and however at the hour of 4 the comforters and the chaplain gathered. They went to the prison of Corte Savella and in our Chapel performed the usual orations and the prisoner fra Celestino otherwise known as Giov. Antonio Veronese was delivered there. He was exhorted by brothers and by two Capuchins, two Jesuit fathers and two from the Vallicella with many very effective reasons for him to remove his false opinions, nonetheless he remained very obstinate, without however giving reasons for his stubbornness but with arrogant presumption persevering in this way until he was led to Justice before daylight in Campo di fiore having however celebrated holy mass in our Chapel in his absence [*sic*] and tied to a bare pole was burned alive, all along with the brothers and the fathers pleading with him up to the final point which he arrived at without showing any sign of repentance. From there the Superintendent with the comforters returned to the Chapel and having changed their clothing returned home.
> The following expenses were incurred:
> To segrestano and fattore [*scudi*] 0:45
> Greek wine and confetti (sugared almonds) [*scudi*] 0:20
> Picking up the ashes [*scudi*] 0:40
> [Total *scudi*] 1:05[34]

The account is sparse, given that its purpose was to certify that the confraternity of San Giovanni's brothers had done everything possible to save the soul of the deceased until the moment of extremity. The realism of the dramatic document goes as far as to certify that the comforters removed the ashes from the burning of the body, to prevent them from being used in magical or diabolical rituals, or sold at a high price for this purpose. Greek wine and sugared almonds (*confetti*) were called for by the rules of the archconfraternity to console the person about to be executed.[35]

A comparison of the account of the accompaniment of Celestino da Verona to his death and the one already reported concerning Giordano Bruno[36] allows us to point out similarities and differences. We will highlight the most important ones.

The two men expired in the same way, burning alive at the stake. Death by burning was an exceptional event, even for the heretics condemned by the Inquisition. The large majority of the offenders sent to the Secular Arm confessed and took communion before their execution, thus removing themselves from the category of "unrepentant" and saving themselves the agony of being burned alive at the stake. This procedure was then replaced by decapitation and the subsequent burning of the cadaver. Giovanni Romeo has counted, among the 3,400 death sentences handed down by all the Neapolitan tribunals in the period 1556–1780, only thirty cases of obstinacy, seven of whom died, like Bruno and Celestino, without the sacraments.[37] And in Rome, over the entire 16th century fewer than 20 were sent to the stake to be burned alive, compared to over 100 individuals who were first hung or decapitated, to be burned *post mortem*.[38]

The opaque Veronese was an informer for the Holy Office and most likely a collaborator with the most powerful inquisitors of the time. He had quickly abjured during his first trial in 1586–1587, and had spontaneously appeared before the Roman tribunal in the summer of 1599. Then, in the last moments of his life he would transform into a heretic of unwavering pertinacity, comparable to Giordano Bruno and just a few others condemned to death in all of the modern age. This is truly astonishing, bordering on unrealistic.

The two records relating to the accompaniment of Bruno and Celestino to the scaffold present the same narrative structure. They open with indication of the hour at which the request for intervention reached the comforters: the members of the confraternity were not involved in the preparations for the execution, and met the condemned only a few hours before his execution. Both accounts narrate the gathering of the comforters, their spiritual preparation in the church of Sant'Orsola and the delivery of the condemned, with indication of the place and his personal information. The central section of the document follows, describing the work of trying to persuade the condemned to choose reconciliation, confession, and communion; this was the comforters' main purpose. Finally the journey to the scaffold is narrated, with reference to the nudity of the bodies and the closeness of the clerics until the victim's last breath.

Celestino and Bruno – who died the same way – appeared to take an attitude that was radically opposed to the comforters who tried to convince them *in extremis* of the fallacy of their ideas and to induce them to reconcile with the Catholic faith. Bruno, as we would expect, spoke with the comforters: "to the end he always stayed in his cursed obstinacy," we read in the registry, "his brain and intellect traversed by a thousand errors and vanities." On the other hand, Celestino's life ends in a sort of stunned silence that he maintained all the way to the scaffold, interpreted by the comforters as an expression of arrogance: "even so he always remained extremely obstinate, without however giving any reasons for his obstinacy but with arrogant presumption went on this way persevering until he was led to Justice before dawn in Campo di fiore." Perhaps that silence is the reason for the missing indication of paternity, which was customarily specified in the journal of the archconfraternity alongside the name of the prisoner they had assisted.[39]

The San Giovanni Decollato journal further reports that the members of the confraternity celebrated the final Mass for Celestino "in his absence."

Another mystery: the celebration of the Eucharistic sacrifice by the chaplain actually required the presence of the condemned prisoner who was to be accompanied to his death. The rules of the archconfraternity precisely prescribe the physical positions that the condemned could take during the three masses planned for his benefit: if the subject's behavior was edifying, he attended while standing; in the opposite case, he could remain lying on a mat, consoled by confetti and drink. During the mass a collection was taken for the victim and his relatives.[40]

As we already know, the comforters were required to make every effort to secure the prisoner's conversion, uninterruptedly and up to the last instant of the condemned man's life. For this reason it is inexplicable that the celebration of the death mass for Celestino would have taken place in the absence of its only potential beneficiary, even if he was unrepentant and obstinately muted in silence.

The journal of San Giovanni Decollato also proves another anomaly involving the execution of Celestino da Verona, one which has never been the subject of historians' attention. According to the confraternity's records, the Veronese Capuchin was delivered to the comforters in the prisons of Corte Savella. Thus the arrangements for delivering the condemned to the comforters directly contravened the aforementioned decree of the Congregation of the Holy Office of September 2, in which the pope personally ordered that Celestino remain in the prisons of the Holy Office until the moment he was taken to Campo de' Fiori (*Sanctissimus D.N. ordinavit quod sententia contra eum legatur in S. Officio ac tradatur locumtenenti R.P.D. Gubernatoris; religiosi theologi accedant ad S. Officium pro eius conversione, ac postea a carceribus S. Officii ducatur ad locum iustitiae et exequatur in Campo Flore*[41]).

The delivery of Celestino to the Secular Arm, although not in the direct form specified by the inquisitorial decrees, is today further proven by the registry of the Tribunale del Governatore of Rome, recently discovered and published by Michele Di Sivo and Orietta Verdi.[42] The record of the friar's delivery to the Secular Arm at Corte Savella is dated September 16: between sundown on the 15th and dawn on the 16th, according to our calendar, after the long meeting with the comforters that the registries of the Archconfraternity date on September 15, and which was therefore under the jurisdiction of the Holy Office.

Someone, violating the strict decree of Clement VIII, had Celestino transported to Corte Savella, a prison considerably farther from the palazzo of the Holy Office than Tor di Nona and Castel Sant'Angelo. Here, within the prison chapel, the friar met the comforters who would accompany him to Campo de' Fiori, after his extraordinary delivery to the Secular Arm *in extremis*.

Now we must find out why this transfer took place and who could have authorized it, in defiance of the will of the pontiff.

Let us review the known elements of the final weeks of Celestino da Verona's life.

On May 6, 1599 the friar sent a request from San Severino Marche to appear before the Congregation of the Holy Office. The supreme inquisitors summoned him at the end of the so-called *feria quinta* weekly meeting,[43] with the pope in attendance: this demonstrates that his request had aroused special attention in Rome.

On June 20 the inquisitor of Venice received an anonymous letter, which someone attributed to Celestino. On July 8 the letter was subjected to handwriting analysis by order of the pontiff, the outcome of which is unknown to us.

On July 9 and 11 the Veronese was subjected to two interrogations, the results of which were read in Congregation the day of the 15th "*per extensum.*" Just 20 days later, on August 5, without the official intervention of any other procedural elements except the accused's futile defense, Clement VIII himself decreed the imposition of the death sentence against the Veronese as a relapsed, unrepentant, and pertinacious heretic.

On August 24 – in the same session that saw the resumption of the hearing of the Giordano Bruno case, with Bellarmino reading the brief Bruno had delivered in April – the Congregation signed Celestino's death sentence. He was then executed at night, between September 15 and 16. Celestino was a heretic who had quickly abjured in his first trial of 1587, and had afterwards behaved in an opaque manner towards his Order and the highest pontifical and inquisitorial offices. His pertinacity supposedly translated, in the moment of extremity, into an absolute and tenacious ideological coherence. Celestino's dedication to his ideals was ostensibly such that he, among very few others in the early modern period, chose to refuse reconciliation with the Catholic faith – which would have normally allowed him to be decapitated before burning – paying for his choice with the terrible death of being burned alive at the stake.

The steps along the inquisitorial path that led to the sentencing of Celestino da Verona to the stake in 1599, decreed by Clement VIII personally, were therefore the defendant's request for a hearing (May 6), the discussion in the Congregation about the anonymous letter received by the inquisitor of Venice (July 8), the two interrogations carried out (July 9 and 11), the reading of the related depositions (July 15), the decision to sentence him to death (August 5), and the signing of the sentence (August 24). This is alongside elements – the defense on August 19, the call for the comforters, and the requirement for secrecy – that appear "minor," but are quite relevant regarding a judgement for capital punishment. At the time of the depositions of July 9 and 11 the Capuchin was already incarcerated at Rome.

First of all, we can see that these timeframes are completely irreconcilable with what we know of the style and ordinary procedures adopted by the tribunals of the Roman Inquisition. It is certain that the Congregation did not have enough time, between July and August 1599, to prepare a proper *ex novo* and *ex officio* proceeding against Celestino da Verona. Even considering Celestino's prior history, this is the only canonical procedure that could have led to such a serious sentence.

Neither can one suppose that the activity in those months was the late consummation of the outcome of the friar's Venetian trial in 1592. On the one hand, as has been argued above, according to the current state of the documentation that trial was not formally completed; on the other hand, it is unrealistic that the death sentence in 1599 was the result of the friar's spontaneous appearance for reasons of conscience in the context of a Venetian trial that was never concluded. If Celestino really had presented himself in Rome in 1599 with the intention of getting himself sentenced to death in order to settle his accounts with the Inquisition and God, in the end he would have accepted reconciliation with the Catholic Church and, taking communion, would not have faced the torment of the stake. In this case, moreover, there would still be no explanation for the secrecy imposed on the last weeks of life and the execution of the accused, nor for the anonymous letter sent to the inquisitor of Venice, nor, on the canonical level, for the imposition of the death sentence as a pertinacious heretic on someone who had recently also appeared *sponte comparens.*

On the formal level, Celestino's sentencing as a relapsed heretic must have been imposed based on elements that emerged from the two letters written between May and June, and from the depositions released on July 9 and 11, 1599. More precisely, since everything that happened after July 11, from what we know from the *Decreta* of the Holy Office, was none other than an unstoppable race towards the death sentence, it was clearly the events of July 8–11 that constitute the point of no return for the case.

Therefore we should focus on the events of those months to try and understand what led to that sentence. Likewise, we should not forget that while these events were developing during the weeks between the beginning of April and end of August 1599, the trial of Giordano Bruno had again come to a halt: the hard to explain period between Bruno's delivery of the brief from prison on April 5 and the later reading of the same, in the Congregation of August 24.

A truly curious coincidence.

Notes

1 S. Ricci, *Giordano Bruno nell'Europa del Cinquecento*, cit., pp. 534–536 has observed:

> It is striking that while Bruno's case seems to be headed for its conclusion, presumably with a complete abjuration, one of his main accusers is taken out of circulation. [...] If Celestino left the scene, and the Bruno trial, with a sinister and sudden change of fate, the [...] disturbing coincidence with the last phase of the Bruno case does not, however, demonstrate definite connections with the latter's end.

In his entry dedicated to Bruno in the *Dizionario storico dell'Inquisizione* Ricci again recalls the curious chronological overlap of the execution of Celestino da Verona and what was perhaps the crucial day for Bruno's fate: "On September 10, [1599, Bruno] stated that he was ready to abjure. On the 16th a note on the subject was read in court. That same night the Capuchin Celestino da Verona was burned at the stake" (Id., *Dizionario storico dell'Inquisizione*, cit., vol. I, *ad vocem*).

2 For more information on the many functions of the "Cardinal Protectors" of religious orders in the Roman Curia of the 16th century, see M. Firpo, G. Maifreda, *L'eretico che salvò la Chiesa*, cit., pp. 742 ff.

3 «[Causa] fratris Celestini de Verona, professi ordinis minorum capuccinorum, carcerati et inquisiti in S. Officio Inquisitionis Veronensis [*this is almost certainly a handwriting error for:* Venetiarum] [note by Luigi Firpo]: examinetur Generalis eius ordinis an unquam penes ipsum et eius religionem fuit inquisitus dictus frater Celestinus; deinde, datis defensionibus, torqueatur arbitrio»: see *Processo*, 140. This document is examined in depth in G. Maifreda, *Giordano Bruno e Celestino da Verona*, cit., pp. 89 ff., advancing the hypothesis that the amendment proposed by Firpo is not necessary, and that the decision correctly refers to the Inquisition of Verona. The decree also does not appear in the official series of the *Decreta*, but does in some minutes of the notary Flaminio Adriani, conserved today in ACDF, So, *Decreta* 029, fascicolo 1, fol. 310 *r–v*.

4 See J. Tedeschi, *The Prosecution of Heresy*, cit., pp. 141–145, also for an analysis of the various cases in which torture was employed.

5 On the term after which the court could reconsider the inquisitorial sentences of perpetual imprisonment that were not considered irremissible, see ivi, p. 147.

6 Regarding the first orientation, see J. Tedeschi, *Il giudice e l'eretico*, cit., pp. 151–152. The famous manual by E. Masini, *Sacro arsenale*, cit., only distinguished between relapsed and not, effectively combining those who had abjured *de vehementi* and *de formali*, both formulas that demanded reconciliation (see for example p. 283, chapter LXVI: "He is presumed to be relapsed, who after having abjured the heresy, receives, leads, visits and accompanies heretics and converses with them"; p. 288, chapter LXXXIII: "He, who falls in to only one heresy, [must] abjure no less than all of it: and thus, if afterwards he falls in another heresy, he must be judged relapsed"; p. 318, chapter CXCVIII: "Aware that the relapsed, whether convinced or confessed, must be given to the secular arm without hearing him, except when he denies being relapsed, and demands to be heard, there is no need to cite him in the sentence").

7 *Processo*, 126, note 5.

8 «Sanctissimus mandavit fieri diligentiam pro reperiendo autore dictarum litterarum per comparationem scripturae, et apud superiores Cappuccinorum, nec non ex scripturis eiusdem fratris Celestini in processu» (ivi, 126, note 6).

9 Ivi, 126, note 7.

10 According to Luigi Firpo, ivi, 45.

11 Ivi, 126, note 10.

12 See Massimo Firpo, *La fase difensiva del processo inquisitoriale del cardinal Morone: documenti e problemi*, in «Critica storica», XXIII, 1986, pp. 121–148, now in Id., *Inquisizione romana e Controriforma*, cit., pp. 371–398.

13 «Circa modum traditionis curiae saecularis fiat verbum coram Sanctissimo» (*ibidem*). Cases of failure to deliver a prisoner to the Secular Arm are recorded in the Republic of Venice, where, as has been discussed, members of a State magistracy took part in inquisitorial trials: thanks to Andrea Del Col for the clarifications in this regard.

14 See V. Lavenia, *Eretici sentenziati e 'reincorporati'*, cit., pp. 153–187, citation from p. 162.

15 *Processo*, 127, note 11 («religiosi theologi accedant ad S. Officium pro eius conversione, ac postea a carceribus S. Officii ducatur ad locum iustitiae et exequatur in Campo Flore»).

16 *Ibidem*.

17 On the detailed informational quality and reliability of the informer from Urbino, with reference to the years we are dealing with, see for example, Artemio Enzo Baldini, *Puntigli spagnoleschi e intrighi politici nella Roma di Clemente VIII. Girolamo Frachetta e la sua relazione del 1603 sui cardinali*, Milan, FrancoAngeli, 1981.

18 Transcribed from BAV, Urb. Lat. 1067, fols. 571*r*–*v* e 592*r*; the first publication was the work of Luigi Amabile, *Fra Tommaso Campanella. La sua congiura, i suoi processi e la sua pazzia*, tome I, Naples, Antonio Morano editore, 1882, p. 69, note a.

19 Brulart de Sillery arrived in Rome April 19, 1599 (see Maximilien de Béthune duc de Sully, *Les oeconomies royales*, edited by David Buisseret, Bernard Barbiche, t. II, *1595-1599*, Paris, Société de l'histoire de France- Klincksieck, 1970–..., 1988, p. 259).

20 As is pointed out by G. Romeo, *Aspettando il boia*, cit., pp. 178 ff. On the "great spectacle of death by the path of justice," see also A. Prosperi, *Morire volentieri: condannati a morte e sacramenti*, in *Misericordie*, cit., pp. 3–70, citation from p. 4.

21 Cited from S. Ricci, *Il sommo inquisitore*, cit., p. 46, translation by the Author. *Pro confutatione articulorum et haeresum recentiorum Haereticorum et pseudo-apostolorum, ex Utriusque Testamenti textu decerpta*, which remained a manuscript, was written by Santori in 1552.

22 The document has been published by G. Romeo, *Aspettando il boia*, cit., pp. 284–285, note 19. The essay masterfully reveals the different public functions of executions:

> Around the scaffold would be built, before and after the execution, many dense plots. A crowd of minor figures pressed in close to the protagonists, carefully observing reactions and attitudes, taking sides for or against them, and tried to insinuate itself in the contradictions that at times would open in the system of the ceremonies, or to bend them to other uses, or to express sentiments and emotions, or to help the condemned to save themselves.
>
> (ivi, pp. 178–179)

See also Carlo De Frede, *Autodafé ed esecuzionidi eretici a Roma nella seconda metà del Cinquecento*, in «Atti dell'Accademia pontaniana», 1990, n. XXXVIII, pp. 271–311 and Id., *Ancora sugli autodafé in Italia durante il Cinquecento. Addenda et corrigenda*, in «Atti dell'Accademia pontaniana», 1997, n. XLV, pp. 53–85, now in Id., *Religiosità e cultura nel Cinquecento italiano*, cit., pp. 297–343 and 345–378.

23 S. Ricci, *Giordano Bruno nell'Europa del Cinquecento*, cit., p. 546. The reliability of the information reported by the "notice" has been questioned in several quarters. For another case, that of Camillo Regoli from Faenza, sentenced to death in 1559, to whom a "muzzle" was affixed, see C. De Frede, *Ancora sugli autodafé in Italia*, cit., p. 355.

24 ASFi, *Mediceo del Principato*, filza 3623, un-numbered pages, p. 2*v* of the letter dated September 24, 1599, capitalized in the original. The passage, with some differences compared to my edition, was published by L. Amabile, *Fra Tommaso Campanella*, cit., p. 69, note a, with the date erroneously given as September 27, 1599, by Domenico Orano, *Liberi pensatori bruciati in Roma dal XVI al XVIII secolo. Da documenti inediti dell'Archivio di Stato in Roma*, Rome, Tipografia dell'Unione cooperativa, 1904, p. 86.

25 The agreement of the three sources on the lay status of the person who was burned at the stake in Rome between September 15 and 16, 1599 was, however, accepted by one of the major historians of the Roman Church, Ludwig von Pastor, who reconstructed: "a heretic, dressed as a Capuchin, was executed in September 1599": *Storia dei papi nel periodo della Riforma e restaurazione cattolica*, vol. XI: *Clemente VIII (1592-1605)*, Rome, Desclée & C., 1958, p. 467.

26 Various examples of the laicization of clerics at Rome in the second half of the 16th century, often at the end of a process guided by Santori, then condemned to perpetual imprisonment or the galleys, are listed in S. Ricci, *Il sommo inquisitore*, cit., p. 64.

27 See the entry by Armando Petrucci in *Dizionario biografico degli italiani*, cit., vol. 1, 1960. A summary examination of the bishop's writings conserved in BAV has unfortunately not brought out information that directly involves our story; see, however, in the «Relatione di quanto ha trattato il Vescovo di Sidonia nella sua missione in Oriente data alla Santità di Nostro Signore Sisto V a 19 aprile 1587», in BAV, Vat. Lat. 841, the references to the "heresies and main errors of the Jacobin nation" (fol. 394*v*), as well as Armenians (fol. 409*r*) and Nestorians (fol. 418*v*) as well as the letters sent by the cardinal of Santa Severina "protector of this Armenian Nation" (fol. 404*r*). A few months later the bishop will baptize five Jews in Saint Peter's "where a great number of people gathered": see the *Avviso* now in BAV, Urb. Lat. 1068, fol. 73*r*, dated January 22, 1600, but refers to the previous Sunday.

28 Transcribed from ASR, *Camerale I*, 1843, fol. 22*r*, I diverge from A. Bertolotti, *Martiri del libero pensiero e vittime della santa Inquisizione nei secoli XVI, XVII e XVIII*, Rome, Tipografia delle Mantellate, 1891 [anastatic reprint by Sala Bolognese, Forni, 1976], p. 110, which reads the date as March 16 (the graphic sign is however to be read "as above," as is made clear by the placement of the two mandates between releases of March 14 and 16); the correct date is reported in *Processo*, doc. 74, p. 356.

29 ASR, *Camerale I*, 1842, fol. 116*v*. Also in this case I diverge from Bertolotti, who transcribes completely erroneously: "1599 8bre To monsignor bishop of Sidonia for compensation for the laicization of Friar Celestino da Verona, a Capuchin, decapitated, *scudi* 2 *baj*[*occhi*] 50."

30 *Ibidem*. For the same payment relative to the January-March 1599 trimester, see for example, ASR, *Camerale I*, 1842, fol. 56*v*.

31 As specified for example by the *Summae theologicae scolasticae et moralis* of the Franciscan Guglielmo Herincx, Antverpiae, apud Petrum Bellerum, 1672, second edition, p. 362, col. 2.

32 Ivi, paragraphs 23–25, p. 156.

> [...] presentibus dictis episcopis, vel dignitatibus in ecclesia publica, vel capella privata assistit indutus omnibus vestimentis, a quo paulatim auferuntur per episcopum, cum certis verbis in caeremoniali postis, ultimo aufertur planeta, dicendo auferimus tibi vestem sacerdotalem, et honore sacerdotali privamus; et ultimo raditur ei caput, ita ut nullum coronae remaneat vestigium, et digiti, et manus (ubi positum fuit chrisma) raduntur, et indutus veste saeculari, traditur Curiae saeculari, ut morti damnetur.

33 See, for example, what is reported in l'*Examen episcoporum et eorum qui approbandi sunt ad administranda sacramenta* di Jeronimo Venero de Leyva, Panormi, apud Ioannem Baptistam Maringum, 1627, chapter XXII, *De degradatione*, paragraph 18, p. 155, cited from here. Among the many canonical treatises of the early modern era that dwell on the subject of laicization, one can also cite Chérubin Mayr, *Trismegistus Juris pontifici universi seu Institutiones canonicae*, t. IV, Augustae Vindelicorum et Oeniponti, sumpibus Josephi Wolf bibliopolae, 1751: «Degradatio celebranda dicitur seculari potestate presente, ad pronuntiandum eidem, cum fuerit celebrata, ut in suum forum recipiat degradatum, et sic intelligitur tradi curae seculari» (paragraph 255, p. 142).

34 ASR, *San Giovanni Decollato*, vol. 16, fols. 68*v*–69*r*. I differ slightly from the edition by D. Orano, *Liberi pensatori bruciati in Roma*, cit. (anastatic reprinting Livorno, U. Bastogi editore, 1971), pp. 86–87.

35 See G. Romeo, *Aspettando il boia*, cit., fols. 165 ff. and Adriano Prosperi, *Il sangue e l'anima. Ricerche sulle compagnie di giustizia in Italia*, in «Quaderni storici», XVII, 1982, n. 3, pp. 959–999. The bibliography on the company of justice is now very broad, as can be inferred from *The Art of Executing Well: Rituals of Execution in Renaissance Italy*, edited by Nicholas Terpstra, Kirksville MO, Truman State University Press, 2008. On the supplying of drinks to the condemned, called for even during the final mass, see Carlo C. Fornili, *Delinquenti e carcerati a Roma alla metà del '600. Opera dei papi nella riforma carceraria*, Rome, Editrice pontificia università gregoriana, 1991, p. 189.

36 See *supra*, p. 166.

37 See A. Prosperi, *Morire volentieri*, cit., p. 37 and R. Romeo, *Aspettando il boia*, cit., p. 146. The exceptional nature of death at the stake has recently been reiterated by Adriano Prosperi in *Delitto e perdono. La pena di morte nell'orizzonte mentale dell'Europa cristiana. XIV-XVIII secolo*, Turin, Einaudi, 2013, pp. 292–293.

38 Tomás A. Mantecón Movellán, *La Ciudad Santa y el martirio de los criminales: justicia e identidad urbana en la Roma moderna*, in *Historia, cultura, violencia. Actas do X Curso de primavera, Lugo, 22-25 de abril de 2014*, edited by Fernando Suárez Golán, Ana Cabana Iglesia, Santiago de Compostela, Universidade de Santiago de Compostela, 2015, p. 133.

39 Many names of those sentenced that appear in the registries of San Giovanni Decollato from the same era, even if not all of them, are accompanied by paternity: see for example the editions given by D. Orano, *Liberi pensatori bruciati in Roma*, cit., *passim*.

40 Regarding the necessity for the nocturnal mass attended also by the condemned, see also V. Paglia, *La morte confortata*, cit., p. 119.

41 *Processo*, 127, note 11.

42 M. Di Sivo, O. Verdi, *Bruno e Celestino da Verona*, cit., pp. 519–527:

> Iovis xvi septembris 1599. Pro Fisco contra fratrem Celestinum de Verona, ordinis fratrum cappuccinorum sancti Francisci subdiaconum, pro criminibus heresis et tamquam per Officium sanctissime Inquisitionis condemnatum et Curie reverendissimi domini alme urbis Gubernatoris tamquam Curie secularis traditum, et in carcere Curie de Sabellis transportatum et carceratum. [...].
>
> (p. 527)

43 The original decree is presented this way: «[In causa] Fratris Celestini da Verona ordinis cappuccinorum, lectis literis F Sti Severini 6a Maij, decreverunt quod veniat ad Sanctum Officium, et deponat quae sibi occurrunt. F datis in Civitate». The notary's insertion is clear, through the symbol "F," from the reference to the location of San Severino Marche, in order to clear up the misunderstanding involving Cardinal Santa Severina. The presence of the pontiff is proven by the phrasing «coram [deleted: Illustrissimus Dominis] Sanctissimum Domini Nostri» (ACDF, So, *Decreta* 037, fol. 679 of the recent numbering).

References

Luigi Amabile, *Fra Tommaso Campanella. La sua congiura, i suoi processi e la sua pazzia*, tome I, Naples, Antonio Morano editore, 1882.

The Art of Executing Well: Rituals of Execution in Renaissance Italy, edited by Nicholas Terpstra, Kirksville, MO, Truman State University Press, 2008.

Artemio Enzo Baldini, *Puntigli spagnoleschi e intrighi politici nella Roma di Clemente VIII. Girolamo Frachetta e la sua relazione del 1603 sui cardinali*, Milan, FrancoAngeli, 1981.

Antonino Bertolotti, *Martiri del libero pensiero e vittime della santa Inquisizione nei secoli XVI, XVII e XVIII*, Rome, Tipografia delle Mantellate, 1891 [anastatic reprint by Forni, Sala Bolognese, 1976].

Maximilien de Béthune duc de Sully, *Les oeconomies royales*, edited by David Buisseret, Bernard Barbiche, t. II, *1595–1599*, Paris, Société de l'histoire de France-Klincksieck, 1970–…, 1988.

Carlo De Frede, *Autodafé ed esecuzionidi eretici a Roma nella seconda metà del Cinquecento*, in «Atti dell'Accademia pontaniana», 1990, n. XXXVIII, pp. 271–311.

Jeronimo Venero de Leyva, *Examen episcoporum et eorum qui approbandi sunt ad administranda sacramenta*, Panormi, CA, apud Ioannem Baptistam Maringum, 1627.

Carlo C. Fornili, *Delinquenti e carcerati a Roma alla metà del '600. Opera dei papi nella riforma carceraria*, Rome, Editrice pontificia università gregoriana, 1991.

Guglielmo Herincx, *Summae theologicae scolasticae et moralis*, Second ed, Antverpiae, apud Petrum Bellerum, 1672.

Tomás A. Mantecón Movellán, *La Ciudad Santa y el martirio de los criminales: justicia e identidad urbana en la Roma moderna*, in *Historia, cultura, violencia. Actas do X Curso de primavera, Lugo, 22–25 de abril de 2014*, edited by Fernando Suárez Golán, Ana Cabana Iglesia, Santiago de Compostela, Universidade de Santiago de Compostela, 2015, pp. 108–40.

Chérubin Mayr, *Trismegistus Juris pontifici universi seu Institutiones canonicae*, t. IV, Augustae Vindelicorum et Oeniponti, sumpibus Josephi Wolf bibliopolae, 1751.

Domenico Orano, *Liberi pensatori bruciati in Roma dal XVI al XVIII secolo. Da documenti inediti dell'Archivio di Stato in Roma*, Rome, Tipografia dell'Unione cooperativa, 1904.

Adriano Prosperi, *Il sangue e l'anima. Ricerche sulle compagnie di giustizia in Italia*, in «Quaderni storici," XVII, 1982, n. 3, pp. 959–999.

Adriano Prosperi, *Delitto e perdono. La pena di morte nell'orizzonte mentale dell'Europa cristiana. XIV-XVIII secolo*, Turin, Einaudi, 2013.

Ludwig von Pastor, *Storia dei papi nel periodo della Riforma e restaurazione cattolica*, vol. XI: *Clemente VIII (1592–1605)*, Rome, Desclée & C., 1958.

11 The Summer of 1599

In the second part of this volume we noted that the figure of Celestino da Verona emerged from the shadows between the second half of the 1580s and the early 1590s, a period in which relations between the papacy and the Capuchin Order experienced profound changes. The trial brought by the Venetian inquisitors against the Venetian Capuchins for magic and witchcraft, held in the same months that Bruno was being detained in the prisons of the Inquisition, is wholly an expression of a murky background in the monasteries, protected by the last margins of jurisdictional autonomy guaranteed to the religious Orders. Measures taken by Clement VIII – a pontiff radically suspicious of the forms of monastery life –would erode this autonomy in the last decade of the 16th century.

As shown by the evidence that emerges in the Venetian trial against the Capuchins in 1592, and as suggested by the slowdown of the canonization process for Felice da Cantalice after the death of Sixtus V, the effort by the papacy and the Holy Office to create a model of Capuchin orthodoxy – through the protector of the Order, the cardinal of Santa Severina – was therefore destined to fall apart in the following decade.

The tensions that ran between the Capuchins and the Venetian Inquisition in the early 1590s stood out in an ecclesiastical and legal landscape by now destined for profound change. The Order, by will of the pope, had to set up procedures of internal justice and tools of investigation similar to those of the episcopal and inquisitorial tribunals – trials, imprisonment, torture – which brought about the definitive alignment of the Capuchins with Roman directives, along the lines laid out by the Canons and Decrees of the Council of Trent.

All this can explain the strict punctuality with which Celestino da Verona's superiors, between 1592 and 1594, tried to break up his ambiguous relations with some inquisitors, the purposes of which were unclear. The Capuchin continued to be empowered for some time by favors guaranteed to him by figures such as Santa Severina, who extended the previous regime of *ad personam* protections and mediation as part of a precise project of propagandistic re-creation of the reputation and memory of the Order. This

DOI: 10.4324/9781003026082-15

was while the Clementine reforms advanced, promoted by a pontiff who had never made any secret of being the "mortal enemy of the friars."[1]

For the remainder of the 1590s – while the trial of Giordano Bruno was underway, the key witness in which was a Capuchin from the much discussed Veronese monastery, who, as many in the Curia well knew, had been involved in ambiguous relations with inquisitors in past years – the pontificate of Clement VIII kept its guard up regarding relations between the Capuchins and the Inquisition. Indirect evidence of this is provided by a letter of May 28, 1599, written by Father Domenico da Costa, already a Provincial and at the time, as definitor of the Province of the Veneto, a very senior figure (just below the provincial himself).

Da Costa was also Procurator of the tribunal of the Capuchin Order. The holder of this office, also called the Procurator General, had the job of handling the general problems of the Capuchins, their provincials, or of individual friars. He worked in dialogue with the Roman Congregations and with the Cardinal Protector of the order, the cardinal of Santa Severina. The Procurator also made decisions when there were petitions to be forwarded to the pontiff or the curial congregations, maintaining correspondence with the various ecclesiastical and civil authorities.

In this capacity Da Costa requested information about the operation of the monastery in Verona and about the case of Vittore da Verona; once again, a friar who had complained about imprisonments and harassment he had suffered because of his relations with the local inquisitor. "Now it seems to me that he is saying that he was put in jail because he had been talking to the most reverend father inquisitor of Verona, which is completely false" we read in the response that came from Verona; "because we have the Holy Office deep in our heart, and in every place and we honor it, we are obedient to it; and to anyone that wants to go is given ease."[2] The almost palpable fear of the Veronese Capuchins of becoming seen as the protectors of heretics emerges clearly from these lines.

Can all this help us to explain what happened to Celestino da Verona in the summer of 1599? Could it involve the trial and decisions made in those same months by Giordano Bruno?

Movements behind the Scenes

Let us return for a moment to Venice. We have already seen[3] that the inquisitor who initiated the Bruno trial, Gabriele da Saluzzo, was replaced by the Dominican friar Giovanni Vincenzo Maria Arrigoni, who was seated in 1595 and remained in office until August 1599, when Clement VIII named him bishop of Sibenik, in Dalmatia.[4] The news of this promotion had already circulated in 1597– we have already learned this as well – when the bishop holding the office at Sibenik, Vincenzo Bassi, appeared to be dying. However, he recovered his health, and Arrigoni – as mentioned previously – could only be consecrated as bishop when Bassi was relocated to the diocese of Andria on May 25, 1599.[5] We also noted that the inquisitor Arrigoni incidentally bore the same name and surname as Celestino da Verona.

Thus Giovanni Vincenzo Arrigoni, inquisitor of Venice, had been in line for promotion to be bishop of Sibenik since 1597. The near certainty that this would happen arrived in May 1599, with Bassi's relocation; in mid-August Arrigoni would then be officially elected by Clement VIII. These events therefore took place in precisely the months (May–August 1599) during which Celestino da Verona reappeared to voluntarily go to Rome, only to be sentenced to death by the pope.

That same summer there was movement within the Capuchin Order, in particular regarding the crucial office of court Procurator. In the summer of 1599 this sensitive assignment was taken on by Anselmo Marzati da Monopoli, nominated at the end of May by the general Chapter of the Order.[6] Marzati, who was part of the Aldobrandini household and deeply involved in the affairs of the Holy Office, became the symbol of the so-called Obedience to Rome in view of the Holy Year of 1600.[7] The Obedience – again by order of Clement VIII – was prefigured in the general decree of June 25, 1599 for the reform of the Regulars (*Nullus omnino*) which called for, among other things, regulating Capuchin access to the city of Rome during the Jubilee. This means that, based on the new rules, Celestino's journey to Rome between June and July 1599 had to be submitted for written, prior approval by the protector of the Order, a cardinal he knew very well: the cardinal of Santa Severina.[8]

The balances of power that affected decisive aspects of the strategy about to be implemented by Celestino da Verona – control of the Venice Inquisition and the Procura of the Order – were changing rapidly. Whatever he had wanted to achieve with his letter of May 6, 1599, which the Congregation responded to on June 3, decreeing "*quod veniat ad S. Officium, et deponat quae sibi occurrunt*,"[9] the friar had to move quickly.

In May 1599 Celestino da Verona requested a spontaneous appearance in Rome. He was then arrested, interrogated, tried, and convicted. In this stereotypical series of events, the sequence of which could be trivialized by a director who influenced the contents of the *Decreta*, one stage stands out as unusual. This is the anonymous letter written by the Capuchin to Arrigoni, the inquisitor of Venice, which was sent at the end of June and debated in Congregation on July 8.

The anonymous letter is the only element of the trial that has any merit among those mentioned by the *Decreta*; the only non-stereotypical piece of a skeletal mosaic, illustrating the last months of Celestino's life from his spontaneous appearance to the death sentence. Mention of the letter is not neutral: the leaders of the Holy Office wanted the information about the anonymous letter to remain permanently in the records, to justify their actions and appear to posterity as one of the fundamental procedural steps. According to the known facts, this was indeed the factor that gave rise to the convulsive steps that followed: thus it had to be mentioned explicitly in the decrees. On the formal level, it must have been the letter – and not the request of May 6, whose only effect was the summons to the Holy Office of June 3 – that sparked the resolve of the pope and the inquisitors. What followed was the offender's arrest, his depositions of July 9 and 11, the death sentence and his execution.

Let us read the decree that emerged from the meeting of the Congregation of the Holy Office on July 8, 1599; when, in the presence of the pope, there was discussion about the anonymous letter sent by Celestino da Verona to the inquisitor of Venice:

> [Causa] Fratris Celestini da Verona cappuccini lecta copia literarum [added with the insertion of a V: «ab ipso ut creditur»] scriptarum 20 junii Inquisitori Venetiarum, Sanctissimus mandavit fieri diligentia pro reperiendo autore literarum, per comparationem scripturae, et apud superiores cappuccinorum nec non ex scripturis eiusdem fratris Celestini in processu.[10]
>
> [In the case] of the Capuchin friar Celestino da Verona a copy was read of the letter [added with the insertion of a V: "believed to be by him"] written on June 20 to the inquisitor of Venice. The pope has ordered that the author of the letter be identified through a handwriting analysis to be conducted with the Capuchin superiors and the writings of Celestino himself in the trial.]

The notation "*ab ipso ut creditur*" was added at a later time, when the notary of the Holy Office had already written the definitive version of the decree. The writer, re-reading the resolution made in a meeting in which he almost certainly had not participated, drawn up based on notes made by others,[11] noticed that the text illogically attributed certain authorship to an anonymous letter for which there was going to be an examination "*per comparationem scripturae*." An anonymous letter could not be attributed to Celestino da Verona in the context of a decree that aimed at identifying the author by ordering a handwriting analysis. The notary thus believed that he was preserving the logical-legal coherence of the decree by his ad hoc addition of the doubtful formula "*ab ipso ut creditur*."

The pontiff and the other members of the Congregation were therefore certain – we do not know on what basis – that the anonymous letter addressed in the session of June 8, 1599 had been written by Celestino da Verona. The fact that the decree in question was left in the *Decreta* series preserved today demonstrates that the tribunal did not feel the need to go back and modify the record, nor did any subsequent decree deny the attribution of the letter contained in the document of June 8. For the Holy Office and for posterity, the letter in question therefore officially remained (and remains) listed under the name of the Veronese friar. The supreme inquisitors, however, required a legally valid certification attesting to the missive's authorship to invoke in the procedure in progress, which would quickly lead to the imposition of the death sentence.

How is it possible, the notary of the Holy Office must have asked that July 1599, that the anonymous letter directed to the inquisitor of Venice could be ascribed to Celestino da Verona before the handwriting analysis was available? If elements such as the penmanship, the writing materials or the language, or the contents of the letter itself made its attribution certain, why order the handwriting examination? And if, on the contrary, the attribution was not certain, why was the letter immediately placed in the *Decreta* under Celestino's name, with the awkward later insertion of "*ut creditur*"?

The entire situation is illogical: a *catch 22* with only two ways out.

The first way out, simpler in appearance, is that the form and/or content of the letter included elements which could unequivocally be recognized as Celestino's work, but that this attribution was not legally unassailable. In that case, the Congregation could have resolved to ask the Capuchin superiors – almost certainly Anselmo Marzati, the court Procurator who had a privileged relationship with the Aldobrandini family – for a handwriting examination and a formal endorsement. All this while the officials of the Holy Office immersed themselves in the Archive, in search of examples of Celestino's writing "*in processu*": therefore from the Roman trial of 1586–1587 or the Venetian documentation of 1592–1593.

However, accepting this hypothesis would leave a considerable set of inconsistencies to work out: how is it possible that someone in the papal Curia knew the Veronese friar so well as to be able to detect familiar elements in an anonymous letter addressed to the inquisitor of Venice? How could Celestino da Verona, who was also not illiterate, have made the naïve mistake of leaving tracks that could clearly identify him in a letter that was intended to be anonymous? Why would Arrigoni, the inquisitor of Venice, have felt the need to send a copy of a simple anonymous letter to the Congregation of the Holy Office, which then judged it to be so important that it should be discussed in the presence of the pope? And, most of all, why would the *sponte comparens* Celestino da Verona have sent an anonymous communication to the judge of the faith of the Serenissima, when the cardinals of the Holy Office had already agreed to hear him in Rome?

The second possible way out of this *catch 22* is that the pontiff and the inquisitors *wanted* the anonymous letter to be from the hand of Celestino da Verona. Or rather that they had used a letter written by someone else, attributing it, for the purposes of the trial, to the Capuchin; or even that they themselves had prepared an anonymous letter addressed to the inquisitor of Venice, perhaps through the "*superiores cappuccinorum*," working based on the same documents in which the handwriting was later found. In this way they would have manufactured evidence against the friar which for some reason could not be signed: perhaps because the tone of the letter implied its anonymity or maybe because the falsification of the signature would have been detectible through the handwriting analysis which at that point would be legally necessary.

This second hypothesis would explain both the certainty of the attribution made before the handwriting analysis as well as the rapidity of the accused's arrest. The day after the inquisitor of Venice received the letter, July 9, Celestino was already being interrogated as a prisoner in the palazzo of the Holy Office.

Accepting this hypothesis we can also identify a reason why the depositions were made secret, and why the pope ordered everyone involved not to talk about the trial in any way. Perhaps Celestino had unequivocally denied authorship of the letter during the interrogations; perhaps it was not even contested, only to then be used as a device in the sentence, which has not survived.

The hypothesis of the forgery of a crucial trial document by the Congregation of the Holy Office in these decades is far from unrealistic: Vittorio Frajese has claimed that the so-called "Seghizzi precept," the notarial document of 1616 that is the foundation of the sentence suffered by Galileo in 1633, is a forgery, assembled by the officials of the Holy Office in order to demonstrate the recidivism of the scientist in propagandizing Copernican theories.[12]

Let us try to attack the problem of attributing the authorship of the anonymous letter written by Celestino da Verona to the inquisitor of Venice by looking at it from another perspective.

The writer of the Holy Office's decree of July 8, 1599 states with certainty that the letter to the inquisitor of Venice, for which there was a handwriting analysis, had been written on June 20: "*litterarum* [...] *scriptarum 20 iunii proxime praeteriti Inquisitori Venetiarum*." We must take the decree literally: the Venetian judge Giovan Vincenzo Arrigoni received, between the end of June and the beginning of July, an anonymous letter which was known to have been written on June 20. That day, June 20, 1599 was in fact a Sunday, a day when postal service was not active, even in the secular Republic of Venice. Mail day was always Saturday in summertime and Thursday in winter. It is therefore very unlikely that "*scriptarum 20 iunii*" referred to the date the letter was received by the inquisitor.[13]

The account books of the Congregation of the Holy Office for the year 1599, until now unexplored, record the list of days that mail from Venice to Rome was received in the summer of 1599. It looks like this:

2, 9, 16, 23, 30 June
7, 14, 21, 28 July
4, 11, 18, 24 August
1, 8, 15, 22, 29 September.

Letters traditionally took five days to travel from Venice to Rome. Looking at the payments "for the dispatch of the trial dossier and letters sent to this S. Offitio" that came from Venice we can also evaluate the physical size of what was sent, given that the cost of each parcel, paid for by the recipient, increased with weight. The Inquisition of Venice sent packages to the Congregation that were heavier than the usual weekly correspondence only on the following dates: February 4 and 18, August 18, November 4 and December 2, 1599. The cardinal of Santa Severina, who signed the expense manifests of the Roman Holy Office, would have authorized payments on those dates for, respectively, 4:45, 4:50, 3:85, 2:40, and again 2:40 *scudi*, while ordinary receipts cost less than one *scudo*.[14]

This shipping weight data seems to suggest that no envelope that was heavier than usual arrived for the Congregation from Venice before August 18, by which date the Capuchin's death sentence had already been decreed. This is obviously very thin evidence, and not sufficient to prove that the handwriting samples deposited on July 8 against Celestino could not have been taken from trial documents sent by the Serenissima.

The postal calendars do reveal another important piece of evidence with greater certainty. If the anonymous letter to the inquisitor of Venice had been written by Celestino on June 20 and immediately sent to Venice, we suppose from San Severino Marche, where the friar was still located on May 6, or from Rome, where he was imprisoned on July 9, it would normally have been received five days later in Venice: June 25.[15] It is completely unrealistic to think that it had been immediately sent by the tribunal of Venice to the Roman Congregation via the June 30 postal delivery, which left Venice on June 26. Given that it was an unsigned letter, no peripheral judge would have considered it necessary to bother the Supreme Inquisition before carrying out the appropriate verifications.[16] If we then assume that the inquisitor had urgently sent the anonymous letter to the Congregation of the Holy Office on July 3, it would not have reached Rome until the July 7 pickup. And even if this whole chain of improbable events took place, it is inadmissible to suppose that this letter was discussed just a day later on July 8, at the *feria quinta* meeting of the Holy Office, in the presence of the pope, with an already certain attribution to Celestino and orders for his immediate arrest.[17]

The available evidence converges around the hypothesis that the anonymous letter allegedly written and sent by Celestino da Verona to the inquisitor of Venice on June 20, 1599 was, in reality, the product of Roman manipulation. The protagonists may have included, in addition to Clement VIII and other members of the Congregation of the Holy Office, the "*superiores cappuccinorum*," behind which it is not hard to glimpse the tribunal Procurator Anselmo Marzato, who was very close to the Aldobrandini household or faction. Without Marzati's endorsement it would have been quite difficult to complete the arrest and trial a Capuchin friar, his special delivery to the Secular Arm, and his mysterious nocturnal execution in the heart of Rome with such unusual speed and secrecy. However, no traces of any information about this are to be found in the surviving documentation or in the tribunal Procurator's work reports for those years.[18]

Becoming a Bishop

At the end of the 16th century it was customary that candidates for the episcopate would go to Rome even before their election and ordination, to champion their cause and offer reliable witnesses. This was necessary to provide information to the preliminary processes carried out in the Apostolic Datary, the Consistorial Congregation and especially in the Congregation of Examination, which usually evaluated the candidacy of prospective bishops through direct interviews. In these years the examination of a candidate for bishop took place about a month before the actual nomination. During that period the Prelates of the Curia, including the consultors and other members of the administration of the Holy Office were also subject to examination.[19]

Normally another month passed between a pontifical nomination and the candidate's investiture as a bishop: the previously cited bishop of Sidone Abel, for example, was made a bishop by Gregory XIII on July 20, 1582 and consecrated by Santa Severina on August 19 of the same year. In those same years about a month separated the Congregation's examination and the provision of the title, both in the case of Guidoni from Mantua (July 29–August 26, 1595, when the office was granted to another ecclesiastic) and of Camillo di Scrivani (September 28–October 30, 1596). This span of time could be shortened or extended for several months by exception.[20]

The decisions of the Congregation of the Holy Office played a determining role in the selection of episcopal nominees, especially regarding areas such as Dalmatia – where Sibenik was located – which exposed the future ordinaries to continuous contact with heterodoxies and infidels. The cardinal inquisitors, *in primis* deacon Santa Severina, who regularly examined the cardinal-nephew Aldobrandini's diplomatic correspondence, exercised an effective preventive veto on the candidacies. Some aspirants to the episcopate were actually examined in the presence of the inquisitors: this happened in August 1598 to Sigismondo Donati, the archdeacon of Ascoli and candidate for the diocese of Venosa.[21]

In all probability the inquisitor of Venice, Giovan Vincenzo Arrigoni, also spent several weeks in Rome before his nomination as bishop on August 18. We also know with certainty that he remained in the city until at least September 22, when the Holy Office sent him back to work at the Venetian office without, for the moment, allowing him to take possession of the Dalmatian diocese.[22] Arrigoni's presence in Rome in the central months of 1599 coincides with the period that sees the reappearance, incarceration, and execution of Celestino da Verona. The summer of that year was therefore decisive, albeit for different reasons, for the life of the Capuchin and for the career of Dominican inquisitor of the same name, who in those months was at the center of the fragile web of relations that supported the nomination of Venetian ordinaries, moving between the Roman Curia, the Venetian ecclesiastical authorities and the government of the Serenissima with a succession of petitions, pressures, coercions and actual extortion.[23]

One can imagine that tangle of meetings and interviews, doubts, and assurances that worried Arrigoni during those middle months of 1599. Perhaps he prostrated himself before Clement VIII, who at the same time had ordered the examination of the anonymous letter attributed to Celestino da Verona, and who had glimpsed the end of the Bruno trial. Both of these trials also concerned the jurisdiction of the tribunal of the Venetian Holy Office, which was still led by Arrigoni. Santa Severina participated in both the Congregation of the Holy Office and that of the bishops and Regulars, so it is plausible that the inquisitor had met him.

Certainly the future bishop of Sibenik had spoken more than once with his relative Pompeo Arrigoni, who was a powerful inquisitor with offices that were in a position to determine the election of a bishop. Already a consistorial lawyer, Pompeo would soon become Datario. It was he who acted as a reference, in the Consistory of August 18, 1599, for the election of his family member to the bishopric of Sibenik; on that occasion he attested that the examination of the future bishop had been done in his presence, not failing to point out the candidate's merits as an inquisitor.[24]

It is difficult to imagine that during the many conversations between the Arrigonis in these months they never addressed the question of the Veronese who bore the same name. He had upset relations between the Capuchins and the Inquisition in the Venetian Republic in the early 1590s; he had also played a decisive role in the never-ending trial against Giordano Bruno. He had been moved with difficulty to the Marches, and was now in Rome for reasons that involved the Holy Office.

It is certain that Arrigoni would have personally discussed the mysterious anonymous letter sent to him by the heretic which had so shaken the pontiff. Or, perhaps, he had consented to its drafting, declaring himself willing to confirm its authenticity.

Life in Prison

The prisons of the majestic palazzo of the Holy Office of Rome, today in the territory of Vatican City, were the scene of the final acts in the lives of Giordano Bruno, Celestino da Verona, and many other unfortunates who were forced to renounce their religious and philosophical conceptions under threat of a horrible death.

The latest and final encounter between the philosopher and the Capuchin in the summer of 1599 also took place within those prisons. Now we will try to better understand the context in which the shrewdly dramatic, as we will see – and for Bruno certainly astonishing – reappearance of the hated Veronese friar took place. Understanding life within those cells a bit better could perhaps also help us to imagine the reactions and outcomes – that may have even affected the trial – which the unexpected reappearance of a virulent accuser might have provoked in the mind of a prisoner who had been confined for eight years. By then Bruno must certainly have been weakened by fatigue, harsh physical conditions, fear, and abandonment.

Previously we recalled that the primary function of prisons in the early modern age was not punishment but rather custody of the accused who was awaiting trial. Moreover, 16th century prisons were a potential source of profit for the contractors who managed them, such as the *birri*. The prison of Corte or Curia Savella, where the comforters of San Giovanni Decollato met Celestino da Verona on his last night alive, was situated adjacent to the Jewish Ghetto. The Tribunal of the Marshall of the Holy Roman Church had direct jurisdiction over it, an office that pontiffs had entrusted to the Savelli family since the Middle Ages. The prison of Tor di Nona, situated on the banks of the Tiber near Castel Sant' Angelo, instead depended directly on the Tribunal of the Governor, the most powerful magistracy in the city.[25] It was also used by the Diocesan (or vicar's) Tribunal and the Tribunal of the *Auditor camerae*. The jurisdiction of the tribunals that corresponded to the two prisons was originally based on an ancient division of the city into two large zones of authority. Normally, someone who was captured in the zone of Tor di Nona or of Corte Savella (or brought into Rome through gates located in one area or the other) had to be secured in the related prison.

To get an idea of the number of detainees in these prisons, we know that a visit in early February 1570 counted 136 people at Tor di Nona, divided in 13 rooms, while on November 29, 1640 57 detainees were registered at Corte Savella: 25 for criminal cases and 32 for civil cases.[26] The conditions of incarceration in Corte Savella were very harsh: Innocent X had the prison demolished in 1652, after an attempt at restoration that proved to be impossible due to the degree to which the space had decayed. Government correspondence of the mid-1600s, recalling the custodial function played by detentions, describes "the great anguish of the prison formerly known as Corte Savella, which was not equipped with courtyards, from which came such a stench, that it gave the poor prisoners more punishment than custody."[27]

The sinister fame of this prison is also owed to the fact that it hosted members of the Cenci family during their famous trial for patricide that took place in 1599. At the time the case was followed by the Roman population with enormous interest, and after the execution a genuine cult sprung up around the remains of the young Beatrice. The story of the trial was revived and narrated several times in the romantic style of the 19th century. The two brothers, Bernardo and Giacomo Cenci, their sister Beatrice and step-mother Lucrezia Petroni were imprisoned, interrogated, and tortured in Corte Savella, accused of having ordered the murder of the father and husband Francesco. The latter was the legitimate son of Count Cristoforo, the General Treasurer of the Camera Apostolica, from whom he had inherited a vast fortune.

The Cenci family's wealth probably played a more than secondary role in the trial and in the imposition of the sentence. Although the case was no more than an ordinary criminal proceeding from a legal point of view, Clement VIII assumed control of it himself, and on September 10, 1599 – a significant date for us – imposed the death penalty on all of the defendants. The awful public execution of Beatrice, Lucrezia and Giacomo Cenci took place the following day: a few days before the burning in which Celestino da Verona died. Only the younger brother Bernardo was pardoned at the last moment, by virtue of the impassioned defense of the most famous Roman lawyer of the time, Prospero Farinacci, who invoked both the boy's young age and mental infirmity as mitigating factors. However, young Bernardo was still forced to follow the procession to the scaffold, and from the platform witness the torture, public killing, and torment of the bodies of his family members. He was condemned to the oar in the papal galleys in perpetuity. The family's belongings were confiscated and sold at auction. Just a few months later, with a *motu proprio* in May of 1600, the pontiff authorized the sale of the Cenci estate, called Torrenova, with over 1,700 hectares of land, to his nephew Giovan Francesco Aldobrandini for 91,000 *scudi*, a sum less than a quarter of its actual value.[28]

The Cenci affair – because of the pope taking control of the sentencing as well as the crude theatricality of the execution he ordered – contributed to creating a climate of fearful apprehension in those months concerning the strict and perhaps equivocal ways in which Clement VIII and his family administered criminal justice. It is said that Caravaggio also attended the execution of the Cencis; he would later depict the terrible massacre in his canvas *Judith and Holofernes*.

In the face of the broad discretion granted to princes in the exercise of criminal justice, and the cruel spectacle of the sentences, testimonies concerning prison life in the old regime can appear reassuring and protective. However, as we have already said, the dignified forms of existence sometimes granted to prisoners in the early modern era are not to be considered an expression of a kind of "clemency" on the part of the secular or ecclesiastical tribunals that administered these prisons. Rather they were only the consequence of the preventive and not punitive function of incarceration. The prisons of the Roman Inquisition were above all specifically conceived as an instrument for conversion, as shown by, among other things, the rules that were in force during the years of Bruno and Celestino's imprisonment:

> In the first place the Captain is notified by the Office of the Inquisition being a Holy Office, and ordered for the health of the soul, and for this much different than other Tribunals, that he has to think of treating them with all secrecy, and to behave with all humanity with the people who are imprisoned, so that in this way they will be more easily made willing to convert, and it being our desire to achieve this, as must be done, it will be necessary to be very solicitous with them, vigilant and diligent, and not rely only on the work of the lower officials (because they are like mercenaries, and more dedicated to profit and so they can

> easily err) but will himself work to supervise, see, and consider things, like this, to which great importance is given, and who however will be always obliged to account for his actions, and those of his officials.[29]

The rules were very insistent about the responsibility and obligation for secrecy imposed on the Captain of the prisons, a title that belonged to the person who had a contract for services managing the prisons. Both he and his guards, "and all those, who help bring meals to the prisoners," had to

> first swear in the hand of the Father Commissioner before a Notary to be faithful, and secret with the Holy Office, and not to bring either certificates or delegates inside, nor outside [...] not things to eat, nor any other sort

without the order of the Commissioner himself. The penalty for offenders was being condemned to the papal galleys, as had been called for by the decrees of the Holy Office since 1573.

After each arrest, a careful search of the offender always fell to the Captain, along with the obligation to deliver money, writings and any other objects found in the prisoner's possession to be deposited with the notary. Monitoring of the employees who cleaned the prisons must have been intense, with orders that they would not dare "under the penalty of the galley, to send delegates to other prisoners or outside the prisons, or send certificates or writings." In the previously referred to case of Pietro Carnesecchi, the prisoner's desperate attempts to communicate with the outside were almost all intercepted in this way.[30]

Other things were just as strictly forbidden, such as "changing a prisoner from one prison to another" or giving them anything ("any commodity of fire, wood, tables, glasses, knives, paper, inkwell, nor other things") without the permission of the Commissioner, "with a penalty of three lashes of the rope and being stripped of the office." It was not permitted for the prisoners to speak with anyone "except about orders, and in the presence of the Father Commissioner." Doctors, barbers, and apothecaries always had to be accompanied in the jail by the Captain or the guards: these, in turn, could not "while in the prisons play, nor eat, nor in any way interact with the prisoners under penalty of three lashes of the rope and expulsion from the office." It was severely prohibited for anyone to accept gifts from the prisoners.

Every three days the contractors for the prisons of the Holy Office were required to

> sweep or have swept the floors and to clean the prisons, and empty the bedpans of the prisoners who do not have the convenience of a toilet, sweep all the stairs of the palazzo and courtyards, change the prisoners' *camisce* and sheets at the prescribed interval, which the Holy Office passes on for washing

the *camisce* were the obligatory uniforms for inmates. Prison employees were required to immediately report an inmate's illness, and to "treat the prisoners with charity, speaking nicely to them, and not insulting them, keeping them, however, as prisoners, as is customary in the Holy Office."

During the years of Celestino da Verona and Giordano Bruno's imprisonment, treatment regarding food was also, like the rest of their maintenance in prison, subject to strict dictates. These rules were established based on the contract that the Captain of the prisons signed when he obtained the position. For the period that interests us, the dietary regime was established in a rule that was set in August 1591 and renewed, in identical form, in August 1601. The Captain, Marco Tullio Valentini, here commits

> to purchase for the prisons good bread and one loaf of *Ripa* without water, and good, and at least a pound of meat a day for each one, and a *foglietta* (about a half liter) of wine with the meal, and to treat them with greater charity, which can be soups, salads and fruits; for these expenses the Holy Office promises to pay 4 *scudi* per month for each prisoner that is poor; but for those that are able to pay, the captain will take care to collect from them, and to get paid the proper 4 and a half *scudi* each month.[31]

The expense of four *scudi* for food, plus ten *baioccihi* for shaving by the barber, is recorded regularly with reference to all the prisoners of the Holy Office at the time. This included Giordano Bruno, who as a "poor" inmate was fed at the expense of the Holy Office during the over seven years of his imprisonment in Rome. The conventions signed by the Captain of the prisons also prescribed what food would be offered to the prisoners for solemn observances and fasts. The contractor had every interest in observing these rules, since any services provided in excess of what was stipulated would not be reimbursed by the Holy Office.

Inmates of means, a majority of whom were aristocrats, could buy supplementary food and the assistance of their servants. The costs of these supplements, which were paid by the inmate through his relatives or friends, were therefore not counted among the Holy Office's expenses. Even these privately paid for supplements were limited in their substance and in the forms of provision. "If some prisoner wants to pay for his own expenses," the contract states,

> the guardians are required to take the aforementioned food, which will be brought to him, and diligently inspect it, that there is no certificate nor other sign, must take it to the prisoner, and for such service the Captain must have a pound of meat per day for each prisoner who will pay expenses themselves, and to the aforementioned prisoner will be granted one, or more servants, and which in any case is a service that can only be done for the prisoners.[32]

However, the food provisions for wealthy inmates were also strictly monitored, in the fear that food coming from outside the palazzo of the Holy Office could be a means for attempts on the lives of the prisoners. A letter from the Congregation of August 1590, for example, enjoined a suburban inquisitor not to feed an inmate "things sent to him by some person outside, so that he was not poisoned."[33]

Finally, the Captain had to keep "a large book," and

> to note in it all the prisoners, and the day, month and year when they enter, and if it was before lunch or after lunch, and opposite the said notations to write all the money that was received from these prisoners, and from others on his behalf, or from the Holy Office.[34]

It is thanks precisely to this meticulous recordkeeping that we are able to discover another important clue.

Notes

1 See *supra*, p. 141.
2 *Acta ordinis. Tabulae capitulorum generalium fratrum Minorum cappuccinorum. I. 1529-1623*, edited by Vincenzo Criscuolo, Rome, Istituto storico dei Cappuccini, 2008, pp. 226–227.
3 See *supra*, p. 143.
4 ASVe, *Savi all'eresia (Sant'Ufficio)*, box 153, list of «Inquisitori domenicani», fol. 1*r*; the date is confirmed at other points in the disordered contents of the same box.
5 See *supra*, p. 144.
6 *Registrum Scripturarum della Procura generale dell'Ordine cappuccino 1599-1613*, cit., pp. 13–14.
7 The quote by Giuseppe Avarucci comes from the *Introduzione* to *Litterae circulares superiorum generalium ordinis fratrum minorum cappuccinorum (1548-1803)*, edited by Melchiorre da Pobladura, Rome, Istituto storico dei Cappuccini, 1960, pp. 5–59, p. 42.
8 The date usually reported for the decree *Nullus omnino* (March 20, 1601) is in reality that of a supplementary decree: see Carlo Bottero, *I conventuali riformati italiani, 1557-1670: vicende e insediamenti*, volume 2, Padua, Centro studi antoniani, 2008, p. 802. However, the author erroneously reports the date as July 25, 1599 (*ibidem*). The correct date is given by *Litterae circulares*, cit., p. 26, which takes if from *Bullarum Ordinis*, volume VI (1750), pp. 324–328. The correct date, along with a collection of the provisions ordered by Clement VIII for the reform of the Regulars from 1596 on, is also reported by Agostino Lauro, *Il costituzionalismo pregiannoniano nel Regno di Napoli. Problema e bibliografia (1563-1723)*, Rome, Edizioni di storia e letteratura, 1974, p. 106, note 2. Regarding Santa Severina's authorization, see the letter «De accessu sodalium religiosorum ad Urbem» of July 16, 1601:

> Veteris legislatores francescani accessum ad Urbem ordinaverant quoad itineris facultatem obtinendam. Ite Clemens VIII decretis pro reformatione regularium promulgatis statuerat die 25 iunii anni 1599 ut nullus sodalis religiosus Romam venire auderet nisi impetrata a superiore generali vel a cad. protectore [il Santa Severina] licentia in scriptis.
>
> (Litterae circulares, cit., p. 26)

9 *Processo*, 126, note 5.
10 ACDF, So, *Decreta*, 037, fol. 710 of the recent numbering, July 8, 1599. I diverge slightly from the transcription reported in *Processo*, 126, note 6.
11 As demonstrated by T.F. Mayer, The Roman Inquisition, cit., pp. 26–36.
12 See V. Frajese, *Il processo a Galileo Galilei*, cit.
13 After 1541 the postal trips between Venice and Rome were changed to an "ordinary" service, that is, with a set weekly schedule that gave the Venetians the advantage over the pontifical service, which was still based on occasional departures. There would be one departure per week on Thursdays in the winter, taking six days, and on Saturday in the summer, in four days. As early as 1550 in Venice the new nuncio, just arrived in his office and tired from the voyage and receptions, it being Saturday had to get to a "table"; he therefore apologized for not being able entertain his interlocutor by letter as he wished, "because today is Saturday and I have much to write." Correspondence also began to come to him from Rome on the Saturday post: "thinking that this has arrived to V.S. [...] I don't want to miss making a priority of the courtesy of writing them each Saturday." See Clemente Fedele, Mario Gallenga, *Per servizio di Nostro Signore. Strade, corrieri e poste dei papi dal Medioevo al 1870*, Prato, Istituto di studi storici postali, 1988, pp. 58 and 67. The same study illustrates the forms of postmarking letters at the moment of consignment by the sender and before, therefore, they are sent.
14 ACDF, *Oeconomica* 24, registro *Mandati 1597-1606*, p. 100*v*.
15 The time of five days is verifiable through various sources: see, for example, C. De Frede, *L'estradizione di Giordano Bruno da Venezia*, cit., pp. 408–409.
16 As already seen, the decree of 1581 still required the inquisitors to inform the Roman Congregation only in reference to "arduous" cases.
17 It is certainly possible to formulate some (mostly convoluted) hypotheses that allow reconciling the time frame of the friar writing a letter to the inquisitor of Venice on June 20 with a discussion of the same in Congregation on July 8. Perhaps the letter was never delivered, but rather intercepted when Celestino tried to send it to Venice from Rome. However, we know from the prison account books, which we will examine in greater detail later, that the Capuchin had not yet been imprisoned on that date. This would have immediately set the machinery in motion leading to discussion of the letter on July 8. However, this scenario makes it hard to explain the inquisitors' doubts about the authorship of the missive. It also does not explain why Celestino would have wanted to communicate anonymously with the inquisitor of Venice, exposing a conversation so compromising as to be grounds for a death sentence. Another idea is that Arrigoni, the recipient of the letter, could have already been in Rome at the end of June, and so could have immediately taken the letter to the Holy Office personally. However, this hypothesis fails to explain Celestino's motivations or his presumed knowledge of Arrigoni's presence in Rome, or why such an expert and prudent judge of the faith considered it proper to concern his superiors with an anonymous letter.
18 Miguel Gotor, author of the recent entry on Marzato, Anselmo for the *Dizionario biografico degli italiani*, cit., has graciously confirmed that he has not found references to Celestino da Verona in documents from the period and in the ancient and modern biographies on Marzato. A summary examination shows that not even the Historic Archive of the Aldobrandini family, to which I had access thanks to the family and the director Antonella Fabriani Rojas, seems to present documents related to the relationship between the Aldobrandini and the leaders of the Capuchin Order, nor documentation that can otherwise illuminate the events dealt with here.
19 On the characteristics of the information process for the nomination of bishops, defined as «instructio, examen et inquisitio» by the bull of 1591 by Gregory

XIV, which reformed its practices and entrusted the foreign investigations of the Curia to apostolic legates or nuncios, or to the candidate's ordinary or the neighboring ordinary, see l'*Introduzione* a *I processi informativi per la nomina dei vescovi di Trento nell'Archivio segreto vaticano (secoli XVII-XVIII)*, edited by Ugo Paoli, Bologna, Il Mulino, 2010, pp. 15–267, especially pp. 23–25.

20 See Armando Petrucci, *Abela, Leonardo*, in *Dizionario biografico degli italiani*, cit., volume I, 1960 and M.T. Fattori, *Clemente VIII e il Sacro collegio 1592-1605*, cit., pp. 184–185, note 115.

21 Regarding these aspects, with different examples of the "extension, the pervasiveness and the overlapping of the power of the Inquisition compared to that of all the other congregations of cardinals," see M.T. Fattori, *Clemente VIII e il Sacro collegio 1592-1605*, cit., pp. 189 ff. and 347 ff. There were 11 inquisitors who were granted episcopal offices under Clement's pontificate. On the case of Sigismondo Donati, see ivi, p. 184, note 115.

22 See the document published in G. Maifreda, *Giordano Bruno e Celestino da Verona*, cit., p. 172.

23 Scroll through the various examples shown in Antonio Menniti Ippolito, *Politica e carriere ecclesiastiche nel secolo XVII. I vescovi veneti tra Roma e Venezia*, Bologna, Il Mulino, 1993.

24 See in particular the undated letter from Cardinal Pompeo Arrigoni which, in view of the Concistory of August 18, proposed the assignment of the episcopate to the inquisitor. In Vatican City, Archivio segreto vaticano (from here on ASV), Misc. Arm. XII, volume 145, fol. 507 old numbering; it can be inferred from here that Giovanni Vincenzo Maria Arrigoni was 44 years old at the time. See the Concistorial minutes of the nomination in ASV, *Arch. Concist.*, *Acta Camerarii*, volume 13, fol. 242 of the old numbering; ASV, *Arch. Concist.*, *Acta Misc.*, volume 37, fol. 144*v* new numbering. See also the brief autograph of December 3, 1600 in ASV, Arm. XXXVIII, t. 3, fol. 212 of the old numbering. August 10, 1599 there was also the foundation of the Congregation *super negotiis Sancta Fidei et Religionis Catholicae* in Rome, at whose first meeting were present the two nephew cardinals and the ubiquitous Santa Severina, his active supporter who became its first prefect: see Marko Jačov, *Clemente VIII e la Sacra Congregazione de Propaganda fide*, in Marco Jačov, Stefano Pifferi, Francesca De Caprio, Jerzy Motylewicz, *Saggi vari*, Viterbo, Sette città, 2004, pp. 7–17, p. 8.

25 See Vincenzo Paglia, *«La pietà dei carcerati». Confraternite e società a Roma nei secoli XVI-XVIII*, Rome, Edizioni di storia e letteratura, 1980, p. 24. On the jurisdictional division between the two prisons, see C.C. Fornili, *Delinquenti e carcerati a Roma alla metà del '600*, cit., p. 144.

26 M. Di Sivo, *Sulle carceri dei tribunali penali a Roma*, cit., p. 15 and V. Paglia, *«La pietà dei carcerati»*, cit., p. 43.

27 Ivi, p. 32, note 108.

28 It must be considered, by way of comparison, that the Papal State spent 150,000 *scudi* for the recovery of Ferrara in 1598. The affair opened a long controversy among the Cenci and Aldobrandini families, which concluded with financial compensation only 30 years later in the time of Urban VIII. The disputes perpetuated the assumption among the Roman people and aristocracy that Clement VIII and his family had manipulated the result of the process for profit. A vast bibliography exists on the Cenci affair, of varying quality and reliability: see Michele Di Sivo, *Vite nefandissime. Il delitto Cenci e altre storie*, in *I Cenci. Nobiltà di sangue*, edited by Id., Rome, Fondazione Marco Besso-Colombo, 2002, pp. 219–255.

29 ACDF, So, St.st., L3c, fol. 378*v*.

30 Ivi, pp. 378*v* ff., also for the citations that follow.

31 ACDF, So, St.st., L3c, *Instrumenta rogati dalla cancelleria del S. Ufficio*, fols. 378*r*–380*v* and 395*r*–397*v*, "*Capitoli*, pacts and conventions to be observed by the Captain, and his guardians of the prisons of the Holy Office, and by his ministers and family," stipulated August 23, 1591 and renewed August 27, 1601 with «Marco Tullio Valentini de Oppido Tarani Sabinensis diocesis», fol. 396*r*.
32 ACDF, So, St.st., L3c, doc. cit., fol. 396*r*–*v*.
33 ACDF, So, St.st., Q3d, fol. 329*r*, August 17, 1590.
34 *Ibidem*.

References

Acta ordinis. Tabulae capitulorum generalium fratrum Minorum cappuccinorum. I. 1529-1623, edited by Vincenzo Criscuolo, Rome, Istituto storico dei Cappuccini, 2008.

Carlo Bottero, *I conventuali riformati italiani, 1557-1670: vicende e insediamenti*, volume 2, Padua, Centro studi antoniani, 2008.

Michele Di Sivo, *Vite nefandissime. Il delitto Cenci e altre storie*, in *I Cenci. Nobiltà di sangue*, edited by Id., Rome, Fondazione Marco Besso-Colombo, 2002.

Clemente Fedele, Mario Gallenga, *Per servizio di Nostro Signore. Strade, corrieri e poste dei papi dal Medioevo al 1870*, Prato, Istituto di studi storici postali, 1988.

I processi informativi per la nomina dei vescovi di Trento nell'Archivio segreto vaticano (secoli XVII-XVIII), edited by Ugo Paoli, Bologna, Il Mulino, 2010.

Antonio Menniti Ippolito, *Politica e carriere ecclesiastiche nel secolo XVII. I vescovi veneti tra Roma e Venezia*, Bologna, Il Mulino, 1993.

Marko Jačov, *Clemente VIII e la Sacra Congregazione de Propaganda fide*, in *Saggi vari*, edited by Marco Jačov, Stefano Pifferi, Francesca De Caprio, Jerzy Motylewicz, Viterbo, Sette città, 2004, pp. 7–17.

Agostino Lauro, *Il costituzionalismo pregiannoniano nel Regno di Napoli. Problema e bibliografia (1563-1723)*, Rome, Edizioni di storia e letteratura, 1974.

Litterae circulares superiorum generalium ordinis fratrum minorum cappuccinorum (1548-1803), edited by Melchiorre da Pobladura, Rome, Istituto storico dei Cappuccini, 1960.Vincenzo Paglia, *«La pietà dei carcerati». Confraternite e società a Roma nei secoli XVI-XVIII*, Rome, Edizioni di storia e letteratura, 1980

Armando Petrucci, *Abela, Leonardo*, in *Dizionario biografico degli italiani*, cit., volume I, 1960.

12 "Perhaps It Is with Greater Fear That You Pronounce the Sentence against Me..."

We will never know with certainty what took place in the prisons of the Roman Holy Office that summer of 1599. It will never really be possible to establish why Bruno decided to voluntarily go to the scaffold, nor if the Veronese friar Celestino's return to the scene had – as I will suggest in this final chapter – in some way influenced, if not actually determined this choice.

The concept of causality itself, if strictly applied, is inadequate for capturing the act and the ways in which we make decisions. Nobody makes their decisions through a clear, logical path and for only one reason. While it is true that the characteristic of human action is almost always rationality and intentional awareness, recent theories and empirical research on choice have deconstructed the idea that the decision maker is a Cartesian "I," with a clear and distinct mental representation of their own goals and the ability to make a rational calculation of the best means to achieve them. In reality, when we make decisions we work in a far less linear fashion, oscillating between conflicts and contradictions. We can also go through phases of *akrasia*: the inability to decide even when our judgement has identified the best choice for us.[1]

The historian, when establishing relationships between the choices and goals of people who lived in the past, must also sometimes work to identify facts and contexts that can reasonably explain individual decisions. It is necessary, then, in the case of the trial of Giordano Bruno and its anguished outcome, to explore all possibilities and submit for debate any hypothesis made plausible by the available documentation. Naturally, one must always be willing to run the risk of making a mistake, and accept the possibility that any effort might be superseded by the emergence of new elements or by more convincing interpretations of known events.

What we now know about Celestino da Verona, his relations with the inquisitors, the procedural style of the Holy Office, and the disconcerting contradictions that almost automatically emerge from the documentation as soon as you go into the details of the Capuchin's life and death, makes it highly improbable that his re-appearance in the prisons of the Inquisition, just as Bruno's trial reached its decisive turning point, was a mere coincidence. It is clear that in 1599 there was an internal dispute within the Holy

DOI: 10.4324/9781003026082-16

Office around his fate. The friar was a heretic who could have easily been passed off as relapsed and a man who, as the record shows, Clement VIII wanted put to death – quickly and secretly.

The pope was traditionally critical towards members of the Orders and skeptical about their morality. He was certainly aware of Celestino da Verona's history of trials and imprisonment, as well as the casual behavior he had shown toward the Holy Office, the papal nuncio in Venice, and the Capuchin Order itself. He also knew about the links between the Veronese and the cardinal of Santa Severina. However, he had to tolerate this as he had more generally tolerated Santori's intrusiveness in carrying out his duties as Cardinal Protector of the Capuchins, which – we know from other sources – had also aroused the vigorous protest of the General Minister of the order, Girolamo da Polizzi.[2] Clement VIII also sought in those years to deeply reform the nearly unlimited functions and assignments of the cardinals who protected the regular clergy. It is not by chance that he failed to nominate new cardinals to the protectorates left vacant by the death of the office holders: those of the Dominicans (vacant since 1598), of the Minor Observant Friars (from 1602) and of the Capuchins themselves (from 1602, after the death of Santa Severina).

Pope Aldobrandini was, by all accounts, convinced that Celestino should suffer the death penalty. If, however, we discard the unverifiable hypothesis that Celestino suffered a self-destructive "madness," it seems evident that the "spontaneous" appearance in Rome of this relapsed heretic – who also had a history of collaboration with the Holy Office – could only have been motivated by good reasons and equally solid support.

The friar knew he was dead weight, in a position to compromise delicate political-curial balances which had been tenuously established over the decade that was now drawing to a close. For this reason he was also sensibly kept at a safe distance from his masters, who – as shown by his bold behavior regarding his transfer to the Marches – he did not completely trust.

Follow the Money!

Historians of the Inquisition do not normally subject the interventions of the holy tribunal to financial analysis. However, this oversight might prevent us from picking up on crucial details, as we learn from the slogan *Follow the Money!*, popularized in the 1970s by the political thriller *All the President's Men*, which explained Richard Nixon's resignation to the world and identified a precise pattern of corruption that was discovered by doing just that; following the money by tracing the channels through which it had moved.[3]

The account books of the inquisitors can reveal previously unseen elements of the history of the Holy Office, starting with the ledger of receipts – which was mentioned earlier – that the Captain of the prisons was required to keep in accordance with his contract. These receipts were included in the tribunal's books of *oecomonica*, which have been preserved. The Inquisition's providential vision and its conviction that it would be eternal, acting to fulfill the will of God, affected, among other things, the material kept in the archives. This produced – fortunately for historians – documents which could have been embarrassing had they been examined by an outsider's eye. At the time, however, nobody could have imagined that the temporal power of the Roman Church and the inquisitorial tribunals themselves would be dismantled everywhere outside the Vatican confines. Likewise it was unimaginable that these registries, along with many other documents produced by the Holy Office over the centuries, would be made freely available for consultation, responding "not only to the legitimate aspirations of scholars," as stated by the Cardinal Prefect of the Congregation for the Doctrine of the Faith in 1998, (now pontiff emeritus Joseph Ratzinger), but also "to the firm intention of the Church to serve Man, helping him to understand himself by reading his own history without prejudice."[4]

The management account books for the prisons of the Holy Office prove that friar Celestino was fed for 23 days in July (costing the tribunal 3:10 *scudi*), for all of August (costing 4:0 *scudi*) and for 13 days in September (costing 2:0 *scudi*).[5] The Capuchin was therefore imprisoned on July 8, plausibly immediately after the request for an examination of the anonymous letter that was ordered in the Congregation. This is further confirmation of the hypothesis that the letter played a central role in the death sentence procedure. Since the decree of the Holy Office that ordered the inspection does not yet define the friar as *carceratus*, we can suppose that at the time it was drafted he was still free. Just a few hours later he was imprisoned, and promptly appeared before the tribunal the following day.

The second element documented in the prison's account books is the extraordinary alimentary hospitality that the Capuchin friar enjoyed in the prisons of the Roman Inquisition.

> To account for what was bought for him in two months: Veal, a pound extra each day for *scudi* 0:60; for the same, purchases of fruit *scudi* 0:40; for the same, giving a half liter of wine extra each day *scudi* 3:0; for the same, the barber shaved, and washed *scudi* 0:10; for the same purchasing a *gabanella* of black twill; for the same buying a pair of cloth pants a pair of twill socks a hat a pair of shoes a belt and a pair of *ligaccie scudi* 1:98.[6]

Celestino da Verona's dietary allotment included supplementary rations of veal and wine, as well as rich supplements of fruit. A simple comparison with the treatment of other prisoners in those decades demonstrates that no other inmate enjoyed such rich provisions,[7] especially in the context of a regime for rations that – as we have seen – was subject to very rigid contractual terms. Giordano Bruno himself, in over seven years of imprisonment, never benefitted from treatment even remotely comparable to that enjoyed by Celestino da Verona during the two months of imprisonment that led up to his execution.[8]

The food purchased for the Veronese could not have been for the purpose of corrupting him, since it appears in the official expense records of the Congregation, meaning the expenses were authorized by payment orders signed, as was customary, by the cardinal of Santa Severina. These expenses related to Celestino's detention were also paid in the normal way, directly to the Captain of the prisons, Marco Tullio Valentini on September 20, 1599, by Santa Severina at his palazzo di Montecitorio, and in the presence of the notary of the Holy Office, Flaminio Adriano.[9] The Capuchin's lavish meals, therefore, can only attest to the favor of the leaders of the Inquisition; a privilege that had to have been obvious to the other inmates as well. Nor is it possible to think that this treatment was granted to Celestino only when his death was imminent. The accounts speak clearly: there was a regular daily supplement of fruit, meat, and wine served through most of the friar's two months of imprisonment.

The Capuchin's Shoes

Two other interesting elements emerge from the account books of Celestino da Verona's imprisonment.

The first is that he was served food for only 13 days in the month of September, even though he was executed during the night between September 15 and 16. It is possible that the prisoner refused food for the last two days of his life, although up to and including September 13 – when the death sentence was already known to him – the Capuchin had eaten voraciously. On the other hand, we cannot easily postulate that the Veronese was moved from the Inquisition prisons to Corte Savella on September 14, where, as we have seen, he was met by the comforters in apparent defiance of Clement VIII's orders. In fact, they met Celestino in Corte Savella just after sundown on September 15, while the record of Celestino's delivery to the Tribunale del Governatore is dated September 16.[10]

A second piece of information presented in the document puts the hypothesis that Celestino fasted during the final days of his life in a peculiar light. For a total cost of about four *scudi* – roughly the amount as the monthly food budget for a prisoner – "a *gabanella* of black twill," "a pair of cloth pants" "a pair of twill socks,"[11] "a hat," "a pair of shoes," "a belt," and "a pair of *ligaccie*" were "purchased" for the friar.

What is this about? The *gabbanella* was a type of overcoat, often richly lined, which at the end of the Middle Ages and into the 15th century was worn by the wealthy classes, later falling into use as an everyday tunic. By way of an example, in the *Storia Fiorentina* by Benedetto Varchi, written in the mid-1500s, we read:

> The dress of Florentines past their eighteenth year is, in summer, when they go to the city, a vest of either black twill or *rascia* (another coarse herringbone wool fabric) almost down to the heels [...]; and underneath

> some wear a robe, and some a *gabbanella*, or another kind of shirt made of silk-lined cloth, which are called "tunics.[12]

It was a light outfit, appropriate for "*la state*" (summer), which in Rome was still hot in September.

Like the *calzette*, the *gabbanella* purchased for Celestino was also of twill: a type of bright fabric that was commonly used in the early Renaissance which mimicked fabric made with wool yarn by using more economical wools mixed with other yarns such as linen or cotton, and woven diagonally.[13] The twill (or herringbone) weaves produced fabrics that were heavy and resistant but soft, good for work and for travel: for example, the weave of today's denim (the fabric used for jeans), tartan, tweed, and gabardine are all twills.

The "*paro di ligaccie*" bought for the Capuchin at the Inquisition's expense consisted of leg wrappings, these also being good for movement. For example, a 17th century description of the mosaic depicting the apostle Peter entrusting the insignia to Emperor Charlemagne, found on the characteristic Roman monument of *Triclinium Leoninum* (the so-called *Nicchione* of the papal Lateran palazzo), reads:

> Whose clothing [...] one sees in this image that he has a tunic, that is a vestment, called a *pretesta*, down to the knee; with *ligaccie* wrapped around the legs down to the feet, according to the old custom; the *ligaccie* were called *fascie crurales*.[14]

In practice a complete travel outfit had been acquired for Celestino (who, according to the regulations was required to wear a *camiscia* in prison, the uniform for prisoners of the Holy Office, and *pianelle*, whose repair so often figured among the tribunal's expenses[15]) and paid for from the coffers of the Inquisition. This purchase was definitely authorized by the Commissioner of the Congregation Alberto Drago – who shortly afterwards, on December 18, 1599, would be nominated bishop of Termoli – and, once again, was backed by a signed order from the cardinal of Santa Severina, without which the related expenses could not have appeared in the formal account books of the Holy Office.

The civilian clothing given to the Veronese friar also contravened the strict rules of the Capuchin Order, which not only required wearing the tunic with the characteristic hood, but also the equally symbolic sandals as footwear. The ordinations of Albacina of 1529 prescribe for the friars

> that those who cannot go barefoot, having first tried, if they cannot resist, they wear sandals, as did the apostles and our ancient fathers, as poorly as possible, as our status requires, and that clogs are not to be worn.

The first constitutions of the Order (1536) reiterate: "And not being able to [go barefoot] they may wear shoes with permission of the prelate, but simple, pure, base and poor, without any curiosity."[16] By all evidence, the "shoes," the clothes, and the "belt" given to the Capuchin by the inquisitors were therefore meant for easy walking among and blending into crowds, discarding the sandals, the habit, and the cord around the hips.

No other case emerges from the account registers of the Roman Inquisition in those years where a complete set of clothing was purchased for a prisoner: not even in reference to Giordano Bruno, who like Celestino was led to the stake just a few months later. The regulations for the management of prisoners of the Holy Office, on the other hand, specify strict rules regarding bringing objects into the jail, preventing the Captain of the prisons and the guards from delivering any potential tools of injury or self-injury to the prisoners. Remember that in those same weeks, on August 24 Giordano Bruno was denied the sharpener and compass he had requested to write his briefs. Nevertheless a potentially dangerous belt and two *ligaccie* were purchased for and given to Celestino.

A Giovan Antonio Arrigoni, now returned to layman status as a consequence of his laicization[17] could have legitimately, canonically speaking, worn a complete suit, even with "a hat" that was convenient for hiding his face. But why would he have had to do so if death by execution awaited him?

Giordano and Celestino

In the scorching heat of July 8, 1599, when the end of the trial was drawing near after exhausting years of imprisonment, Giordano Bruno must have been utterly astonished to witness the arrival of his old fellow prisoner, Celestino da Verona, in the prisons of the Holy Office; the man who had become his mortal accuser. The friar who had overwhelmed him with damning accusations reappeared just as Bruno, bowed by the long loss of freedom, was engaged in an extreme battle against abjuration. Everything about the case: the temporizing, the tactics, the efforts at writing and rewriting briefs, the doubts about the use of "criminal" evidence to support the impending sentence, shared by some in the Congregation, Bellarmino's insistence, not to mention the philosophical and moral viability itself of the relationship established over the years between the tribunal and the accused, must have all been thrown under unexpected shadows.

We have formulated some hypotheses about the reasons for which Celestino might have thought that the late spring of 1599 was the right time to return to Rome. It is hard to imagine that Cardinal Santori – protector of the Capuchins, the friar's perpetual master and the prime mover of his transfer to the prison in the Marches at the end of the hectic circumstances of 1593–1594 – did not have a role in this decision. At the end of the decade, however, the Curia was no longer that of the late Sixtine pontificate and the anti-Navarran fervor of the early 1590s. The Capuchin thus found himself trapped in yet another inquisitorial trial that the pope intended to bring to an immediate conclusion, even at the cost of forcing canonical procedures in the utmost secrecy.

Giordano Bruno knew all too well who Celestino da Verona was. He must have asked himself if the hostile Capuchin's reappearance and brazenly privileged treatment were a message that someone really intended to send to him.

The special food enjoyed by the Veronese friar, the anomaly of his hasty death sentence, and the strange gift of clothing, so different from the outfit required by the Inquisition's prison rules and the constitutions of the Capuchins, better suited instead to traveling the peninsula in the heat of September; these glaring exceptions cannot have gone unnoticed by Bruno, and likewise by the few dozen other prisoners that occupied the cells of the palazzo of the Holy Office in those weeks. The account books for these months show that the tribunal had expenses for 19 inmates in the month of July 1599, and for 28 prisoners in August, in addition to which were an unknown number of prisoners that were able to pay for their own support, and were therefore not included in the registers of expenses authorized by Santa Severina.[18]

The ostentatious privileges granted to Celestino da Verona by the inquisitors can only be explained by two hypotheses: either the leadership of the Holy Office wanted to demonstrate the favor he enjoyed with them, or the friar was in a position to extort those same leaders to the point of obtaining such blatant privileges. Both possibilities must lead us, one more time, to conclude that Celestino da Verona was a central figure in the logic of the Holy Office and, consequently, among the concerns of the pope. Throughout the history of the Church in the second half of the 16th century, many very serious disagreements arose between the pontiffs and the cardinals who guided the action of the Congregation of the Holy Office. Nobody could have known this better than Giulio Antonio Santori, who had previously worked as an inquisitor under Julius III, and who believed he knew, better than anyone else, that while popes were destined for succession, the Holy Office would fulfill its providential function until the end of time.

The imprisonment and death sentence of Celestino da Verona, perhaps for the charge of having written a compromising anonymous letter to an inquisitor who was awaiting election as bishop, once again brought the Capuchin into the same prison as Bruno. It is impossible not to believe that at this point the inquisitors close to Santa Severina tried to use their old collaborator – even if only by exhibiting him – just as they had a few years earlier in Venice. To once again make him the instrument of unblocking the legally shaky trial of a well-known philosopher, formerly protected by kings and by an emperor, who was rebellious and even harder to deal with since he had taken up the intelligent strategy of submitting briefs in his own defense, potentially a harbinger of other delays and unpredictable developments.

The use of hidden persuaders recruited to secretly provoke heretics and induce them to recantation was not without precedents. We can invoke the case of Cardinal Gaetano, a Dominican theologian who arrived in Augusta in 1518 with the task of convincing Luther to abjure, on pain of arrest and being taken to Rome in shackles. After multiple official meetings achieved nothing, the cardinal privately sent a member of his delegation – Urbano da Serralonga – to the monastery where the reformer lived. During this visit the emissary first reminded Luther of the example of Gioacchino da Fiore's abjuration; he then mocked him for his stubbornness, telling him that a false declaration of repentance was not such a big thing: there was fake money in circulation, but everyone took it for real.[19]

Giordano Bruno could have ascribed a variety of meanings to the return of his bitter accuser to the prisons of the Holy Office, placed in the cells next to his. He may have interpreted it as the outcome of the Capuchin's effort to retract the accusations against him; or as the result of his desire to give the inquisitors new elements of proof against him; as a punishment for the friar's foolish ambitions to blackmail the judges; or as a means to allow Santa Severina's trusted collaborator to carry messages not dignified enough to be spoken by the lips of a cardinal. Certainly it was this very plurality of possible meanings that the imprisonment of his main accuser could assume in Bruno's eyes, this game of mirrors into which the philosopher could not help but fall, that made Celestino's mere presence a tool of psychological pressure to be exploited by the judges. The pressure was only enhanced by the ostentation of the favor lavished upon the informer.

Then there is the question of what Bruno thought of Celestino's death sentence itself. Imposed directly by the pope with atypical speed and process, the condemnation to death of someone who was so openly a beneficiary of the inquisitors, and who – the acute Bruno must have realized this – had so commendably collaborated with the judges by becoming the crucial witness in his own trial, must have begged for an explanation in Bruno's mind. Perhaps, by imposing an exemplary sentence on Celestino the pope or the inquisitors wanted to show Bruno the futility of his obstinate self-defense from abjuration? To make him understand that he must submit himself to the superior will of the pontiff and the Holy Office, in an era that – at least in Italy – had by now abandoned humanistic disputation on the subject of religion and embraced the obligation for unconditional obedience based on faith?

We will never know what Celestino and Bruno said during the weeks between July and September 1599, when they certainly had the opportunity to speak to each other. We will never be able to verify if Celestino might have been the bearer of a secret or a message which he passed on to Bruno to induce him to change his attitude towards his jailers. It is possible that the Capuchin became the mouthpiece for words instilled by his superiors, aimed at weakening Bruno's tactics with the briefs. Perhaps he divulged some background aspect of the trial to Bruno which the philosopher could have only supposed until then, and which no inquisitor could have revealed to him directly without undermining the legal validity of the trial with an admission of its flawed assumptions. These unmentionable details could, on the other hand, be communicated by an informer who visibly remained in the graces of the judges, even after being sentenced to death by the pope himself: such a man might to some extent be considered a credible spokesman on behalf of the inquisitors.

This would explain why someone in the Holy Office made Celestino's dietary privileges so extravagant: such anomalous luxury was meant to legitimize him in the eyes of his fellow prisoners – of *one* fellow prisoner – as a representative of the inquisitors. He had been so in the past, and continued to be so in the present.

These efforts do not appear to have been completely successful: once again on September 10, when Celestino was headed for the stake, Bruno stated his willingness to do «*totum et quicquid ei iniunctum fuerit*» – whatever he was ordered to – by his judges, but only after another desperate attempt to present a final brief addressed directly to the pope. The philosopher's stubborn confidence in the possibility of negotiating his fate had not been affected. At that moment, even after two months in prison with the ostentatiously overfed and provocative Veronese friar, Bruno still believed he had a chance of getting out of the trial alive: he still believed that the trial made *sense*.

If a relationship did exist between Celestino's re-emergence and the end of the Bruno trial, it must therefore be looked for in some event that took place between the end of September 10 and the day of the Capuchin's death – in the space of just under a week.

Squaring the Circle

Earlier we described the proceeding against Giordano Bruno as being divided into five phases, punctuated by four periods of stalemate, each accompanied by Celestino da Verona breaking in on the scene of the trial.

The first round of witness and prisoner interrogations failed to produce any evidence to support Mocenigo's accusations. When this led the trial's first stalemate, Celestino da Verona intervened for the first time: he entered the Inquisitorial prison in Venice, but was not formally tried, despite the fact that he had abjured once before, in Rome in 1587.

After Bruno's transfer and entry to the Roman prisons the stalemate resumed, for the same reason that had caused so much trouble for the Venetian inquisitors: the lack of any available evidence. Then Celestino da Verona's second intervention arrived, in the form of written testimony against Bruno, containing accusations which turned out to be decisive in setting up the trial.

In April 1599, while the inquisitorial tribunal found itself stalled again, this time by Bruno's tactic of submitting written briefs in his defense which the tribunal was forced to consider, the Capuchin suddenly reappeared on the scene with his "spontaneous" request to be heard by the Roman Holy Office. Once again, he entered the prison where Bruno already languished, and this time he enjoyed ostentatiously privileged treatment.

After the resumption of internal discussions at the Holy Office on August 24, 1599, Bruno's appearance before the inquisitors on September 10 halted the proceeding anew, as the defendant again linked his willingness to abjure to the presentation of a new written brief, this time addressed directly to the pope. In the meantime Celestina da Verona had been burned alive at the stake, inexplicably receiving a complete layman's traveling outfit as a gift from the inquisitors. We cannot demonstrate conclusively that these events contributed to the final resumption of the trial. Nevertheless, at the same time or immediately afterwards, Giordano Bruno, despite multiple injunctions ordering his retraction, withdrew his stated willingness to abjure and was condemned to death.

These events make it more than plausible to suspect that somebody's skillful direction had organized Celestino's interventions in the trial against Bruno in his capacity as a collaborator of the Holy Office, at least since 1592. Consequently they throw a disturbing light on what happened in the summer of 1599.

It is possible that Celestino da Verona had actually been received by the Congregation several weeks after June 3 and had made requests, or advanced demands to be freed from his exile in the Marches, having now passed the canonical five years of segregation in the little monastery of Colpersito. Perhaps he may have reminded them of the merits of the denunciation he had made against Giordano Bruno six years earlier, now that the trial of the philosopher was reaching its end. In June 1599 Celestino's denunciation against Bruno was still a fundamental premise of the trial: a failsafe cornerstone of the prosecution.

Threats made by the friar could have set the inquisitorial machine in motion, with its now inconvenient collaborator seen a threat to its authority and credibility. In canon law, an attack on the jurisdiction, life, assets, or the dignity of the Holy Office or its officials and their families was equivalent to heresy, and sanctioned as such. The bull *Si de protegendis*, issued by Pius V in 1569, excommunicated anyone who intimidated ("*perterrefecerit*") inquisitors and those in charge of cases at the Holy Office, and made offenders eligible for prosecution. We cannot exclude the possibility that this was the actual charge for which Clement VIII sentenced Celestino da Verona to death as a relapsed heretic.[20] It is a charge whose disclosure would have involved making it known that the inquisitors were being blackmailed: perhaps this was why the pope felt such an urgent need for the final acts of the trial to be held in absolute secrecy, and to prevent the public reading of the sentence.

It is not at all plausible to believe that a trusted assistant of the Holy Office, who had long been protected by the Inquisition and granted special treatment, even during his final months of imprisonment, was sent to his death following a spontaneous appearance for a case of faith. This would imply that the shrewd Veronese friar reported himself to the Holy Office only to then fail to reconcile with the Catholic Church, even *in extremis*, instead seeing himself condemned to death without a real trial, behind a veil of inexplicable secrecy. Then there was the mysterious last minute defiance of the pope's orders that he be brought directly to Campo de' Fiori from the Inquisition's prisons, which lead to the scene in Corte Savella, which itself was full of anomalies. Furthermore, no hypothesis explains why the Capuchin was given a full civilian traveling outfit, nor the spiral of ambiguities within which almost all the written testimonies concerning the laicization and burning of Celestino da Verona converge.

On that subject, the recent discovery of yet another abnormality involving Celestino's death should be mentioned. The notary's sketch of the burning was recently found alongside the official record at the Tribunale del Governatore.[21] Unlike the previously cited drawing depicting the execution of Giordano Bruno (Figure 12.1), and for that matter, unlike any other image seen to date in research on this type of representation (see another example in Figure 12.2),[22] this sketch does not trace the flames in a few brush strokes that approach, but do not overlap the figure of the condemned. Instead it shows the scaffold completely wrapped in and overcome by fire, in a fury of lines (Figure 12.3). A dense curtain of flames renders the dying man indistinguishable: perhaps with the purpose of making the graphic certification uncontestable, and to protect the notary in case of future disputes.[23]

Figure 12.1 Notarial representation of the execution of Giordano Bruno

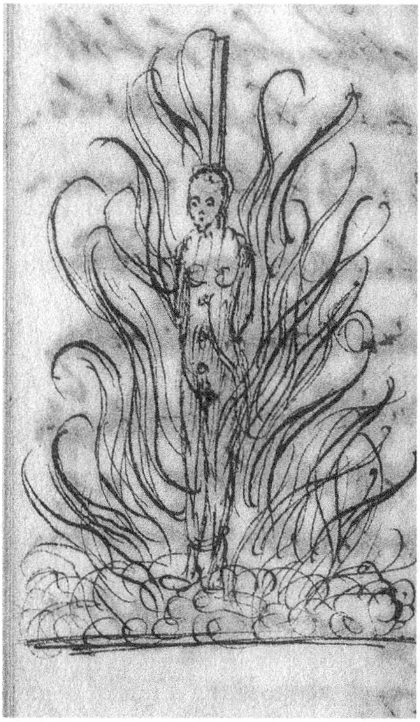

Figure 12.2 Notarial representation of another person condemned to the stake in the same years

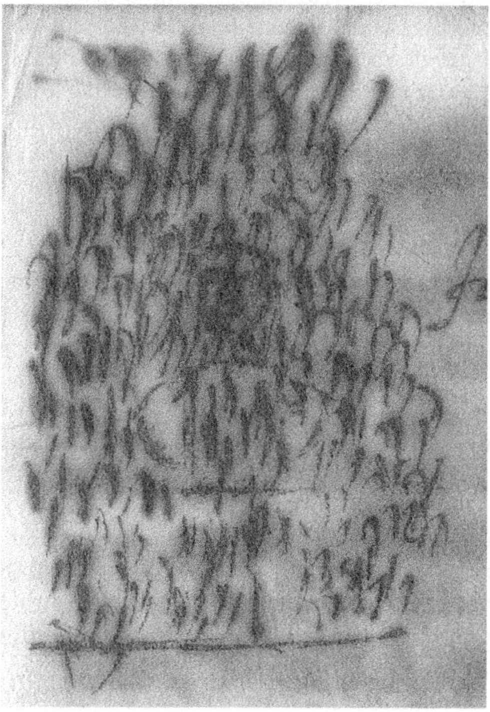

Figure 12.3 Notarial representation of Celestino da Verona burning at the stake

The only viable hypothesis that can settle the interpretive problems that the centuries and the operational secrecy of the inquisitorial tribunals have placed between us and the facts surrounding the death of Celestino da Verona is that he did not in fact die: he was never sent to the stake. Instead, he was provided with civilian clothing and freed directly from the prisons of the Holy Office, while a non-existent "Cristoffaro da Verona" was laicized by the bishop of Sidone, an old protégé of Santa Severina's. In Celestino's place an unfortunate substitute layman was sent from Corte Savella among many precautions, and at night – as the reporters clearly inform us – to be burned at the stake.

Having been fed for only 13 days in September 1599, the friar could have been released on the day of the 14th, with the Tribunale del Governatore taking charge of a prisoner after sundown on September 15, officially dated September 16. The call for the comforters, as proven by the registries of San Giovanni Decollato, came that same September 15. The men could have therefore been switched in the palazzo of the Holy Office, a space within which the inquisitors could act with ease and discretion. However, carrying out the articulated and prolonged ceremony of administering comforts to a replacement prisoner would have been too risky had he remained at the Holy Office; thus the need to stage the comforting in Corte Savella.

During the night of September 15 the brothers of San Giovanni Decollato found themselves faced with a person who would not repent, choosing to die impenitent. "He was always very obstinate, without however giving reason for his obstinacy," the registries of the Archconfraternity report: a lethargic silence that was taken for "arrogant presumptuousness," but which perhaps had been induced by a state of semi-consciousness. A poor, drugged derelict, however, could not stage a reconciliation and eventual communion in someone's place as a substitute. This would have subverted two sacraments that no comforter would have been willing to violate. Thus we have the celebration of the mass in the absence of the condemned, and the terrible necessity of sending the wretch the stake to be burned alive.

Simply restoring Celestino da Verona's freedom meant facing the opposition of Clement VIII, who was convinced of the need to send the Capuchin to his death, even at the cost of forcing the ordinary canonical and inquisitorial procedure. Perhaps this was to punish the Capuchin's actual relapse into heresy, or perhaps to sever the dangerous ties that had connected him with the Holy Office; perhaps it was a reaction to the friar's requests, demands, or attempts at blackmail, any of which could have tainted the inquisitorial tribunal and compromised the outcome of the Bruno trial, which had reached a very delicate phase. Perhaps it was only for some of these reasons, or for all of them together.

Celestino da Verona's protectors may have engineered his return to the scene while the trial of Giordano Bruno had again ground to a halt in order to once more use him to disrupt Bruno's defensive strategies; perhaps by threatening him, perhaps by flattering him, or perhaps by pressuring him with elements of the trial about which it is difficult to conjecture today. This side of the chessboard had every interest in Celestino remaining alive, not only so he could continue to serve as an informant, but also so his release from prison could testify to the solidity of the protection that the inquisitors granted to their present and future collaborators.

In the preceding days Clement VIII had imposed a decisive and cruel turn in the Cenci trial, sentencing all of the defendants to death, and having them executed in theatrical style on September 11.[24] This example of brutal pontifical resolve may have convinced Celestino da Verona's protectors of the need to stage the burning the pope had ordered, providing cover for the Capuchin's release. The secrecy that Aldobrandini had imposed around the execution of Celestino da Verona would at that point turn out to be an important advantage.

Substitutions

Exchanges of persons and the related deception was a phenomenon that was anything but rare in the Old Regime, an era of constant uncertainty around identity, which of course lacked citizenship bureaus or personal and photographic certifications. In an era when imposters were punished very severely, at least on paper, substitutions and disguises were as common in real life as they were in the theater and short stories, and were also used to allow women to travel and live in dangerous contexts by passing for men.[25]

The case of Arnaud du Tilh was famous – Montaigne also described it this way. In the mid-1500s du Tilh appeared in a village in the Pyrenees, presenting himself as Martin Guerre, a soldier of the royal French Army, long lost in war and presumed deceased. Guerre's wife and sisters recognized him, as did his neighbors, friends, and relatives. However, a case was opened against him by some of du Tilh's heirs who were financially harmed by his reappearance. To the shock of all, the real Martin Guerre, who had fought alongside du Tilh, reappeared at a certain point in the proceeding. The business ended with impostor being hung in front of Guerre's house, who returned to his wife and full possession of his assets.[26]

Precisely to avoid this type of problem canon law had addressed the exchange of persona in a marriage in detail, sanctioning its annulment. Second marriages based on the loss of a spouse – in cases of distant separation, imprisonment, or presumed death in war – and later contested upon his return were a genuine social and literary *leitmotiv* in the Europe of those centuries.[27]

Cases of impersonation even ended up involving royal families. The King of Portugal, Sebastiano I, was killed in battle during the invasion of Morocco in 1578, but his body was never found. Playing on fears that Phillip II of Spain would annex the Lusitanian kingdom, as actually happened in 1580, at least four impostors appeared, all claiming to be Sebastiano.[28] The most able of these was the Calabrian Marco Tullio Catizone, who presented himself at court after learning a convincing degree of information about recent events in Portuguese history and having his appearance changed to that of the deceased ruler: he had an arm stretched out and an ankle inflated among other things. Catizone was later arrested in Venice at the end of the 16th century, but his detention became an international affair: the King of France, Henry IV, requested his release from prison, and in December 1600 Catizone – dressed as a wayfarer – was freed. Imprisoned again in Florence and then brought to Naples by the Spanish, he met the astute Viceroy Count di Lemos, who had his portrait done by the painter Fabrizio Santafede, sending the image, with a detailed report on his continuous changes of identity to the new King Phillip III. In the end Catizone was executed in Andalusia in 1603, where he had found a way to re-establish relations with Portuguese who were hostile to Habsburg domination. Nevertheless, rumors spread that the imposter had secretly been freed from Castel dell'Ovo, with a hapless victim executed in his place, and so continued to represent a threat to the Spanish domination over Portugal.[29]

In the secular prisons of the early modern era the exchange of a free person and a released prisoner was permitted – and regulated by city statutes – to collect the money needed to satisfy a financial penalty or a debt. The exchange of Christian and Muslim prisoners and slaves in the Mediterranean during the 16th–17th centuries, or their redemption by ransom is another phenomenon well known to historians.[30] Regarding the Inquisition, the phenomenon of substituting people while the sentence was still being served has not yet been sufficiently investigated. However, there are traces of evidence that suggest the possibility. There is, for example, the documented case of a Ligurian merchant, Carlo Chiavello, who in 1581 was sentenced to 20 years on the galleys of the Inquisitor of Genoa. He applied to the pope to plead for an exemption, and following this the Roman Holy Office wrote to the Genovese judge of faith urging clemency. The inquisitor stated that he was willing to tolerate a replacement, responding:

> He [Chiavello] is very industrious [...] he is a man forty years of age, more or less [...] and for all this there is a remedy. [...] Let him buy a Muslim slave to row for him. He has the means to do it.

John Tedeschi has concluded that individuals destined to the galleys actually may never have set foot aboard one[31].

In essence, it's a matter of contextualizing – while certainly avoiding anything forced – events that took place in an era that has been called the "*ancien regime* of identity": an age in which the category of individuality was more fluid than it is in comparison with today. The modern concept of identity emerged after the political and cultural turn in the Europe of the late 18th century, which signaled the passage from "intersubjective identicality" to the "individual identity" which is now an essential trait of our society.[32]

In reality, the entire affair we have examined in this book is disorienting, projecting us into a world that is in so many aspects – legal, institutional, social, cultural, and symbolic – profoundly distant from what we know today. On one hand, it was precisely the irreducibility of this past to our present that long excluded the questions that now seemed necessary to begin asking from the historiographic panorama. Even if only some of these questions become part of the agenda for studies on Bruno, on his life and philosophy, this research will have achieved its main objective. On the other hand, that same irreducibility, combined with the desperately fragmentary and dispersed condition of the surviving historical sources, has inevitably led to misunderstandings, anachronisms, and simplifications in today's interpretations. This book has tried to offer some remedy, and in doing so has raised more questions than it has provided answers. The hope is that philosophers and historians who are aware of the centrality of Bruno's journey in the European and extra-European past and present will be able to build, on the terrain of doubt, new opportunities for dialogue.

Notes

1 For more on these subjects one can start with *The Routledge Handbook of Social Epistemology*, edited by Miranda Fricker, Peter J. Graham, David Henderson, Nikolaj J.L.L. Pedersen, New York and London, Routledge, 2021.

2 See Massimo Carlo Giannini, *Politica curiale e mondo dei regolari: per una storia dei cardinali protettori nel Seicento*, in *Religione, conflittualità e cultura. Il clero regolare nell'Europa d'antico regime*, edited by Id., a monograph edition of «Cheiron», 2005, n. 43–44, pp. 241–302, p. 248 (also for the information about the protectorates that follows).

3 I tried to go down this road in G. Maifreda, *The Business of the Roman Inquisition*, cit.

4 See what is reported in *La soglia della verità*, in «Avvenire», XXXI, 23 January 1998, n. 19, p. 21.

5 ACDF, *Oeconomica* 24, register *Mandati 1597-1606*, p. 89r; I published this document in G. Maifreda, *Giordano Bruno e Celestino da Verona*, cit., pp. 175–176.

6 *Ibidem*.

7 Only with reference to November 1580 can one find the exceptional case of a certain "woman Livia da Valomontone," who was probably afflicted by mental and health problems. After having been fed, shaved and dressed with "a black garment bought for her and two strings to attach a crown," she was brought "in the home of m[ister] Guerra to be watched over together with her bed," where she was fed with "two pounds of mongana veal to make the broth," and then brought back with her bed to the prisons, "guarded" by several women who had to be supplied and compensated, and fed with "fresh eggs," for an overall cost of 7:15 scudi: ACDF, *Oeconomica* 15, register «Primo di ottobre 1577. Registro dei mandati di danari che riceverà et pagarà il Depositario del Santo Officio», un-numbered pages, accounts referring to November 1580.

8 The expenses for Bruno's monthly sustenance starting in 1593 have been partially published: see for example Angelo Mercati, *Il sommario del processo di Giordano Bruno. Con appendice di documenti sull'eresia e l'Inquisizione a Modena nel secolo XVI*, Città del Vaticano, Biblioteca apostolica vaticana, 1942, pp. 121 ff. and *Processo*, 237–240. The systematic exploration of *Oeconomica* 24 allows

us to follow Bruno's nutritional and barbering upkeep month after month for the period covered by the registry.

9 On Santori's role as guarantor of the accounts in those months, see for example ACDF, *Oeconomica* 24, register *Mandati 1597-1606*, fol. 88*r*, where the certification related to Celestino's account can be found.

10 As is now demonstrated by the documents published by M. Di Sivo, O. Verdi, *Bruno e Celestino da Verona*, cit. In ASR, *Tribunale criminale del Governatore*, Congregazione per la visita alle carceri, box 137, folder 1599, doc. 22, there is an account of a visit to the prison of Corte Savella carried out in the 13th hour, which lists the names of the 35 detainees plus four "Spaniards," but does not include the name of Celestino da Verona.

11 See for example Gian Galeazzo Scorza, *Pesaro fine secolo XVI. Clemente VIII e Francesco Maria II della Rovere*, Venice, Marsilio, 1980 («calzetti di saia incarnata et scarpe bianche», p. 94); Augusto Ferraiuolo, *«Pro exoneratione sua propria conscientia». Le accuse per stregoneria nella Capua del XVII-XVIII secolo*, Milano, FrancoAngeli, 2000 («le diedi per remuneratione due para di calzetti di saia», p. 138).

12 Benedetto Varchi, *Storia fiorentina*, edited by Gaetano Milanesi, t. II, Florence, Le Monnier, 1858, book IX, section XLVII, p. 85.

13 See also the recent Mark Greengrass, *Christendom Destroyed: Europe 1517-1648*, London, Penguin, 2017, p. 96 of the Italian edn.

14 Giovanni Severano, *Memorie sacre delle sette chiese di Roma*, part I, Rome, per Giacomo Mascardi, 1630, p. 554.

15 See for example in ACDF, *Oeconomica* 24, register *Mandati 1597-1606*, fol. 83*v*, the expense of six and a half baiocchi for the repair of Giordano Bruno's "*pianelle*" in June 1599.

16 *I cappuccini. Fonti documentarie e narrative del primo secolo (1525-1619)*, edited by Vincenzo Criscuolo, Rome, Curia generale dei Cappuccini, 1994, pp. 148–149 and 180.

17 It would appear that we can infer from the record of the Tribunale del Governatore that the laicization of Celestino took place before his delivery to the Secular Arm:

> [...] Magnificus et excellentissimus dominus Iohannes Baptista Goctarellius locumtenens criminalis, visa sententia, per illustrissimos et reverendissimos dominos cardinales Inquisitionis, contra eundem lata, quam dominus Franciscus Petrucius, substitutus fiscalis, facta exibuit tenoris etc., nec non remissione de ipso fratre Celestino facta Curie eiusdem reverendissimi domini Gubernatoris nec non fide degradationis eiusdem actualiter facta, subscripta per dictum Arcangelum Callist[uum], substitutum in officio domini Hieronimi Mazziocti, quam idem substitutus fiscalis facta pariter exibuit, mandavit eiusdem Celestinum per ministrum iustitiae in platea Campi Flore duci, et ibidem igne flammis accensis penitus comburi et concremari, omni meliori modo, super quibus presentibus sociis testibus.
>
> (published in M. Di Sivo, O. Verdi, *Bruno e Celestino da Verona*, cit., p. 527)

18 ACDF, *Oeconomica* 24, register *Mandati 1597-1606*, fols. 81*v* ff.

19 Adriano Prosperi, *Lutero. Gli anni della fede e della libertà*, Milan, Mondadori, 2017, p. 244.

20 Herman H. Schwedt, *Conflitti e violenze intorno a Girolamo M. Zambeccari OP, inquisitore di Reggio Emilia nel Seicento*, in *L'inquisizione e l'eresia in Italia. Medioevo ed età moderna. Omaggio a Andrea Del Col*, edited by Giuliana Ancona, Dario Visintin, Montereale Valcellina, Circolo culturale Menocchio, 2013, pp. 207–252, which also cites the authoritative Cesare Carena, *Tractatus de Officio Sanctissimae Inquisitionis, et modo procedendi in causis fidei*, Lugduni,

Sumptibus Laurentii Anisson, 1669, pp. 84–85. Since Lateran IV (1215) the plenary indulgence was guaranteed to the inquisitor in the performance of their work, and was extendable to their vicars, notaries, accountants, consultants and any other official. See also E. Masini, *Sacro arsenale*, cit., p. 5.

21 See M. Di Sivo, O. Verdi, *Bruno e Celestino da Verona*, cit. The image is also reported in G. Maifreda, *Giordano Bruno e Celestino da Verona*, cit., p. 197.

22 Thanks to Michele Di Sivio for the information provided to me.

23 M. Di Sivo, O. Verdi, *Bruno e Celestino da Verona*, cit., p. 527. On the other hand, while the daytime execution of Bruno was attended, in addition to the crowd in Campo de' Fiori – as stated by the documents – by two official witnesses from the tribunal, among which were the notary of Governor Giuseppe de Angelis, the official certification of the nighttime burning of Celestino concludes with a concise «super quibus presentibus sociis testibus». The notary, therefore, was not – or did not want to officially appear – among the eye witnesses of the event. The tribunal record relative to Bruno instead makes explicit: «Presentibus dominis Julian Santar[...]o et Josepho de Angelis testis adhibitis etc.» (ivi, p. 526). Even the record of the Tribunale del Governatore, as previously with that of San Giovanni Decollato, does not indicate Celestino da Verona's paternity, while both specify this in the case of Giordano Bruno.

24 Regarding the severity of punishments by Aldobrandini, see the entry by A. Borromeo, *Clemente VIII, papa*, cit. and Simona Feci, *Violenza nobiliare e giustizia nella Roma di Clemente VIII*, in *I Cenci. Nobiltà di sangue*, cit., pp. 321–337.

25 See Rudolf M. Dekker, Lotte C. van de Pol, *The Tradition of Female Transvestism in Early Modern Europe*, London, Macmillan, 1989 and the stimulating Tobias B. Hug, *Impostures in Early Modern England: Representations and Perceptions of Fraudulent Identities*, Manchester, Manchester University Press, 2009.

26 Natalie Zemon Davis, *The Return of Martin Guerre*. Cambridge, MA, Harvard University Press, 1983.

27 Gilles Lecuppre, *L'imposture politique au Moyen Âge: La seconde vie des rois*, Paris, Presses universitaires de France, 2005, pp. 115–116 of the Italian edn.

28 See also, for example, the observations of Alessandro Barbero on the exchanges of people included in Id. and Piero Angela, *Dietro le quinte della storia. La vita quotidiana attraverso il tempo*, Milan, Rizzoli, 2012.

29 See the entry by Franca Petrucci, *Catizone, Marco Tullio*, in *Dizionario biografico degli italiani*, cit., vol. XXII, 1979. The affair has recently been taken up again by Bruno Forte, *Il libro del viandante e dell'amore divino. Opera poetica*, Brescia, Morcelliana, 2016, especially p. 180.

30 For the first point, see for example the cases studied by Marina Gazzini, *Storie di vita e di malavita. Criminali, poveri e altri miserabili nelle carceri di Milano alla fine del Medioevo*, Florence, Firenze University Press, 2017, p. 73; for the second point one can start with Giovanna Fiume, *Schiavitù mediterranee. Corsari, rinnegati e santi di età moderna*, Milan, Bruno Mondadori, 2009.

31 Cited by J. Tedeschi, *The Prosecution of Heresy*, cit., p. 151.

32 The reference is to the studies of Dror Wahrman (starting from *The Making of the Modern Self: Identity and Culture in Eighteenth-Century England*, New Haven, CT and London, Yale University Press, 2004), about which see also discussion by Simon Gunn, *History and Cultural Theory*, Harlow, Pearson Education, 2006, especially pp. 151–152.

References

Piero Angela, *Dietro le quinte della storia. La vita quotidiana attraverso il tempo*, Milan, Rizzoli, 2012.

Cesare Carena, *Tractatus de Officio Sanctissimae Inquisitionis, et modo procedendi in causis fidei*, Lugduni, Sumptibus Laurentii Anisson, 1669.

Rudolf M. Dekker, Lotte C. van de Pol, *The Tradition of Female Transvestism in Early Modern Europe*, London, Macmillan, 1989.

Augusto Ferraiuolo, *«Pro exoneratione sua propria conscientia». Le accuse per stregoneria nella Capua del XVII-XVIII secolo*, Milan, FrancoAngeli, 2000.

Giovanna Fiume, *Schiavitù mediterranee. Corsari, rinnegati e santi di età moderna*, Milano, Bruno Mondadori, 2009.

Bruno Forte, *Il libro del viandante e dell'amore divino. Opera poetica*, Brescia, Morcelliana, 2016.

Marina Gazzini, *Storie di vita e di malavita. Criminali, poveri e altri miserabili nelle carceri di Milano alla fine del Medioevo*, Florence, Firenze University Press, 2017.

Massimo Carlo Giannini, *Politica curiale e mondo dei regolari: per una storia dei cardinali protettori nel Seicento*, in *Religione, conflittualità e cultura. Il clero regolare nell'Europa d'antico regime*, edited by Id., a monograph edition of «Cheiron», 2005, nn. 43–44, pp. 241–302.

Mark Greengrass, *Christendom Destroyed: Europe 1517–1648*, London, Penguin, 2017.

Simon Gunn, *History and Cultural Theory*, Harlow, Pearson Education, 2006.

Tobias B. Hug, *Impostures in Early Modern England: Representations and Perceptions of Fraudulent Identities*, Manchester, Manchester University Press, 2009.

I cappuccini. Fonti documentarie e narrative del primo secolo (1525–1619), edited by Vincenzo Criscuolo, Rome, Curia generale dei Cappuccini, 1994.

Gilles Lecuppre, *L'imposture politique au Moyen Âge: La seconde vie des rois*, Paris, Presses universitaires de France, 2005.

Adriano Prosperi, *Lutero. Gli anni della fede e della libertà*, Milan, Mondadori, 2017.

Joseph Ratzinger, *La soglia della verità*, in «Avvenire», XXXI, 23 January 1998, n. 19, p. 21.

The Routledge Handbook of Social Epistemology, edited by Miranda Fricker, Peter J. Graham, David Henderson, Nikolaj J.L.L. Pedersen, New York and London, Routledge, 2021.

Herman H. Schwedt, *Conflitti e violenze intorno a Girolamo M. Zambeccari OP, inquisitore di Reggio Emilia nel Seicento*, in *L'inquisizione e l'eresia in Italia. Medioevo ed età moderna. Omaggio a Andrea Del Col*, edited by Giuliana Ancona, Dario Visintin, Montereale Valcellina, Circolo culturale Menocchio, 2013, pp. 207–252.

Gian Galeazzo Scorza, *Pesaro fine secolo XVI. Clemente VIII e Francesco Maria II della Rovere*, Venice, Marsilio, 1980.

Giovanni Severano, *Memorie sacre delle sette chiese di Roma*, part I, Rome, per Giacomo Mascardi, 1630.

Benedetto Varchi, *Storia fiorentina*, edited by Gaetano Milanesi, t. II, Florence, Le Monnier, 1858.

Dror Wahrman, *The Making of the Modern Self: Identity and Culture in Eighteenth-Century England*, New Haven, CT and London, Yale University Press, 2004.

Natalie Zemon Davis, *The Return of Martin Guerre*, Cambridge, MA, Harvard University Press, 1983.

Epilogue. On the Ground of Truth

Giordano Bruno's key accuser was once again caught in the nets of the Inquisition at exactly the moment in which Bruno was pursuing a line of defense that intertwined with his hope of being able to plant the first seeds of his program of political-religious reform in the heart of Catholicism. He had worked and traveled a great deal to prepare for this, and – as he himself said – had returned to Italy for that purpose. It was a great battle, fought with the weapons of philosophy and waged, in spite of everything, through a primarily humanist appeal to debate and persuasion, on the ground of truth.

Whatever the reason was for the Capuchin's return to the prisons of the Holy Office, his presence was once again injected into the Bruno trial: even if only through the hidden meanings that Bruno could project on that undoubtedly shocking and unwelcome reunion, and their unknowable influences on his actions in the trial. Whatever the two prisoners might have said to each other in those summertime weeks, and whatever they may have done to each other, it is certain that at the beginning of September 1599 Giordano Bruno remained deferential to the tribunal, but was still determined to pursue his line of confrontation with his judges.

There was, however, a very slight variation in how Bruno executed his tactic of writing briefs before and after Celestino da Verona's entry to the prison. The first two briefs were not addressed to anyone specific, just the tribunal as a whole. However, starting in August 1599 the philosopher began to address his writings to Clement VIII himself: a pope who since his election to the throne had been opposed to the Holy Office's symbolic papal candidate, the cardinal of Santa Severina, and who recently had not hesitated to summarily condemn Severina's protégé, as well as Bruno's bitter adversary, Celestino da Verona.

Both texts written by Bruno after August 24, the first of which was only read in the Congregation on September 16, 1599 ("*coeptum legi memoriale missum sanctissimo Domino Nostro*"), and the "*memoriale directum Sanctissimo*" which on January 20, 1600 was opened, but not read ("*fuit apertum, non tamen lectum*"[1]), were placed in the records of meetings held in the presence of Clement VIII. But neither of the two – unlike the statements written

DOI: 10.4324/9781003026082-17

by Bruno earlier in the year – was read in its entirety. Why, although the trial was at its decisive moment, and while every effort was being made to induce Bruno to repent and reconcile, even turning to Dominican superiors, theologians, and comforters, did the judges stop reading the defendant's own written defenses in the Congregation? These were potentially important texts, which could have presented signs of repentance or even unearthed new charges. We can only conjecture that perhaps those two texts contained appeals to the pope, referring to events that took place in the summer of 1599 that the pope should not know about. Or that he did not officially want to know about.

During the months of Bruno and Celestino's renewed coexistence within the Inquisitorial cells, Bruno must have intuited that an internal conflict regarding the Capuchin's fate was underway within the Holy Office. He may have believed that the pontiff, as evidenced by his firm intention to condemn the Veronese to death, was unaware of what was happening in the prisons of the palazzo of the Holy Office: or of the fact that the informer's protectors meant to continue their protection, perhaps with the intention of freeing him once their purposes had been served. It had already happened in Venice in the fall of 1592; it could happen again.

With the passing of the days and weeks between August and September 1599, the suspicion that the Holy Office did not intend, not even this time, to punish its faithful collaborator must at some point have transformed into certainty.

The bleak astonishment Bruno must have experienced upon learning of the imprisonment and death sentence of his enemy, along with the sentiments aroused by their discussions in a tense shared confinement, were perhaps at some point later followed by the news, maybe stolen or artfully leaked, of Celestino's release from prison disguised in layman's clothing, and of a feeble stand-in being sent to burn in his place.

In July and August 1599, the question of the truth became for Giordano Bruno, one brief after the other, the heart of the trial and the key to its possible final resolution. His judges, however, perhaps meant to remind him that the game was being played on an altogether different field: that of unconditional submission to the Church of the Counter-Reformation. To this end they first used the one person who had contributed to Bruno's disgrace more than anyone else: Celestino da Verona, the living image of the *arbitrium* inquisitors had claimed for centuries, was perfectly suited to convince the philosopher to lay down the arms of his humanist dispute with the Inquisition and accept the harsh objectivity of the Tridentine faith.

After this effort foundered, the friar's liberation and his replacement at the stake by some poor unknown soul was a clear signal intended to reinforce the message that the power of the inquisitors, and the need to bow before them, was absolute. In terms of finally shifting Bruno's vision of the trial and his position, this may have succeeded where the Capuchin's presence had failed. However, the trial resumed heading in the opposite direction from what the judges had hoped for.

This new, awful demonstration of what could be perpetrated by a Church whose transformation Bruno had believed could begin a new era of continental religious and political pacification, but which by now had closed off every opening for authentic reform in a hierocratic entrenchment, may well have struck a mortal blow to the philosopher's convictions. Bruno's battle for his physical and intellectual survival, the entire story of his trial, his search for the truth and the historic mission of his philosophy itself might have all appeared powerless, hopeless to him. At that point, the urge to turn the tables on his judges and make his death the ultimate instrument of protest and a spark of future change must have become irresistible.

"Perhaps it is with greater fear that you pronounce the sentence against me, than what I feel in receiving it."

Note

1 *Processo*, doc. 62, p. 331 and doc. 65, p. 338.

Index

Note: Page numbers followed by "n" denote endnotes.

For Product Safety Concerns and Information please contact our EU representative GPSR@taylorandfrancis.com Taylor & Francis Verlag GmbH, Kaufingerstraße 24, 80331 München, Germany

Printed and bound by CPI Group (UK) Ltd, Croydon, CR0 4YY
30/09/2026
02225126-0008